Matthew & Dennis Linn

DELIVERANCE PRAYER

Experiential, Psychological
and Theological Approaches

PAULIST PRESS • *New York/Ramsey*

Book design by Theresa M. Sparacio

IMPRIMI POTEST
Joseph J. Labaj, S.J.
Provincial, Wisconsin Province
Society of Jesus
September 22, 1980

Library of Congress
Catalog Card Number: 81-82334

ISBN: 0-8091-2385-1

Published by **Paulist Press**
545 Island Road, Ramsey, N.J. 07446

Printed and bound in the
United States of America

Contents

Section Three
PSYCHOLOGICAL PERSPECTIVES
ON DELIVERANCE PRAYER

Section Four
CONCLUSIONS AND GUIDELINES
FOR DELIVERANCE PRAYER

Appendices

Foreword

by Most Rev. Joseph C. McKinney

"Bishop, can you get the bishops to teach us the wisdom of the Church on how we should deal with Satan and evil spirits?" That question was put to me on January 1, 1971. I had just agreed to act as a bishop advisor to the new spiritual phenomenon then known as Catholic Pentecostalism. I considered the question "strange" and chose to ignore it. In the decade since then, I have watched the development of overt devil worship, witchcraft is on the rise, and many in our country have pursued a false worship that comes from turning to Eastern religions. People are fascinated by horoscopes, going to fortune tellers, playing with ouija boards, turning to palm reading, etc., while dope, orgies, violence, and horror abound.

As young people with their characteristic curiosity were duped into trying such practices, they experienced a form of spiritual bondage. When they came to the moment of spiritual conversion and decided to be followers of the Lord, sincere level-headed pastoral leaders began to run into situations that will-power and prayer could not conquer. They discovered that only a special deliverance prayer could break the bondage and bring a freedom to the human spirit that enabled individuals to pursue the full Christian life. Many were helped, some were hurt. Deliverance ministries started to spring up. Some had disastrous fruits and some had very good fruits.

On November 15, 1972 Pope Paul VI had numbered this among the greatest needs of the Church today. "This question of the devil and the influence he can exert on individual persons, as well as on communities, whole societies or events, is a very important chapter of Catholic doctrine, which is given lit-

1

tle attention today, though it should be studied again." The charism of the Petrine office was evident to me. I began to echo the challenge of the Holy Father.

Each year his challenge became more relevant. I started to search for good, sound teaching. One could gain insights from a variety of pastoral leaders who were working in the charismatic renewal but it all needed to be evaluated, refined and brought together. As the need continued to grow, I found myself saying to small groups of proven leaders, "The Church needs the wisdom of your experience. We need sound teaching on how to deal with evil spirits."

In my estimation this book is the best response to date. The introduction tells its origins. Bishops' representatives called for up-to-date teaching. Theologians and pastoral leaders came together. I am especially grateful that Fathers Matt and Dennis Linn accepted the challenge of editing the material. I consider them God's men for this task. Not only have they gained a wealth of experience through their pastoral practice but they are highly trained in many areas of theology and contemporary sciences that deal with the human spirit. They are men of prayer, common sense and science.

Father James O'Brien accepted the responsibility for this theological project three years ago. This book is a lasting memorial of his efforts to bring together theologians and pastoral leaders. Good theologians study the past teaching of the Church and reflect upon the present religious experience of men. As they integrate the two, the wisdom of the Church grows. This is good theology and this work is a gift that the Church needs.

While I am delighted with the pastoral wisdom of these pages, I consider it more as a beginning than as a final word. The image of surgery comes to mind. Man has long tried to deal with disease by cutting it out, but it has taken much learning from experience to bring surgery to the perfection we know today. I predict that deliverance prayer will have a similar history. We have to perfect diagnostic skills for the discernment of spirits. We have to learn what can be healed through the medicine of prayer, life style, sacraments and sacramentals, and what can be healed only through deliverance prayer.

When deliverance is called for, it is ordinarily after a long case study. As surgery requires teams, so does deliverance; as surgery can be minor or major, so can deliverance; as surgery requires trained people, so also does deliverance; as surgery is aimed at healing, so also is deliverance; as surgery has a variety of procedures, so also has deliverance; as surgery has become highly specialized, so also will deliverance. At present deliverance is most often like exploratory surgery, and the deliverance team must be ready to deal with the unexpected. Even after long discernment, the unexpected often happens.

Surgery is not really successful until the person is nursed back to a healthy life. If this after-care is vital to surgery, it is even more necessary when deliverance is involved. Probably the most complicated part of deliverance is after-care. The most successful surgeon is useless without the help of those who can care for the patient when the surgeon is finished. The after-care aspect of deliverance was obviously a deep concern of the first generation of Christians. Their concern is reflected in the Gospel. If the evil spirits return, the person is worse off than before.

This book answers a critical need. While we still have much to learn about deliverance, it is obviously a skill to be learned through doing. Quacks abound. They need to be identified. Gifted pastoral leaders also abound and they need to be encouraged. This book should help in both instances. It is a good start but there is much more to be learned. The best wisdom from the past can be found in the Roman Ritual. This book takes that wisdom one step forward as it reflects upon present-day practice and integrates it with the wisdom of the ages.

Many questions remain, many more will be raised, and I pray that wise, gifted leaders will build upon the wisdom that is contained here. I especially hope that theologians will put aside their questions about the existence of evil spirits and advance our learning about demonology. Jesus did not question their existence. He dealt with them convincingly and commissioned his followers to do the same. We, who are his followers, need to imitate him and know that he has won the victory. He has entrusted us with the mop-up operation.

Freedom to embrace the cross and live the full Christian life is our goal. Healing makes that freedom possible, and sometimes healing through deliverance prayer is needed. That need is intensified by the strange practices of our times that bring bondage to the human spirit. This book addresses the need of the individual. The Holy Father's question about demons in communities and societies is not treated here. I am grateful for this book because it does answer the question, "Where can we gain some current wisdom about how to deal with Satan and evil spirits?"

Introduction

by Matt Linn, S.J.

I. MY DOUBTS ABOUT EVIL SPIRITS

Ten years ago I could not have edited this book. I knew that Christ called us to preach, heal and cast out demons in his name (Mk. 6:12–13; 16:15–18). I was willing to do the first two but didn't believe at all in demons. My graduate studies in anthropology, psychology and theology convinced me that demons were only to be found as gargoyles on medieval cathedrals or fantasies created by too much demon rum.

Anthropology showed how cultures such as the Navajo needed a belief in evil spirits both to explain the origin of illnesses that medicine now cures and to keep social order. Today if someone breaks the social order by stealing our sheep, we take him to court rather than, as the Navajo did, place a hex on him or an evil spirit on his trail. I knew that the Navajo could remain externally a peaceful people because their aggression had a well-controlled outlet through belief in evil spirits.

Having completed anthropological studies, I began psychological studies that revealed the psychological dynamics behind the need of people, such as the Navajo, to believe in evil spirits. Some of my psychotherapy clients also needed to find evil spirits, although I tried not to focus on the demon but rather on the real issues and especially on the client's strengths. One college student shared how in the middle of taking LSD he experienced being taken over by a frightening presence and since that time had bouts with suicidal ideation and had almost succeeded in taking his life. In therapy we worked through many hypotheses: that the demon was an image from

5

the collective unconscious or from early conflicts with an authoritarian father, that the demon was an internalization of his fear of having no future career and was being used to avoid responsibility to create that future, that the demon was simply caused by the drug or by suggestion while on LSD, and that conflict with his girl friend and not the demon triggered the suicide attempt. After a few sessions he dropped out of therapy, claiming that he received healing through a deliverance prayer (i.e., prayer in Jesus' name commanding the evil spirit(s) to leave peacefully). But I knew he was free because he finally faced the real demon. Even today I believe that demons are seldom the only cause of emotional illness and not present in every emotional illness.

Studying Scripture strengthened my demythologizing of demons. Some Scripture scholars claimed that the boy who had a "mute and deaf spirit" that caused him to foam at the mouth and grind his teeth was only suffering modern epilepsy (Mk. 9:14). In casting out the spirit, Jesus was just accommodating himself to his contemporaries who mistakenly thought that illness could be caused by spirits. New Testament studies further showed how the story of the epileptic boy's deliverance from an evil spirit was really two stories: one about a deaf mute and one about an epileptic. The redactor intertwined a second story because the early Church was finding that deliverance from evil spirits didn't always happen immediately and needed the explanation that it was because people were not praying (and fasting) enough (Mk. 9:29, Mt. 17:21). Form criticism added that any great religious figure had to do exorcisms and that the exorcism stories in other cultures followed the same basic pattern. A demon was always driven out with a violent reaction to show that this was a demon that only a great man could cast out.[1]

I also learned that a focus on personal demons only led to medieval witch hunts and kept people from taking responsibility to change the social structures that caused poverty and war. Again there is much truth in this, and I still believe that the evil one wants us to be more concerned about how he possesses people than about how he possesses unjust social structures through unfree hearts. He would rather have us worry about being possessed as in the film "The Exorcist" than have us worry about how to free our hearts to vote fairly or to share our surplus with a starving world.

II. SEEING THE NEED FOR DELIVERANCE PRAYER

To free hearts, I now find myself cautious about finding a demon behind every bush, but I am equally cautious about beating around the bush when it is really a case of demonic bondage needing prayer for deliverance. Those who see a need only for deliverance err just as greatly as those who see a need only for medicine, only for psychiatric treatment, or only for environmental change when several or all of these factors may contribute to a person's suffering. A growing number of doctors, psychiatrists and social workers now know that it is sometimes as necessary to treat demonic bondage with deliverance prayer as it is to treat bacteria with penicillin, a manic-depressive neurosis with therapy and drugs, or an alcoholic with AA and environmental change.

Through the Association of Christian Therapists I have come to know over twelve hundred professionals who combine healing prayer, of which deliverance prayer is a small but important part, with their professional practice.[2] Many of these therapists report that not only does prayer bring more depth to their therapy but also that the time needed with a patient seems to be cut by a third. The high point of a recent conference was a day on deliverance prayer during which three hundred professionals shared how through such prayer they had found freedom for themselves or their clients. Even professional journals are beginning to document how, through prayer for deliverance from evil spirits, clients received healing where conventional treatment alone failed.[3]

My openness to praying at times for deliverance from evil spirits came before I met these professionals. It came mainly through spiritual direction and directing retreats. In spiritual direction I met Julie, a school teacher who would have violent fits during which she would find herself throwing objects at friends or turning the violence inward with self-hatred and attempts to take her own life. For this she had been receiving psychiatric help but nothing seemed to help. After I asked her when the violent fits began, she shared how they came during a session of primal scream therapy. In that session she had reached such despair during a primal scream that she had invited Satan to help and gave herself to him. Since then she had a sense of his presence within, could not pray, and found that the violent fits came on especially when others were praying. Even while listening to her, if I started to pray mentally, she would stop in the middle of a sentence and begin to go into a trance or start shaking.

Since this was my first experience, I immediately called up the local chancery to ask to see an exorcist. The priest replied that they had no exorcist, nor would they appoint one since exorcists went out with medieval belief in demons. It was just as well since this was not a case of possession (total bondage) needing solemn exorcism but a case of oppression (partial bondage) needing only deliverance prayer. So with two gifted professionals we informally prayed for Julie to be freed from demonic bondage and for the love of Jesus to heal her emotional wounds.

During the prayer she would be taken over by another hateful personality that knew the difference between regular and holy water, that knew when and for what we were mentally praying, and even knew the next sentence I was about to read. But just as real was the power of the Lord protecting us and bringing Julie to the point where she could finally say "Jesus Christ" without choking and being tortured every time she struggled to say a syllable. With those words the evil one's power broke. Four years later Julie reports that from that time on she was freed and was able to drop therapy, and that she has had no return of the violence or other problems. Because of her restored health Julie was able to return to her religious order which she had left several years earlier for reasons of health.

My openness to praying at times for deliverance came not

just from the Julies who chose Satan but even from balanced people who prayed daily and were close to the Lord. Beth was a religious sister who prayed and received the Eucharist daily. She came to me well rested and looking forward to an eight-day directed retreat. But to her surprise each time she tried to pray, she experienced a tremendous fear and evil presence that made her want to quit the retreat. For four days we tried every spiritual and psychological approach I knew but nothing helped. Finally in desperation I blessed some salt and told her that if this happened again, she should sprinkle the salt in the form of a cross and say simply, "In the name of the Father, Son, and Holy Spirit, I command any evil to leave and only Jesus Christ to be present." She laughed and told me that she didn't really believe in evil spirits and certainly didn't expect this to work. To humor me, she prayed as I instructed, and to her surprise, and, I must confess, to mine too, she found that the attack immediately broke. She finished the retreat with peace.

I don't think this is an isolated incident since other retreat directors have shared such examples. One professor of spiritual theology received a call from another retreat director asking for advice on how to help a retreatant who was reaching panic and despair. When the theology teacher hung up the phone, he was led to pray for the retreatant a prayer of deliverance from demonic attack. A few minutes later he received another call from the director who said the retreatant had called to say that the attack had just then mysteriously vanished. The retreatant had not known that anyone was praying for her. I know that this still takes faith to see more than ESP bringing suggestion, but what accounts for suggestion not working until deliverance prayer is said?

III. OPENNESS TO DELIVERANCE PRAYER

Spiritual directees and retreatants began to change the way I viewed deliverance. At the same time, the Catholic Church reaffirmed its view of deliverance. On November 15,

1972 in a general audience address Pope Paul VI focused on the existence and danger of the devil.

> What are the greatest needs of the Church today? Do not let our answer surprise you as being oversimple or even superstitious and unreal: one of the greatest needs is defense from that evil which is called the devil. . . . Evil is not merely a lack of something, but an effective agent, a living, spiritual being, perverted and perverting. . . . It is a departure from the picture provided by biblical and Church teaching to refuse to acknowledge the devil's existence . . . or to explain the devil as a pseudo-reality, a conceptual, fanciful personification of the unknown causes of our misfortunes. . . . We are dealing not just with one devil, but with many. . . .
>
> This question of the devil and the influence he can exert on individual persons as well as on communities, whole societies or events, is a very important chapter of Catholic doctrine which is given little attention today, though it should be studied again. Some people think a sufficient compensation can be found in psychoanalytical and psychiatric studies or in spiritualistic experiences. . . . People are afraid of falling into old Manichaean theories again, or into frightening deviations of fancy and superstition. Today people prefer to appear strong and unprejudiced.
>
> Our doctrine becomes uncertain, obscured as it is by the darkness surrounding the devil. But our curiosity, excited by the certainty of his multiple existence, justifies two questions: Are there signs, and what are they, of the presence of diabolical action? And what are the means of defense against such an insidious danger?[4]

Three years later the Sacred Congregation for the Doctrine of the Faith backed the Pope's words with "Christian Faith and Demonology," outlining the traditional teaching on the existence of Satan and demons.[5]

Pope Paul VI's emphasis on the reality of the devil and the need to be freed from the evil one's power found expression in the newly revised *Rite of Christian Initiation of Adults.*[6] This rite outlines for adults a process over months or years of instruction and spiritual formation leading eventually to baptism. At all stages the rite relies heavily upon deliverance prayers called "exorcisms" which can be done by priests, deacons, or even lay catechists appointed by the bishop (n. 44). Even inquiring adult non-Christians can receive this exorcism prayer before they begin their baptismal instructions (n. 111). Then, once they have entered the first baptismal instruction, the rite invites those once involved in the occult to enter into a newly introduced special deliverance prayer and renunciation of non-Christian worship (n. 79). Finally, after the adult candidates complete their course of instruction, they enter into a period of final spiritual preparation and purification, the core of which is three deliverance prayers or "exorcisms" held during the Sundays of Lent (n. 154). Through these exorcisms, the adult candidates "are freed from the effects of sin and from the influence of the devil. They are strengthened in their spiritual journey and open their hearts to receive the gifts of the Savior" (n. 156).

The baptismal rite further suggests that deliverance prayer can strengthen our spiritual journey outside the context of the baptismal process since deliverance prayers can be prayed "more than once and in various circumstances" (n. 112). The rite is a model of deliverance prayer. It teaches that deliverance prayer is necessary, that it can be led by the laity, that it should be peaceful and positive, and that it should occur over a period of time in order to allow for proper instruction and the building of a strong spiritual life. The focus in both deliverance prayer and the new rite is not on battling evil spirits but on delivering the candidate into a loving and committed relationship with Christ and his community who are "revealing anything that is weak, defective or sinful in the hearts of the elect, so that it may be healed, and revealing what is upright, strong, and holy, so that it may be strengthened" (n. 25).

IV. PASTORAL PRACTICE TODAY

Many voices joined those of the Church leadership to acknowledge the devil's existence. Even those who demythologized Scripture were admitting that Jesus and the early Christians really did heal and cast out demons even if not exactly as written. For example, James Dunn writes:

> That Jesus healed mentally deranged and/or demon possessed people belongs to the base-rock historicity of the Gospels. Exorcisms were the one group of miracles to which D.F. Strauss, in his epochal work on the mythical nature of the miracle stories in the gospels, attached a high degree of historical probability. And no developments in gospel criticism since then have given any reason to question his judgment. On the contrary, they have reinforced the essential historicity of Jesus' work as an exorcist.[7]

The Anglican Church too, recognizing that such events still happen, produced a new rite of exorcism, recommended an exorcist for every diocese and published guidelines for freeing both people and places from evil spirits.[8] Both in England and in the United States the explosion of the drug and occult worlds demanded pastoral ministry from those who included deliverance prayer in their total care. Such groups as David Wilkerson's Teen Challenge, with its stress on deliverance prayer and Christian community, had higher success rates with drug addicts (77%) than the best New York State program (29%). In Roman Catholic circles, the Catholic charismatic movement seemed especially able to deal with those emerging from the drug and occult worlds on campuses such as the University of Michigan at Ann Arbor. While some Church authorities were debating the existence and nature of evil spirits, many lay people were confronting them in deliverance prayer and finding new freedom to live the Gospel.

In the midst of trying to come to terms with evil spirits, many made mistakes. The film, "The Exorcist," created demonomania, leading to pandemonium. Some suggestible viewers joined groups that saw evil spirits everywhere without the help of a movie screen. Eventually many of these groups broke up but not before they left behind a wake of people emotionally scarred and sinking into despair because nothing had rid them of their "demon." In the wake of such destruction, even those who did need deliverance prayer feared that it would be like the horrible experience of the film or of some groups rather than the normal, simple deliverance that occurs unnoticed when we really pray the Our Father's "but deliver us from evil." If these did receive deliverance prayer, others wondered what great sin had invited the evil one. They ignored the possibility that much bondage is uninvited and that the evil one can enter during an emotional wound such as a traumatic birth or the death of a loved one. By searching for what great sin had invited the evil one, they also missed seeing the spiritual growth in the person which made it impossible now for the evil one to remain. Fortunately the abuses were not as widespread as the groups that were doing deliverance well, such as the Anglican Cathedral in Atlanta where, during the past six years, hundreds have received, when needed, mature deliverance ministry without a known casualty.

Because the prayer for deliverance from evil spirits has the potential for much good or much harm, it has been closely monitored by the bishops of the United States and especially by their appointed liaisons to the charismatic renewal. Since they and the bishops saw deliverance prayer as crucial for the Church's growth, the National Steering Committee of Diocesan Liaisons for the Charismatic Renewal invited seventeen professionals to write papers directed at the issues involved in praying for deliverance from the bondage of evil spirits.

The committee chose these seventeen to author papers because of the diversity of their backgrounds. The seventeen represented various disciplines (theology, psychology, sociology), various backgrounds (eight university professors, five pastors or directors of Christian communities, four priests full-time in the healing-deliverance ministry), and various faiths (Roman Catholic, Episcopalian, Methodist). They also came from different places, not only geographically (from eleven states, Italy and England), but also philosophically (in previous writing some had strongly doubted while others strongly supported the personal existence of the devil).

On January 24, 1980 these authors met in Houston for a symposium to present and discuss their papers. Twenty others, many with sound healing-deliverance ministries, also received invitations. After three days of discussions and refining the papers, the thirty-seven participants chose to publish the nine papers in this volume as a response to the Church's plea for sound teaching on deliverance.[9]

The papers are divided into four sections. The first studies the tradition of deliverance prayer, the second studies the present practice, and the third studies the psychological perspective on deliverance prayer. In the fourth section the National Steering Committee of Diocesan Liaisons for Charismatic Renewal presents a set of conclusions and tentative guidelines. These guidelines are essential because while there is need for deliverance prayer, it should be done only by mature Christians under the direction of an authority so that it remains a very small part of a complete healing ministry. By being attentive to all these perspectives, hopefully the following papers will further the dialogue toward a sound healing-deliverance ministry.

Finally, special thanks to Selina Forrest, Linda Rovder, and Mary Kotch who worked so hard in preparing for the theological symposium entitled "The Ministry of Deliverance in the Charismatic Renewal" and typed the present manuscript.

NOTES

1. After seeing prayer for deliverance in many cultures throughout the world, it seems usually to have the cross-cultural pattern of reactions described in the Gospels, and perhaps this accounts for the common pattern in other exorcism stories contemporary to the Gospels. The more extensive studies in English on possession, Osterreich's *Possession, Demoniacal and Other* and *Demon Possession* by John Nevius, both conclude that the New Testament exorcism stories describe typical states reproduced in present possessions; cf. John Richards, *But Deliver Us From Evil* (New York: Seabury, 1974).

2. For further information write: Association of Christian Therapists, 3700 East Ave., Rochester, N.Y. 14618.

3. Some professional writings verifying the good effects of deliverance are the following: R. Mackarness, "Occultism and Psychiatry, *The Practitioner* (March 1974); Barlow, Abel and Blanchard, "Gender

Identity Change in a Transsexual: An Exorcism," *Archives of Sexual Behavior* VI:5 (1977); Conrad Baars, M.D., *Feeling and Healing the Emotions* (Plainfield: Logos, 1979).

4. "Deliver Us from Evil," General Audience of Pope Paul VI, November 15, 1972 as reprinted in *L'Osservatore Romano* (November 23, 1972).

5. "Christian Faith and Demonology," document commissioned by the Sacred Congregation for the Doctrine of the Faith, *The Pope Speaks*, XX:3–4 (1975), pp. 209–233.

6. *Rite of Christian Initiation of Adults* (Washington, D.C.: U.S. Catholic Conference, 1974).

7. James D. Dunn, *Jesus and the Spirit* (London, 1975), p. 44.

8. For Anglican guidelines, see Dom Robert Petitpierre, *Exorcism—The Findings of a Commission Convened by the Bishop of Exeter* (London: SPCK, 1972).

9. Another paper by Randall Cirner was later with Michael Scanlan, T.O.R. published in *Deliverance From Evil Spirits* (Ann Arbor: Servants, 1980) which is a well-balanced, practical guide to deliverance prayer.

Section One

The Tradition for Deliverance Prayer

Introduction

Although the devil isn't behind every temptation, the Church teaches that he does tempt, oppress, and possess. Possession—where the evil spirit is in complete control and often exercising great strength, familiar with previously unlearned languages, and able to foretell the future—is very rare and is not the focus of this book. Such cases of solemn exorcism should be left to priests who have permission from the bishop. In contrast to rare *possession* needing solemn *exorcism* by a priest are the many cases of *oppression* where an evil spirit is in partial control (e.g., a sexual compulsion) and the person needs *deliverance* prayer by any Christian open to the power of Jesus Christ. Its Christian tradition goes back to Jesus teaching his disciples to pray the Our Father's "but deliver us from the evil one" and then sending them out to cast out unclean spirits. Jesus asked the Church to continue this deliverance mission through the centuries in order to proclaim that the "reign of God is at hand" (Lk.11:20; Mk.6:7).

The following four articles examine the Church's tradition of praying deliverance prayer. Because many readers may not be familiar with deliverance prayer, we begin with our article which presents a case study illustrating how each step and obstacle of deliverance prayer can bring deep growth. The final part of our article examines the tradition of the Lord's Prayer to shed light on the modern question: How can deliverance prayer be done with the greatest fruit and least harm? The Our Father is Jesus' model for what needs to be done before one can finally at the end pray, "deliver us from evil." For as Fr. Dennis Hamm points out in his article, the original way Jesus prayed the Our Father was probably "deliver us from the evil *one.*" This tradition of praying the Our Father as a prayer of deliverance from the evil *one* was favored by the Greek Fathers and many Western writers such as Tertullian, Ambrose and Cassian. Only with St. Augustine and the *Libera nos* prayer of the Roman Mass did we come to our present impersonal interpretation of "deliver us from evil."[1]

The second article, by Fr. Dennis Hamm, professor of Scripture at Creighton University, explores not just the Our Father but the entire biblical tradition supporting and negating deliverance prayer. He raises key questions. Is there a decreasing emphasis on deliverance in the New Testament since a later writer, John, has no mention of casting out evil spirits? Was Jesus really casting out evil spirits or simply accommodating himself to Jewish understanding that disease and mental illness came from evil spirits? Are our present speculations on the origin and structure of the demonic world unbiblical? The Bible says little about the nature of demons other than that they are personal (intelligent, free), malevolent, and conquered by all who preach and call upon the risen Jesus. As with the nature of God, there is more that we don't know than that we know. The Scriptures are not concerned that we discover the nature of these evil spirits, but that we conquer the evil one. This is done by preaching the Gospel, by forgiving and serving one another in a full Christian life, and by bringing the reign of God through prayer for healing and deliverance.

Christian prayer for deliverance from evil spirits continued through the centuries. Around A.D. 150 Justin Martyr in his *Dialogue with Trypho* stated that every evil spirit exorcised in the name of Jesus Christ was overcome and expelled.[2] In the third century, the *Apostolic Tradition of Hippolytus* has baptismal candidates go through exorcisms by their godparents, by their teacher at the end of each weekly instruction, and before baptism by the bishop. Today's adult new rite for the catechumenate follows this by introducing "minor" exorcisms through the period of the catechumenate before the "major" exorcisms.

But as time went on, people lost the tradition of lay exorcism (deliverance) and thought that it could be done only by very holy saints such as Francis of Assisi and Teresa of Avila, and eventually only by priests. Fr. Robert Faricy, S.J., professor of spiritual theology at the Gregorian University in Rome, in the third article summarizes the tradition of the Church for clergy or laity praying private exorcism (deliverance). Though deliverance prayer can be prayed aloud, Fr. Faricy suggests that the normal prayer of deliverance be done peacefully and silently, usually without even being noticed.

But deliverance prayer is noticed because it is prayed aloud by many in the charismatic renewal. In the fourth article Fr. John Healey, liaison to the bishop of Brooklyn for Catholic charismatic prayer groups, reveals the traditional roots for the present practice of deliverance prayer. Fr. John brings together many resources: the rich tradition of the Catholic Church, the practical wisdom culled from training deliverance teams in Brooklyn, and the wider experience of Fr. Paul Schaaf who has done deliverances throughout the world. In addition when writing this paper, John was living in a community with other families who practiced a simple form of deliverance prayer. Children were taught to pray for protection through Jesus, their guardian angel, or Michael the archangel, just as the Catholic Church did after each Mass. They also found that parents particularly have power to silently bind the evil one and deliver their children into the protective hands of Jesus. If parents were experiencing hassles, their children would pray for them because the freedom of Jesus flows from any baptized heart. The focus was not on the evil one lurking everywhere but on Jesus' protective love and power that was everywhere when called upon.

The following four articles will explore how deliverance prayer is founded not just on the parental instinct to pray for a child's protection but is firmly rooted in centuries of Church tradition.

NOTES

1. Sacred Congregation for the Doctrine of the Faith, "Christian Faith and Demonology," The Pope Speaks, XX:3–4 (1975), p. 213.

2. Justin Martyr claims that the name of Jesus delivered even when no other way brought freedom (*The Second Apology,* The Fathers of the Church, VI, pp. 125–26). Irenaeus also underscores the power of Jesus' name (*Proof of the Apostolic Preaching,* Ancient Christian Writers, Newman, 1952, XVI, p. 107). Later in the fourth century Athanasius extols the power of the cross for deliverance (*Treatise on the Incarnation of the Word,* p. 322).

1
Deliverance in the Tradition of Our Father: A Case Study

by Matt and Dennis Linn, S.J.

I. A CASE STUDY: GEORGIA

Perhaps no prayer ministry can do as much harm and as much good as prayer for deliverance from the influence of evil spirits. The mistakes make headlines such as about a young woman in Germany who starved herself to death during exorcism prayer. But we seldom read of the numerous, quiet successes where people are released to live a full life again. Yet these can teach us how to pray in a manner bringing the greatest amount of freedom and the least harm. This article then will focus on the question: How can prayer for deliverance be done in a more healing way? Suggestions will be offered in three parts: first, an actual case study of a deliverance; second, the results of this case in four years of follow-up; third, some general guidelines to maximize the healing and to minimize the harm in deliverance prayer.

In selecting a case, we asked ourselves: What do people fear in praying for deliverance? We made a brief list: violent manifestations, long duration, many blocks to work through, occult bondage, team disunity, periods of depression, fears preventing sleep, and wrong discernment. Then we searched for a difficult case that could illustrate how we handled these problems. Thus the following case of Georgia is not the typical deliverance that occurs easily, quickly and with little outward manifestations. It is presented to illustrate that even in a deliverance having many obstacles, the power of the Lord overcomes every obstacle and even uses the obstacle to bring new gifts of freedom.

Georgia seemed an unlikely candidate for deliverance prayer. She had never heard of deliverance and was a pillar of the Church who attended daily Mass and frequently prayed the rosary. Out of curiosity she attended a prayer meeting in which the participants were praying with one another for physical healing. As some prayed to heal a disc in Georgia's back, her arms, shoulders, and face began going into contortions. A voice spoke through her twisted lips, "I've got her. Get away, all of you!"

As I approached Georgia's group, her behavior was difficult to differentiate from hysteria. But several things indicated to me that this was probably not hysteria. First, when I was behind her, I put a few grains of blessed salt on the back of her sweater. Though she could not see me do this nor could she feel the few grains of salt through her sweater, the voice through those trembling lips shouted, "Stop that! It burns!" The same thing happened when I blessed her with holy water, though nothing happened when I used regular water. I was dealing with something that knew the power of blessed salt and could tell the difference between holy water and regular water.

I looked her in the eyes and commanded every spirit not of God to leave. But she only became more agitated as people spontaneously tried to call out different spirits. I held up my hand and asked everyone to be quiet. As the people quieted down, so did Georgia's agitation. I asked her what she was experiencing. Georgia answered, "I feel so frightened. It feels like animals crawling around inside of me. I don't know what is happening. I've never felt this way before." Then seeing most of the people in the room gathered around her, she added, "I'm so embarrassed." I was annoyed. Everyone in the room was watching her, with no one still praying for physical healing. I thought: The devil has had his day at the expense of this woman.

Feeling her embarrassment and my annoyance, I asked her if she would like to move to another room. When she responded "yes," I asked her if she would mind if four or five others joined us. Though she didn't respond "yes," I had the feeling that she wanted whatever could help her through this frightening experience. So I asked a clinical psychologist, two people gifted in discernment, and several others gifted in prayer to join us privately upstairs. These were all people with whom I had worked previously.

We then prayed for protection and explained briefly what was happening to her: "Sometimes when a person is growing and becoming stronger inside, that person may feel the agitation of certain dark spirits trying to leave. If you wish, we will simply pray Jesus' light into you and ask that those spirits leave so that you can go home not feeling so agitated inside." Though she had never heard of such a thing, Georgia told us to go ahead, since she felt as if "animals were crawling inside." I was hoping, as we filled her with Jesus' light, that all the evil spirits would leave. Several weeks ago I was in a similar situation and all the spirits had left as I prayed light into the person's eyes.

But as I asked Jesus' light to flood into Georgia's eyes, all the contortions and voices started again. They persisted even as we commanded them to be quiet and to leave peacefully. Finally, we decided to command spirits one by one to leave. We had Georgia in the name of Jesus Christ renounce the first spirit, gluttony. But the contortions started and prevented Georgia from either saying the name of the spirit or the name of Jesus Christ. However, with the use of blessed salt and the prayer of command, we were able to free Georgia that night from the spirit of gluttony. She, too, was soon able to say, "In the name of Jesus Christ, I renounce, bind, and command you, spirit of gluttony, to go peacefully to Jesus now."

But the next spirit, a spirit of hypocrisy agitating her hands, did not leave despite thirty minutes of prayer. Since Georgia had to return home, we prayed for advice as to what we should do. The answer we received was to give her the Eucharist to bind the spirits. As we gave her the Eucharist, the activity in her body quieted down. She said she would be fine. We drove her home, and after staying there for a half hour, we left, since she appeared settled but wanting to return in the morning.

Second Day

When Georgia came the next morning, the wrinkles on her forehead spoke of fright and her barely open eyes of tired-ness. She shared that she had spent the entire night pacing, as she was unable to sleep. Then she complained about all the people the night before who "looked at me as if I were a side-show. They seemed to be saying to me, 'You had all that in you.' And I wanted to say back, 'You'd better believe it, but look at yourself.' Those hypocrites!" As I had some other things to do that day and as I could see that Georgia had strong feel-ings about those hypocrites, I suggested that she write down, starting with last night, those who had treated her like a hypo-crite.

When I returned a few hours later, Georgia had a page and a half full of names. We spoke about forgiveness, and she decided to try to forgive them at Mass that evening where some of them would be present. After struggling through the Eucharist, she returned and, partially because of her aching back, stretched herself out on the floor and cried out to God her frustration at not being able to forgive. When she finished crying out, it was as if she were empty enough now for God to fill her with his love. When Georgia stood up, her face looked radiant with no trace of fear. She felt as if she could fly. I hoped that perhaps the Eucharist and this prayer had taken care of whatever had needed to be done.

Third Day

When Georgia returned the next morning, she looked al-most as depressed as the day before. Much to my surprise she hadn't slept. I asked her to return to the position that had giv-en her the Lord's consolation the previous night. So she stretched out again in prayer on the floor. There she had an image of a black dog and a hand with cards in each of the fingers. She shared that the cards reminded her of those used by a fortune teller she occasionally sought out for entertainment. This fortune teller had correctly predicted her husband's death in an auto accident and also had predicted that Georgia would have an affair. Several times she had come close to having an affair.

This filled her with a sense of dirtiness and of being a hypocrite. To deal with this she spent a few hours writing down the ways she experienced herself as a hypocrite and in need of forgiveness which she then received in the sacrament of reconciliation. Then she again received the Eucharist, but this time she felt a closeness to the people and even to those she had previously experienced as hypocrites. That evening she looked strong and full of life. Yet she said, "I think there is still something within me." I felt so, too. But I also felt that forgiveness and inner healing prayer had given her the interior resources to now deal with whatever was left inside. Georgia asked if the team could come back and finish praying with her.

When we assembled as a team later that evening, we first took time to praise the Father, especially thanking him for the growth we saw in Georgia. Then we took time to ask the Father's blessing and protection upon the room and upon each person whom we anointed with oil for a specific task: one for intercessory prayer, another to hear the Lord in the Scriptures, two others to discern spirits, and the clinical psychologist for the gift of authority. He would command evil spirits to leave. Having prayed with him before, I knew that he had that gift more than I did. I asked forgiveness for not being aware of his gift the previous night. We also asked forgiveness of Georgia for leaving her so long the other night in front of "gawking people." The time for deliverance seems to be remarkably shortened when issues of forgiveness are dealt with before praying. I found that I was present that evening to anoint each and to affirm in the name of the Church all that was to happen. During the prayer my role was to use blessed salt and the power of the cross to hasten out whatever spirit was being commanded to leave.

Whenever the cross was touched to a given area, Georgia said that it became so hot that you could "fry an egg with it." But more than just a sacramental, the cross was a sign of an interior journey that Georgia was sharing with Christ. During the entire session Georgia was aware of Jesus either as he underwent his agony or as he carried his cross. As he carried his cross, she experienced with him the crowd of gawkers. "Is that what you went through, too? But I have friends here helping me and you have none." Several hours into the deliverance, because of the contortions, her back pain increased. But she refused pillows to support her aching back in order to be with Christ in his pain. At the time, her refusal seemed appropriate because the gift of her deliverance was to be one with Jesus as they climbed Calvary.

That climb lasted almost five hours for Georgia. During that time nine spirits left, often with a peaceful yawn or cough, beginning with the spirit of fortune telling and then the spirit of hypocrisy. Some spirits left immediately as Georgia would say, "Spirit of _____, in the name of Jesus Christ, I renounce you, bind you, and command you to go peacefully to Jesus Christ." If the spirit did not leave, or if the spirit prevented Georgia from saying any part of that statement, then the clinical psychologist would look into Georgia's eyes and command the spirit to leave. He would say, "Spirit of _____, in the name of Jesus Christ, I bind you and command you, go peacefully to Jesus now."

During impasses, several things helped. First, we found it helpful to stop at times for about ten minutes to let Georgia be with Jesus on the way to Calvary and to quietly fill her with Jesus' love and light. Second, words of the Lord often gave new strength and direction. For example, after a prophecy about her hands becoming healing hands purified through the deliverance, the spirit of jealousy left immediately. Third, inner healing helped as when Georgia again pictured that black dog. This time its image dissolved into her father being put into a straitjacket and taken away to a mental hospital. "In that straitjacket, he looks just like that black dog." As a resentment welled up in her that no one had helped her father, we stopped for a few minutes to let Jesus in his passion touch these wounds. She experienced with Jesus how he too looked like an animal, "a worm and not a man," and yet how he too reached out and forgave the thief and those who "did not know what they were doing." As Georgia drew strength from Jesus, she began also to forgive and the spirit of resentment lost its foothold.

After resentment, the final spirit to lose its foothold was the spirit of self-centeredness. Again the agitation centered in the hands. Georgia was reminded of all the times she hadn't reached out or shared her resources. Perhaps these feelings were accentuated this evening as she experienced both Jesus and the team reaching out so freely to her. Georgia slid into a depression, losing all the ground she had gained. When we asked her to join Jesus at the cross, she saw the Lord reaching down to take her burdens like stones. But she refused to give him permission to take the burdens. She had been with him as he experienced so much suffering; she didn't want to add more. The breakthrough came when reading Hosea 2:16–22. Because of his word, she no longer had the sense of overburdening a friend, but of being espoused forever "in love and mercy" to the man she had followed all evening. As she saw the Lord again reach down for her burdens, she put the stones one by one in his hands. Then we prayed for protection and arranged an appointment for the next day. She returned feeling freed and alive, so we simply thanked the Lord and exchanged phone numbers for future follow-up and a friendship that has grown over the years.

What counts is not how many spirits go or what prophecy is heard or even that Georgia had followed the Lord all evening. Some deliverances could be helpful and yet have no startling prophecy or Scripture passages. Perhaps the experience of the person going through the deliverance might even be one of desolation and dryness. What counts is the effect that a deliverance has in opening a person to love more not only God but also her neighbor and herself. What follows is an account of the changes in Georgia's life as a result of her deliverance.

II. GEORGIA'S GROWTH

The following is an account of some of the new ways that Georgia found herself loving God, others, and herself after the deliverance.

Love of God

Before the deliverance, even though many may have considered her a pillar of the Church, Georgia found herself focused on high society values. The major events of the week frequently centered around finding the right outfit to wear, feeling hurt about not being included on a guest list, and keeping her cleaning lady busy so that both her beach home and city home would look presentable. The deliverance marked the first time for Georgia that she felt every ounce of her energy focused and moving with Jesus, especially as the team encouraged her to climb Calvary with Jesus. The support she received from the deliverance team gave Georgia a desire to no longer live life alone, but rather to have a team in her life who could pray with her and help her stay focused on Jesus. This section on love of God will show first how her deliverance gave her the gifts to gather this team together, and, second, how this team has helped her continue her deliverance experience of focusing on Jesus.

Deliverance gave Georgia the gift of listening and of healing which she used in gathering a team. The deliverance attuned Georgia to new ways of listening such as through prophecy, visions, discernment of spirits—the whole intuitive side she hadn't used before. After her deliverance Georgia continued to pay her cleaning lady, Carol, but instead of washing windows or washing clothes, Carol began praying with Georgia and using the new ways of listening to try to find out the next step.

The next step was revealed to Georgia through one of the new intuitive ways of listening—the dream. After the deliverance, Georgia had a dream of a woman wearing a gold filigree bracelet above her stunted hand. Several days later at a prayer meeting, she spotted this woman, Nancy, wearing the same bracelet above her stunted hand. Georgia asked Nancy if she could pray with her for that hand. As Georgia held that hand and prayed, Nancy felt growth in her stunted hand. Then Georgia understood the prophecy that her deliverance would free her own hands to heal many people.

Almost daily over the past three years she has met with Nancy and her husband. Frequently the cleaning woman, Carol, joins them to form a team of four. They usually begin by praying a few minutes for Nancy's hand. Then they ask Jesus how they can deepen their relationship with him today. Each day Nancy's hand, which had stopped developing fifty years ago at the age of twelve and was therefore about one-half the size of the other hand, continues to grow and is now about four-fifths the size of her other hand. Just as Georgia found lack of forgiveness impeding her deliverance, when there is some conflict between the members of the team, Nancy's hand will not grow. After they work the conflict out and forgive each other, the hand will usually begin to grow again as they start praying for it. Thus Georgia's deliverance gave her a desire for a team, the gift of listening to contact the right team members, and the gift to heal a hand and the conflicts that make hands withdraw rather than reach out for Jesus in each other.

As this team of four has reached out to Georgia, they have enabled her to continue the experience of the deliverance by helping her to focus her entire life on Jesus. Together they have "tuned in" to ask Jesus about every aspect of Georgia's life. When asking, for example, about what she should do with her beach house, the response was to share it with others seeking a quiet place for prayer. As a result, about ten people have keys to her beach home. So, too, with regard to finances, they ask in prayer what stocks Georgia should buy and also where

Jesus would like them to spend the profits from those stocks. Stockbrokers are amazed that in years of decline, Georgia's stocks climb. Before the deliverance she had no idea that Jesus was so personal and wanted so much to communicate. Ever since the deliverance, she has communicated with him just as she did on the way to Calvary.

Her deliverance encounter at Calvary is now a key for Georgia to discern. Georgia recalls one time when she thought the Lord was telling her that she would win a new car in a raffle. Therefore she asked him how many tickets to buy and went out and bought them, and she was shocked when her name wasn't drawn. Later in prayer she heard, "You were looking at the new car and not my cross when you asked. My voice is not the excitement that comes from new cars but the gentle voice heard when you were with me and ready to carry my cross." Georgia has learned that her choices are the Lord's choices when she goes back to her deliverance and walks again with the Lord.

Love of Others

Georgia's deliverance not only gave her the gifts to develop a team that would pray with her and help her to stay focused on Jesus, but it also gave her gifts for loving her team and the several hundred people they have touched through both prayer ministry and day-to-day living. Due to her gifts we come for prayer, send others—especially priests—and sometimes call her for discernment. At times when we are faced with a deliverance and feel that a person is prepared, we will call Georgia and ask how we are to pray in a loving way. We do that because we know that Georgia has as keen a sense of discerning spirits and of timing as anyone we know. When we call, she will listen to Jesus as he tells her which evil spirits we are to deal with now or later, the order in which to call them out, and which ones may require forgiveness or inner healing prayer. Usually the deliverance will proceed just as she said it would.

Though we can implement a thousand miles away what Georgia tells us over the phone, what we miss is Georgia's presence. Her presence, like that of others who have been through deliverance, breaks down denial and allows a person to be at home with weakness. After ten minutes a stranger frequently feels free to share with Georgia things never shared with anyone else. He knows he will be understood and not judged.

Three things happened in the deliverance that gave Georgia the gift of now being present to another without judging that person. First, when she felt "gawked at," she became sensitive to the need to never point a finger at another. Second, seeing the harm that resulted from the time she visited the fortune teller just for entertainment has helped her to understand that actions which invite the evil one are not always intentional. Third, Georgia says that the deliverance put her in touch with both more sin and more love than at any time in her life. Being loved by Jesus and the team during those times when she felt her worst side exposed has gifted Georgia to love others as they come in touch with their worst side.

Her non-judgmental presence is reflected in the loving way Georgia prays deliverance as well as in her day-to-day living. When facing hypocrisy in another and in herself, Georgia learned that what she sees in another is usually hidden in herself, too. For instance, in praying with a mother who couldn't let go of her children, Georgia soon began to see herself also as an overprotective mother who did too much to earn her children's love. She saw how her children, who would soon be married, had not yet learned how to cook and wash. As she began letting her children take responsibilities and make mistakes in order to learn, she also began to even look forward to visits from her overprotective mother. Now that she sees overprotection in both herself and her mother, she understands and loves her mother. Thus Georgia's deliverance has gifted her to not only pray for deliverance in a loving way but also to love others day-by-day, even people like her mother who previously upset her.

Love of Self

Georgia could love her mother only because after the deliverance she found that she could love herself as Jesus does, even with her overprotectiveness. Though now Georgia doesn't consciously go about saying "Now I love myself" she lives differently. Loving herself as Jesus does makes it easier for Georgia to be alone, easier to allow others to help her, and easier to trust that every moment can be a gift.

First, Georgia finds that she need no longer fill her day with activity but can enjoy drawing away and being alone. Before she had hesitated to draw away alone since she feared loneliness, especially a loneliness in which she might discover her worst side. But now she knows that in solitude she can go back and be with the Lord at Calvary, even with her worst side, just as during her deliverance.

Second, after deliverance Georgia finds it easier to allow others to do things for her. Even when for the first time she allowed people to pray for her disc problem (which began the deliverance process), she was less interested in having her disc healed than in learning about physical healing so that she could help her niece who was suffering from encephalitis. Now Georgia finds that she loves who she is, even to the point of saying that she is worth receiving love and ministry from others. She especially takes time to do this for a weekend each month with the team. During that weekend together, they try to do the most loving thing with each other, which may be ministering to each other, enjoying a pizza, or perhaps even taking time to wash windows together.

Third, since her deliverance where even being gawked at helped her to walk up Calvary with Jesus, she knows that every moment can be a gift. She wondered why after the deliverance and a year and a half of praying her back was not healed. Then one day a woman with the same kind of back pain prayed for and healed Georgia's back. That taught Georgia and the team something they have frequently used: people hurting in the same way usually have the gift to heal each other in that area. In knowing that everything from being gawked at to even a back that is not immediately healed can be gift, Georgia has found it easier to live in the present moment rather than always waiting for tomorrow and for things to change.

In short, Georgia has become strong as a result of her deliverance. This has happened not because she keeps praying for protection that the evil spirits don't return—though she does that daily. Rather Georgia's deliverance has strengthened her because she has kept her eyes focused on Jesus and continued to ask him how to use the gifts of her deliverance to love God, others, and herself.

III. GENERAL OBSERVATIONS

Although Georgia and others have found much growth through deliverance, others have been hurt through deliverance prayer. The misuse of deliverance prayer has led to the breakup of prayer groups that find evil spirits everywhere. Many people focus away from the power of Jesus to the power of evil; those in the ministry fall into a "battle fatigue" personality, and those ministered to are left feeling empty and evil for even needing such ministry. Perhaps no other ministry can help or hurt a person so much.

If Jesus continues to heal powerfully through deliverance, he must want us to pray in a more healing way rather than to abandon the ministry because some have been hurt. Just as the Pharisees were wrong to suppress healing on the Sabbath, so, too, we would be wrong to suppress deliverance where Jesus is desiring to release his healing power. Rather than ask if there should be a deliverance ministry, we need to ask how can this ministry be exercised with the greatest healing and least harm.

When Jesus taught us how to pray, he taught the Lord's Prayer. Perhaps in leaving "deliver us from the evil one" as the last petition, Jesus was also teaching us the preparation for healthy deliverance prayer. Until the time of St. Augustine,

Christians prayed the Lord's Prayer as a prayer of deliverance from a personal "evil one." This use of the Lord's Prayer as a deliverance prayer continued in the baptismal liturgy up to modern times. The remainder of this article will use the Lord's Prayer as a framework for discussing how to pray deliverance prayer in as healthy a way as Jesus did and as he asked us to do, too (Mt. 10:1; Mk. 16:17; Lk. 10:19–20). In this section "deliverance prayer" will mean the prayer of command that frees another from the influence of evil spirits. The steps are not a rigid framework but simply ways that may be helpful to rely more on the discernment and power of Jesus so that he might increase and we might decrease. Deliverance prayer will be healing to the degree that it becomes the prayer of Jesus.

"Our Father"

Jesus prays "our" rather than "my" Father. Deliverance prayer whenever possible should be the prayer of a community rather than an individual. Praying deliverance prayer alone invites the dangers of less power, weaker discernment, and possible physical harm. When there are times that a person must pray alone as in confession, then he should draw on the prayer of the Church and others who are praising and interceding. But the ideal way is to pray as a team of mature Christians gifted with authority, love, and discernment which are often found in different personality types. The different personality types add to the richness but also make it easy for deliverance teams to fracture. This was prevented when the team praying for Georgia's deliverance anointed one another for the release of their gifts and asked forgiveness for not using one another's gifts. One of the most powerful deliverance teams has cuts its ministry time in half since they have taken time to become one by asking forgiveness of one another, praying for each other's gifts to grow, and just enjoying each other at picnics. The deliverance team that only prays together is usually in trouble.

Not every personality has the maturity needed for deliverance team prayer. This ministry attracts the authoritarian personality that sees all in black and white, needs to dominate, and has pools of anger that seek a target like Satan. Such a person might have difficulty working as a team member needing to submit to the group's discernment. All in deliverance should be in submission to another mature director who knows his or her strengths and weaknesses. The authoritarian personality also has an insecurity fostering a need to succeed and to see deliverance as complete when it is not. The authoritarian need to be in control and to succeed may also prevent making needed referrals to AA or those with counseling skills. In contrast, the ideal team member does rely on the authority of Jesus Christ but can discern with others, loves the wounded with a healing compassion that perseveres through setbacks, prays readily for inner healing rather than only for deliverance, and relies on the gifts of others that are fostered in deep relationships. Where such a team member is, others feel more alive.

The person being delivered should be also not an individual praying "my" Father but a person in community praying "our" Father. Some covenant communities have asked that a person seeking deliverance first live in community to be built up through love. Not everyone can live in a covenant community, but those being delivered should have at least one friend with whom they share their life and draw life. If, as in Georgia's case, this has not happened before the deliverance, they should commit themselves to finding a friend after their deliverance. This may be difficult since some in need of deliverance have a dependent personality needing to be dominated by spirits or by another person so that they don't have to take responsibility. This drives friends away or attracts the dominating friend who fails to develop the other's gifts. If this dependency is left unhealed, those praying for deliverance will have their phone ringing day and night. Slowly Jesus must become the one those being ministered to depend upon and who through a community's love calls them to step out and to take new risks. Spiritual direction focusing on developing a personal relationship with Jesus and competent professionals such as those in the Association of Christian Therapists can help with this process.

"Our Father, Who Art in Heaven"

Because we have the Spirit in our heart, we can say "Abba" and trust in the care of our Father who will not give us a stone when we ask for bread (Mt. 7:9). If he is the Father who protects the birds of the air, will he not protect us when we pray a prayer of protection (Mt. 6:26–27)? Yet those in the deliverance ministry can pray a prayer of protection and return home to find that their family has been hassled and the television no longer works.

We have never experienced the evil one's backlash, the price that Malachi Martin claims the exorcist must pay.[1] Perhaps it is because we spend time really praying for protection: each morning and night, when daily receiving the Eucharist, and especially before and after a deliverance. We invoke the protection of Mary, Michael the archangel, and the whole heavenly court who are with the Father in heaven.

Yet many others pray as much for protection and still get hurt. Much of this is mystery. But perhaps one possibility is that because many are praying for us and our ministry, we are constantly open to the Father's protective love. Not only do we have people who commit themselves to pray daily for us, but, as in the case of Georgia's deliverance, we frequently anoint people to do intercessory prayer during the deliverance. Their prayer is so important that often we can tell the intercessors when they took their breaks, since these were the times of greatest struggle in the deliverance. All those in the deliverance ministry need someone else praying for them. Where others intercede, the Father's protective love surrounds those ministering and receiving ministry. The Father will protect those who are doing his will, submissive to his guidance through another, filled daily with Jesus' life through the sacraments and prayer, and asking for his protection through Mary, Michael, the Precious Blood of Jesus, and others joined in prayer. This will not eliminate all suffering any more than the Father's love eliminated Jesus' redemptive suffering when Jesus prayed, "Let this cup pass from me; yet not my will but thine be done" (Lk. 22:42–43). Prayer of protection assures that the Father's hand is present in any suffering.

"Hallowed Be Thy Name"

Too often groups involved in deliverance find their prayer changing from predominantly praising the Father to angrily battling spirits. This happened on the first evening when Georgia felt fear and agitation as the gawkers tried to battle and call out spirits. Deliverance prayer should begin instead with praising the Father for his protection, wisdom and power that in Jesus defeats Satan each time. Thus deliverance prayer was most effective for Georgia the night we began by praising the Father especially for Georgia's growth and then anointed each to bring the Father's presence. The deliverance moves forward to the degree that there is a focus on the power of God rather than on the difficulty of the deliverance and the power of Satan. When a spirit leaves, a mature team will spontaneously break out with praise of God rather than mark their scorecard with a "We got that one" or "That one is gone."

Deep praise also leads to a calm, peaceful atmosphere suffused with the Father's powerful presence and love rather than the fearful, battlefield atmosphere where one tries to outwit and outshout Satan. A wise woman who prays powerfully for deliverance once said that she would not pray for deliverance until she first experienced the powerful, loving presence of the Father. For her and for the Jew to hallow the Father's name was not to pronounce his name but to reverence his personal presence. Too often we are ready to battle before the Father is with us.

"Thy Kingdom Come"

It is difficult to tell some others that they need deliverance because they may immediately feel guilty of doing a great evil that opened the door to an evil spirit. Moral fault such as allowing a habit of sin to grow or taking part in the occult does invite evil spirits. But in some of his deliverances Jesus did not mention sin as a factor, yet he did with others like the paralytic, the adultress, or the man at the pool. In one of his deliverances Jesus freed an epileptic boy who seems to have been possessed from early in childhood before he could even commit serious sin (Mk. 9:22). The Church recognized this in exorcising infants at baptism. In our practice it seems that most spirits have entered without the person's moral fault, e.g., in traumas, parental involvement in the occult, curses, etc. In many cases a person's guilt feelings about having an evil spirit are not warranted.

Rather than stress that an evil spirit is present because a person has fallen into evil, it would seem better to stress that an evil spirit can no longer hide because the person has grown stronger with Jesus' life spreading the kingdom of God within. For example, as Georgia grew in forgiveness, walking with Jesus to Calvary, the kingdom of God grew, making it impossible for even the more rooted evil spirits to maintain their foothold. Sometimes no deliverance prayer is needed, since the spirits are forced out by a person's spiritual growth or the presence of God's power brought on by praise, the Eucharist, resting in the spirit, tongues, etc. The more we are filled with God's life, the more peaceful deliverance will occur as with a simple yawn during the Eucharist. Rather than worry about whether more deliverance is ahead, it is better to focus instead on building up Christ's life which will peacefully force out all that is not of Jesus.

This is not to say that all spirits will leave simply by growing in God's life, and we need never use formal deliverance prayer to command them to leave. The danger lies in saying that deliverance must come only through deliverance prayer or only without it rather than in the most loving way Jesus may want the kingdom of God to come. As with Georgia who went to daily Eucharist, some spirits seem able to resist daily Eucharists but leave when commanded to go to Jesus. However, in other deliverance cases, the spirits resisted the command and left when a person received new life in the Eucharist. It was disappointing that Georgia's deliverance was not quietly taken care of the first night by receiving the Eucharist. But if it had, she would have missed the struggle of Calvary and what she considers to be the most loving and powerful act of God in her life. Going through the struggle with Jesus led her to commit herself more deeply at any cost to Jesus and to working for his kingdom to come.

Unlike Georgia some want only deliverances from smoking or an exploding temper and are not seeking a deeper relationship with Jesus. When a person has no freedom to choose Jesus, the Lord often honors this first step, but at other times he asks for a person to choose him with whatever freedom remains. Those ministered to can give their freedom to Jesus by renouncing all willing or unwilling involvement in the occult, renewing their baptismal promises, and in their own words offering their entire life to Jesus. When the deliverance proceeds to focus on a particular spirit, they should also say, "Spirit of _____, in the name of Jesus Christ I renounce you, bind you, and command you go peacefully to Jesus now!" The more they line up their will with Jesus' kingdom, the more Jesus can come.

"Thy Will Be Done"

Formal deliverance prayer should be done only by the mature who can discern when and how to pray for deliverance. Sometimes, as with Georgia, the time is ripe and the deliverance will begin during a prayer for physical healing or any other time the power of the Lord is present. Even when the Lord begins the deliverance, discernment is needed to determine in what private place it should be done, who should pray, when it should be stopped for rest, and how the Lord wants each step to occur. As with Georgia who needed three days of ministering, the Lord often wants us to build up the person's life before all the spirits will leave. One community built up a person through prayer and love for three years before they discerned that it was finally the Lord's moment to deliver that person from spirits that were known to be present from the start. They have a powerful healing-deliverance ministry because they ask, "Is this the Lord's moment and is this his next step?"

How can we tell if it is the Lord's moment? Sometimes the team and the person prayed for intuitively know. At other times I am led to simply pray in tongues, fill the person with light and ask the Lord to quietly drive out all darkness or to warm the parts of the person that need to be healed first with his love. That leaves the next move up to the Lord. If the person or I begin to sense that a deliverance is taking place, I then might look into his (her) eyes and, silently praying in tongues, continue to fill the person with the Lord's light and love. I vary this with times when I am looking but not praying and with times when I am looking and commanding. If the manifestations are turned on and off with prayer and get more pronounced at each command (e.g., "Spirit of fear, I bind you and command you, go peacefully to Jesus now"), then it may be time for deliverance prayer since there is enough life present to disturb the spirits. There is something present that knows the difference between when I silently am looking and praying and when I silently am looking and not praying. There is something that is responding only to hidden prayer. If it is not immediately taken care of by silent commands, then I ask the person if it would be all right for me to get others to help discern how to pray with him (her).

Even when the team discerns it is the Lord's moment to begin the deliverance prayer, they can easily be deceived each step of the way. Ideally they should begin by binding all spirits of false prophecy, deceit, confusion, etc., before they even begin to discern. They should bind every evil spirit present, forbidding them to interact or act out in any way but the way of Jesus. As in the case of Georgia's deliverance, persons with special gifts of discernment, prophecy, and listening to Scripture should be on the team or at least available through a phone call. It is sometimes helpful to keep one person discerning outside the room where he (she) is not distracted by anything happening in the room.

There are many ways of discerning. Most of the spirits involved in Georgia's deliverance were directly revealed to the discerners as they prayed. However, to help clarify their discernment, the team would sometimes ask Georgia what she was experiencing (e.g., an image of a black dog which eventually pointed to the spirit of resentment). At other times they would command the spirits to identify themselves (e.g., anger, self-centeredness), and at still other times they would watch the physical and emotional behavior manifested during prayer (e.g., spirit activity in the stomach for gluttony or in hands for fortune telling, and sudden fear of continuing deliverance for fear). But even information gained in these ways needs to be discerned. For example, when Georgia was depressed she thought that the deliverance was finished, but instead the spirit of self-centeredness needed to leave.

To avoid being misled, one should ask, "Does this new direction bring the same feelings of peace, commitment, faith, hope, and love that flow when I am most listening to the Lord and saying the deepest 'yes' to him?" We will know this only if we often ask the Lord to reveal to us the times we most heard his voice in our life and during that day. To grow in discernment, it is helpful to ask each night, "When did I most hear the Lord today and how did I feel?" This yields a set of feelings that can serve as a measuring stick for whether one is hearing the Lord, oneself, or the evil spirit.

"Give Us This Day Our Daily Bread"

Before starting to command a spirit to leave, I ask what is necessary for this person to have Jesus as fully within as when receiving the daily bread of the Eucharist. Sometimes we are led to simply fill the person with the blood of Jesus or to pray in an area of inner healing. But I wait until either I sense that Jesus is really present or that deliverance is needed now to remove the barrier blocking his presence. Sometimes receiving the Eucharist brings Jesus' presence that breaks through barriers. One man who was tortured by a spirit of homosexuality for twenty years was freed as he received the Eucharist after six hours of fruitless deliverance prayer.

Sometimes the bondage seems not to be with an evil spirit but with a familial spirit. One lady sensed the presence of her deceased grandfather and frequently saw him in her dreams. After offering the Eucharist for him she found that she no longer had a phobia of falling nor fits of paralysis. Further research revealed that the grandfather had died in service after falling off a ladder and breaking his neck. Sometimes what people sense as an evil controlling spirit may be a familial spirit. For familial spirits, deliverance is often not necessary, and new freedom comes when offering the Eucharist for a deceased grandfather or whoever is sensed to be involved and needing prayer. We can bring new freedom by offering prayer especially for the following deceased: those we love or dislike the most, babies that have been aborted or have not lived long enough to receive much love, others (suicides, the emotionally ill) in our family tree who have died without experiencing much love, and others the Lord places in our heart. At the Eucharist, we can take some of these deceased, give them Jesus' forgiveness, offer them to Jesus, and then receive Communion for them so that they can become one with Jesus. This may have to be repeated until we sense that the person is really one with Jesus. This is simply praying for a soul that may be in purgatory, but often it brings freedom in areas that were bound.

"And Forgive Us Our Trespasses As We Forgive Those Who Trespass Against Us"

One of the most frequent barriers to deliverance is that those seeking deliverance either cannot accept the Lord's forgiveness or cannot give the Lord's total forgiveness to another who has hurt them. In the case of Georgia, the deliverance could not proceed until she forgave those gawking at her like self-righteous hypocrites. This forgiveness deepened as she saw her own need to be forgiven as a hypocrite professing commitment to Jesus and yet on the verge of having an affair. After she forgave others and herself for hypocrisy, the spirit of hypocrisy was easily delivered because there was no psychological need for it.

This may have to be done with each stubborn spirit, as later occurred when the spirit of resentment would not leave until Gloria forgave those she resented for not helping her father. The inner healing through forgiveness and love leads to deliverance which leads to further inner healing and further deliverance. Deliverance teams which do not allow time for forgiveness and inner healing to be worked through leave open doors for the spirits to return. If possible the forgiveness should be deepened through the sacrament of reconciliation and through further prayer extending the forgiveness to others living and dead who have hurt us or been hurt by us. Of all the petitions in the Lord's Prayer, Matthew chose to repeat his emphasis on forgiving and being forgiven: "Yes, if you forgive others their failings, your heavenly Father will forgive you yours; but if you do not forgive others, your Father will not forgive your failings either" (Mt. 6:14–15).

"And Lead Us Not into Temptation"

Deliverance sometimes seems to lead to more temptation rather than less. Those delivered from lust, for example, may be tempted in all the old ways and even some new ones since their growth has ranked them higher on the evil one's list of targets. As they grow healthier and no longer need to fearfully deny their feelings, they may have even stronger sexual desires. They may thus think that nothing other than wishful thinking happened during deliverance prayer. But if they reflect, they will find new strength in saying "no" to sexual temptations and in saying "yes" to healthy ways of transforming sexual drives into creative activity. They will be more alive not just with sexual desires but with all their emotions—compassion, joy, gratitude, hope, and anger at not making more progress. Deliverance doesn't stop temptations and feelings but gives new freedom and the drive of awakened feelings to break old habits and begin anew.

To help persons through this time of struggle, it is necessary to follow up. After a deliverance, especially where there
has not been enough inner healing, they may experience a
frightening emptiness. Sometimes they may need to stay over-
night with a team member or at least be told that they can call
any time of the day or night just as alcoholics may need to call
an AA member when they feel like drinking. If they have a
strong Christian life with daily prayer, Scripture reading, the
sacraments, and a loving community, then they often need little help but should check back after a week. If these are missing, then these should be introduced along with other helps
such as AA or counseling. Those delivered should also pray daily for protection and say a simple prayer of self-deliverance
when bothered. This prayer can be a brief "Spirit of
_____, in the name of Jesus Christ I bind
you and command you, go peacefully to Jesus Christ now"
while breathing out all evil darkness and filling oneself with
the light and breath of the Holy Spirit. This prayer can be repeated until filled again with peace and Jesus' desires. The Jesus Prayer can also be a simple, positive way to breathe in
Jesus' light and desires while exhaling all darkness that is not of
Jesus.

Not only those delivered but also the deliverance team
faces temptation. As they minister more they may begin to
have more confidence in their technique and listen less to how
the Lord wants to minister uniquely to this person. They may
tend to treat the spirit of lust in Joe as they treated the spirit of
lust in John. They may also be tempted to share with others
their successes and what should remain confidential. Whatever
happened during the prayer should be treated with the same
confidentiality that a priest observes in confession. Even in this
article we changed the names of the spirits and other identify-
ing details and finally had Georgia read and give permission
for the final version.

However, the main temptation for a deliverance team
usually does not center around technique or confidentiality.
The evil one's chief temptation and weapon to destroy a deliverance team is overextension. If they see the Lord's victory,

they will be tempted to pray with many others and to forget about ministering to one another and just enjoying a movie or pizza together. Even before they leave for home, a deliverance team should take time to fill one another with new life and to deal with whatever needs surfaced during the deliverance. If one member became fearful, found it hard to be loving, or found an area lacking freedom, then this should be shared and given to the Lord. This happens frequently as when Georgia discovered in praying for an overprotective mother that she herself needed ministry for being overprotective. One of the main gifts of ministering to others is that we discover where we need ministry.

"But Deliver Us from the Evil One"

Only in the last petition does Jesus pray for deliverance. It is as if Jesus were saying that deliverance depends on all that has been requested in the other petitions of the Lord's Prayer. To the degree that we are bonded to our Father by praying as Jesus did, we cannot be bonded to the evil one. To the degree that we have taken on the mind and heart of Jesus, the light of the world, we will be delivered from the darkness of the evil one. Darkness goes not by shouting at it but by turning on the light.

Note too that the Our Father finishes as it started by praying for "us" rather than for "me." As Georgia found, the focus should be on daily asking Jesus how to use for "us" the gifts flowing from deliverance rather than constantly focusing on the evil spirit and his possible return to "me." For Georgia to remain free from the evil one, she had to begin to reach out and bring others into a closer relationship with Jesus Christ just as the alcoholic must try to bring another into AA. The test for complete deliverance is not whether a person feels more free but rather Georgia's question: How have I used the gifts of my deliverance to love God, others and myself? "What the Spirit brings is love, joy, peace, patience, kindness, goodness, trustfulness, gentleness, and self-control" (Gal. 5:22). The test for deliverance *from* the evil spirit is the degree of deliverance *into* the Holy Spirit.

"For Yours Is the Kingdom, the Power and the Glory Now and Forever"

This phrase was added in the third century by the Christian Church familiar with how God's kingdom, power and glory comes through deliverance from the evil one. I can understand why deliverances might have led to this addition, because when praying for deliverance, I find that God manifests his kingdom, power, and glory more than perhaps at any other time.

In deliverance prayer the Father openly battles with the kingdom of evil in order to manifest his own kingdom. For example, when I see him use the Eucharist to drive out a spirit of homosexuality rooted despite twenty years of struggle, I see how anxious the Father is to establish his kingdom in every area of life. That is not to say that every homosexual has an evil spirit. But sometimes through deliverance freedom can come into areas that appeared to be a psychological burden for life.

As the Father establishes his kingdom through deliverance, I see that though there is an evil one, the Father is even more powerful. In Georgia's deliverance, I saw the power of God manifest itself through blessed salt as it agitated and loosened the foothold of evil spirits, and through the cross "you could fry an egg with." The Father's power also conquered through prophecy a spirit of jealousy, through forgiveness a spirit of resentment, and through Scripture a spirit of self-centeredness. In other deliverances the Father's power may manifest itself in another way.

In the most powerful deliverance I have seen, the Father's power was manifested through blessed oil. That deliverance occurred when I was with a man seconds after his wife released him from a curse. Though I did not know about the curse, I saw the man suddenly become cold in all parts of the body and then unable to move. Then in fifteen minutes I saw the power of God especially through blessed oil deliver him from twelve evil spirits and fill him with new life. I find myself using prayer, sacraments, and sacramentals with more conviction because of the way deliverance has shown me the reality of the evil one and of the Father's unlimited power to bring new life.

When I see the Father's new life that deliverance brings to Georgia, a homosexual or a man bound by a curse, my heart wants to respond much as Bethlehem's angels did to the Father's new life: "Glory to God in the highest." Even though healthy communities, inner healing prayer, and other ways may manifest God's kingdom, power, and glory, a powerful manifestation of them may be missing where deliverance prayer is not an option.

Before Georgia's deliverance I hoped that I would never need deliverance prayer. I now know that each time the Lord may invite me to go through deliverance, it can be an invitation for me to experience the kingdom, the power, and the glory now and forever. Amen.

NOTE

1. Malachi Martin, *Hostage to the Devil* (New York: Thomas Crowell, 1976).

2

The Ministry of Deliverance and the Biblical Data: A Preliminary Report

by Dennis Hamm, S.J.

I should first state how I perceive the deliverance ministry currently practiced in the charismatic renewal. My knowledge of this ministry is mainly vicarious. I have witnessed directly very little deliverance during the periods that I have been active in charismatic renewal—in St. Louis around 1969–71 and in the Berkeley prayer group with which I prayed regularly in 1978–1979. But persons I know and trust—for example, my former St. Louis neighbor Francis MacNutt and my fellow Jesuits Matt and Dennis Linn—have, over the years, shared some of their experiences with me. The pattern of their experience seems to be this: first there was an initial skepticism, regarding the ready demonic interpretations and the use of informal exorcism as practices within some fundamentalist groups; then, as they grew in their own healing ministry, there was the meeting up with "hard cases," persons whom no conventional medical or psychiatric therapy seemed to help, who seemed to experience a kind of bondage not simply explainable as personal sinfulness or mental illness and yet not so severe as to be called demonic possession and thus warrant formal exorcism; then there was the move from simple prayer of petition to a format of commanding in the name of Jesus that the apparently personal evil force leave. It worked. In this experimental way, they came to judge that where nothing else worked, the interpretation of demonic obsession or oppression (as distinguished from possession) and the command in the name of Jesus (as distinct from the full ritual of exorcism) was pastorally appropriate—one tool in the kit, as it were.

I respect their judgment and their decision in this matter, though nothing in my admittedly more limited ministry has led me to the same perceptions and practice. This understanding of deliverance has been confirmed by talks I have heard in person or on tape by Fr. Francis Martin, Bishop Joseph McKinney, Fr. Paul Schaaf, Mr. Bobby Cavnar, and Pastor Prange of St. Paul. The impression I get is that of persons, open to the Spirit, developing a pastoral practice that is effective and, increasingly, carried out with sensitivity to the need for discernment, coordination with other therapies, privacy, team complementarity, orderly procedure, integration with the need for repentance and conversion, and an awareness of the need for after-care and community support. So the practice is already there. Good is being achieved. Abuses, at least in the ministries of those I know, are being avoided.

This is the perception of the ministry of deliverance that I bring to my biblical question. The question itself is this: Does Scripture, in its presentation of evil and in its protrayal of the ministries of Jesus and the Church, say anything to legitimate and guide the contemporary ministry of deliverance? To sort out the beginnings of an answer to that question, I shall use the medieval pedagogical device of marshaling arguments on both sides of the question. I shall discuss in Part I the biblical data which seem *not* to support the contemporary ministry of deliverance. Then in Part II, I shall present the biblical material which does seem to support such a ministry. While this method will not serve to advance a clear, tightly-argued thesis, it will, I think, more accurately represent the current state of the question.

PART I: BIBLICAL DATA WHICH SEEM NOT TO SUPPORT THE CONTEMPORARY MINISTRY OF DELIVERANCE

1. The Old Testament provides little support for the world view embracing a highly developed demonology and sa-

tanology. Nowhere in the Hebrew Old Testament does Satan appear as a distinctive demonic figure, opposed to God and responsible for all evil.[1] A figure called "the satan" (*ha satan* in Hebrew, *ho diabolos* in the Greek version) appears several times—in the prologue to the Book of Job and in the third chapter of Zechariah. In these passages, the word *ha satan* is a role description, not a proper name (it becomes a name in the Latin Vulgate), and the role is that of prosecuting attorney in the divine court. In Job he is given leave by God to test the virtue of the book's hero. In the vision of Zechariah 3:1ff, the satan is standing in the presence of the Lord, at the right hand of Joshua, apparently to challenge his fitness.[2] In 1 Chronicles 21:1, "a satan" is said to incite David to take the census; here the chronicler, rewriting the history of the Books of Samuel and Kings, ascribes to this agent of the divine court an action, which, in 2 Samuel 24:1, is attributed to Yahweh himself.

This reluctance to attribute negative activity to the Lord God also gives rise to the few examples of evil spirit talk in the Old Testament. In 1 Kings 22:17–23 we hear the prophet Micaiah tell King Ahab of a vision of the heavenly court in which the Lord asks for volunteers to deceive Ahab, to which one of the spirits responds, "I will go forth and become a lying spirit in the mouths of all his prophets." And the Lord sends him off to do just that. Another example of an evil spirit sent from the Lord occurs in 1 Samuel 16:14–23, which also provides the only example of anything close to a deliverance (at least as we are using the term here) in the Old Testament: "The spirit of the Lord had departed from Saul, and he was tormented by an evil spirit sent by the Lord." The problem appears to be a kind of depression or melancholy, for the remedy turns out to be the music therapy of young David's harp playing.

These references to human evils and suffering as somehow attributable to the agency of Satans and evil spirits operating out of the divine court serve a double purpose in the Old Testament: they preserve the autonomy and supremacy of the one God, and they avoid the embarrassment of attributing such negative activity directly to the divinity. These Old Testament passages do not, however, present a picture of a vast array of demonic forces organized under the headship of a supreme evil one and directly antagonistic to the purposes of God. For this we must look to the Jewish literature that develops between the Testaments.

Most of this literature was written between 200 B.C. and A.D. 100. Its best known and most important examples are 1 Enoch, The Book of Jubilees, The Assumption of Moses, The Books of Adam and Eve, and our canonical Daniel.[3]

In these writings, the devil (alias Mastema, Satan, Semyaza, Azazel, Beliel) and his forces, their fall, and their relation to human history are described in a great variety of ways. For example, 1 Enoch 6, inspired by Genesis 6:1–4, takes that mythic fragment about the "sons of heaven" taking as wives the daughters of men, and retells it as a story of angels lusting after women. Out of these unions spring a bloody and unrighteous generation of giants. Meanwhile, some of the angels, "fallen" in the sense just described but as yet unpunished, teach the use of cosmetics and various occult practices (1 Enoch 8). The archangels bring this situation to the attention of the Lord (ch. 9), who responds by dispatching various angels to warn Noah of the flood, and to bind and imprison the bad angels, now called Watchers, who are to stay thus incarcerated until the final judgment. Enoch is sent to reprimand the doomed Watchers (ch. 12), who, in turn, ask him to carry a petition back to the Lord of heaven. But Enoch falls asleep and is given a dream vision of further reprimand to carry back to the Watchers. The message is that their petition regarding their offspring, the giants, shall not be honored and that, moreover, from those children of the Watchers and the daughters of men shall issue evil spirits. About those spirits the apocalyptist says:

> [They] afflict, oppress, destroy, attack, do battle, and work destruction on the earth, and cause trouble: they take not food, but nevertheless hunger and thirst, and cause offenses. And these spirits shall rise up against the children of men and against the women, because they have proceeded from them (1 Enoch 16:11ff).

This, then, was one story of the fall of the angels. Note that the fallen angels, or Watchers, are distinguished from demons. Later, in 1 Enoch 65, the evil of which the bad angels (here called the Satans) are accused is that of leaking to mankind the secrets of witchcraft and metallurgy.

The Book of Jubilees (ca. 150 B.C.), a hard-line Pharisaical interpretation of the history of Israel celebrating the primacy of the Law, elaborates an angelology and demonology beyond that of 1 Ënoch. In chapter 10 of Jubilees, we hear more about the evil spirits who emerged from the sons of the Watchers. They are called both evil spirits and demons; they are said to lead astray and to blind the sons of Noah; they are subject to Mastema, also called Satan. In answer to the prayer of Noah, the Lord God commands the good angels to bind them. But at the request of Mastema/Satan, one-tenth are left free to carry out his will against the sons of men. For our purposes, some of the words of the oracle of the angel are worth quoting in full:

> And one of us he commanded that we should teach Noah all their medicines; for he knew that they would not walk in uprightness, nor strive in righteousness. And we did according to all his words: all the malignant evil ones we bound in the place of condemnation and a tenth part of them we left that they might be subject before Satan on the earth. And we explained to Noah all the medicines of their diseases, together with their seductions, how he might heal them with herbs of the earth (Jubilees 10:10–12).

Scholars agree that the version of the fall of the angels found in 1 Enoch and Jubilees takes its inspiration from Genesis 6:1–4, which itself is now recognized to be a fragment of a myth common in the ancient world. The purpose of the biblical author was, to quote Vawter's comment, "not to provide an etiology for a race of giants but rather to continue his representation of man as a creature constantly trying to overstep the boundaries that separate him from God and to usurp the divine prerogatives."[5] Clearly, the later apocalyptic writers have developed this fragment in quite another way for their own purposes.

Another Old Testament text that provided imagery for the fall of Satan was Isaiah 14:12ff. Here Isaiah used the Canaanite myth of Athtar (a god who was identified with the morning star in Canaanite religion; he attempted to take over Baal's position after Baal was temporarily conquered by Mot) and applied it to the arrogant king of Babylon.[6] The further application of this myth to the fall of Satan (helped especially by the Vulgate translation of "morning star" as Lucifer) does not seem to have been Isaiah's intention.

Still another component which becomes important for the world view of Jewish apocalyptic literature is that of the "guardian angels of the nations." These beings seem to be the Canaanite pantheon demoted to serve Yahweh in the administration of universal history. Deuteronomy 32:8f is a key expression of this notion. They become corrupt insofar as the nations become corrupt through idolatry. They are destined for destruction (Is. 24:21ff; 34:2, 4). As heavenly counterparts of the Gentile nations, they are enemies of Israel, but deliverance from their power is out of the hands of the people of God; that battle is fought by the Lord and his archangels.

Nothing, then, in the Old Testament references to satan figures and evil spirits, or in the intertestamental angelology and demonology, or even in the Old Testament seed texts which inspired them (e.g., Gen. 6:1–4; Dt. 32:8f; Is. 14), would seem to support a deliverance ministry.

2. The New Testament writings very much reflect the demonolgy of Jewish apocalyptic,[7] but the New Testament nowhere describes the origin of Satan or demons. When it alludes to the story of the fallen Watchers in Jude 6 and 2 Peter 2:4, it is not done to explain the origins of evil in the world but to evoke a powerful image of divine punishment to reinforce the ethical exhortation that provides the contexts of those passages.

3. In the New Testament picture of the developing Church, we find, as we read through those twenty-seven books, a decreasing emphasis on ministry dealing directly with the demonic. The Synoptic Gospels and Acts, to be sure, insist on the centrality of the exorcism/deliverance ministries of Je-

sus and the disciples (and that will be a major consideration in the second part of this article). But when we move from the Synoptics to John, we find, surprisingly, no narrative or even a summary description in which Jesus is said to drive out demons. In John the conflict with Satan is couched in different terms: Jesus' hour of glory, the death-resurrection, is spoken of as a victory against the evil one, the enemy, the prince of this world. For the Fourth Gospel, the Christ event itself is the definitive and sole act of deliverance.

When we search the letters of Paul (even the Corinthian correspondence, that privileged window upon the intimate details of that community's life), we find no mention of anything that sounds like a deliverance ministry. The only instances of the word *daimonia* in Paul occur at 1 Corinthians 10:20f. He is surely asserting the reality of *daimonia* here, but since he seems to be alluding to Deuteronomy 32:17, the word appears to refer to pagan gods, much as the word *daimonia* is used in Acts 17:18. (We shall discuss his other ways of referring to cosmic evil in the second section; here it is enough to note that the *daimonia* in question are not for him the objects of a deliverance ministry.)

4. The language of the New Testament sometimes blurs the distinction between healing and exorcism. Often it refers to the casting out of demons as a kind of healing, e.g., Matthew 4:24, where Jesus is said to heal (*etherapeusen*) all, including the demonized; Matthew 15:28, where the demonized daughter of the Canaanite woman is said to be healed (*iathē*); Matthew 17:17f, where *theapeuein* is again used of an exorcism; Luke 6:18 and 8:2, the same use of language; Luke 9:42, where *iathē* is used of the demonized lad; and Acts 5:16, which refers to those afflicted with unclean spirits (*etherapeuonto*).

At other times New Testament authors reverse the above process and speak of healing as a kind of exorcism, as, for example, Luke 4:39, where a fever is rebuked as if it were a demon, and Acts 10:38, where Jesus' whole healing ministry is spoken of as going about healing (*iōmenos*) those who were oppressed by the devil. Even the calming of the storm is described in language proper to an exorcism: compare Mark 1:25

and 4:39, where the same Greek words describe Jesus' action (he rebuked—*epetimesen*—both the demon and the wind) and his command ("Be muzzled!"—*Phimōthēti, pephimōsō*); and in both cases the witnesses marvel that the threatening agents (unclean spirits, wind, sea) obey him.

On the one hand, such passages make it difficult to appreciate deliverance/exorcism as a distinct ministry; on the other hand, some of the passages tempt one to think that *all* healing is a kind of deliverance.

5. As regards a distinction between formal and informal exorcism, while we must admit that the expulsion of evil spirits by means of scarves and handkerchiefs that had touched Paul's skin (Acts 19:12) is a method that lacks some of the "formality" of Jesus' commanding the departure of the unclean spirit of the Capernaum demoniac, there is in the New Testament no distinction that appears to anticipate the later distinction between formal and informal exorcism or, to use the contemporary charismatic terms, between exorcism and deliverance.

6. One of the classic biblical passages used to support the deliverance ministry, Ephesians 6:10–17, does not describe a specific ministry of deliverance; rather it uses military metaphors from the Old Testament to describe the whole of Christian life. The devil, the principalities, the powers, the world rulers of this present darkness, and the spiritual hosts of wickedness in the heavenly places are indeed demonic realities for the author (and this will be important for Part II of our discussion), but the imagery of the full armor of God, spelled out in verses 14–17, points to something broader than a deliverance ministry. The weapons of God himself (the breastplate and helmet of Isaiah 59:17) and of the Messiah (portrayed in Isaiah 11:2–5) are said to be transferred to the faithful for use in their spiritual warfare. The next verses, Ephesians 6:18–20, translate the military metaphors of verses 11–17. As Markus Barth puts it in his masterly commentary, "The armed struggle of the Christians consists only of their prayer and their participation in spreading the Gospel of Jesus."[8] The passage describes a struggle with very real forces of evil, but it indicates the ordinary activities of Christian life as the weapons of that struggle.

7. The same is true of another classic passage used to support the deliverance ministry, 1 Peter 5:8f:

> Be sober, be watchful. Your adversary the devil prowls around like a lion seeking someone to devour. Resist him, firm in your faith, knowing that the same experience of suffering is required of your brethren throughout the world.

In the context of this letter, the sufferings in question are those of persecution, not direct diabolic oppression. See 1 Peter 3:13f and 4:12ff where persecution—suffering for being a Christian—is described by another bold image, a "trial by fire." In our passage, language from Psalm 22:14 is used to speak of the persecutors of Christians as doing the devil's work. Accordingly, the resistance to the devil urged in 1 Peter 5:9 is spelled out in 4:12–19 as rejoicing, keeping the commandments, doing good deeds, and entrusting one's life to a faithful Creator. A specific deliverance ministry, therefore, is not the immediate concern of 1 Peter 5:8f.

8. Many other New Testament references to Satan, the demonic, and fallen angels are incidental, or geared to a point other than deliverance itself. I'll mention them briefly.

In the Synoptic tradition, most of the texts where Satan (or the devil) appears do not point to a ministry of deliverance but to more indirect forms of resistance. Jesus meets the temptations in the desert through fidelity to his true messianic call. The implied antidote to the power of Satan described in the interpretation of the sower parable (Mk. 4:15ff) is simply avoiding the distractions of the world, receiving the word deeply, and being fruitful. In the description of the sin of Judas, the contrast between him and Peter implies that repentance, not deliverance, is what is ordinarily required when one abandons the Master. Of the passages mentioning Satan in the Synoptic tradition, only the language of the Beelzebul controversy (Mk. 3:20–30 and par.) and the word of Jesus at Luke 10:18f seem to point toward a deliverance ministry, and we shall discuss these texts in Part II of this article.

The reference to the exorcised man whose last state becomes worse than his first (Mt. 12:43–45; Lk. 11:24ff) surely draws upon the experience of exorcism/deliverance, but it is clear that Matthew means it to be understood as a parable, as he indicates with his words, "Thus shall it be with this wicked generation, too." C. K. Barrett suggests that its meaning, as applied to the ministry of Jesus, is that those who do not take full advantage of the deliverance made available for them by Jesus will find their last state worse than the first. In the Lukan context, the parable seems to apply more to the Christian experience, saying that this is what happens to those who do not "hear the word of God and keep it."[9]

In Acts, none of the full narratives portraying encounters with the satanic or demonic describe a deliverance ministry. The lie of Ananias and Sapphira to the community (Acts 5) is indeed described as a free yielding to Satan, but what the account tells is the story of their punishment, not an instance of deliverance. The Cypriot magus, Elymas bar-Jesus (Acts 13:4–12), is called a son of Satan, but there is no talk of evil spirits in this account, and Paul's response to the man is not an exorcism but a curse.

The Philippian slave girl with the soothsaying spirit, Python (Acts 16:16–18), is a unique case. As Haenchen comments, "Luke neither considered the slave girl sick nor did the thought of help enter as a motive for the act."[10] This is the only full narrative of exorcism in Acts and it cannot be seen as an act of ministry. Otherwise Paul would not have waited "many days." As Luke tells it, Paul is mainly delivering himself of an annoyance.

The story about the sons of the high priest Sceva (Acts 19:14–16) shows them trying to exorcise in the name of Jesus, and failing. No exorcism is in fact performed here. The point is the superiority of the power of the name of Jesus in the ministry of a Christian.

Nor do any of the Pauline references to Satan point directly to a deliverance/exorcism ministry. In Romans 16:20, he assures his readers that if they obey, do good, and avoid evil, then the God of peace will crush Satan under their feet. In 1

Corinthians 5:5, "I hand him [the incestuous man] over to Satan" seems to be a way of referring to excommunication, the realm of Satan being the world outside of Christian community (cf. 1 Tim. 1:20).

In the spirit of Ephesians 4:26f (don't give an opportunity to the devil through unresolved anger), 1 Corinthians 7:5 (don't let lack of sexual self-control provide an occasion for Satan's temptation) and 2 Corinthians 2:11 (forgiveness in the community is a defense against Satan's designs) are both texts which speak of the ordinary dynamics of Christian life as tools against Satan. More clearly metaphorical references to Satan are 2 Corinthians 11:14 (false apostles are like Satan disguising himself as an angel of light) and 2 Corinthians 12:7 (where a persecution or physical malady hindering Paul's mission is described under two images—a thorn for the flesh and a messenger of Satan). The reference to Satan blocking Paul's projected visits back to Thessalonica (1 Thes. 2:18) may also refer to physical sickness.[11] None of the Pauline references to Satan, then, occur in context with a deliverance/exorcism approach to evil.

9. The New Testament Book of Revelation, with all its focus on the conquest of Satan, is nevertheless not a book about demonic deliverance; rather it is a book about the battle between the Church and the forces of evil embodied in the Roman empire. The deliverance is the cosmic deliverance worked by the Lord of history; the strategy advocated for the people of God is simply religious fidelity and, on the political level, passive resistance.[12] The ministry of deliverance nowhere appears as a tool against the power of Satan and his beast.[13]

10. Finally, to name last what is usually mentioned first in this discussion, in the culture of first-century Palestine much of what we would today diagnose as mental illness was then attributed to demonic possession.[14]

All of the above, of course, is one-sided and incomplete. To fill out the picture, we turn now to the biblical data which seem at least to be open to the contemporary deliverance ministry.

PART II: BIBLICAL DATA WHICH APPEAR TO SUPPORT THE CONTEMPORARY MINISTRY OF DELIVERANCE

1. The devil and his kingdom are central to Jesus' understanding of his ministry. That this ministry included exorcism "belongs to the base-rock historicity of the Gospels."[15] The central saying of Jesus in this matter is Matthew 12:28/Luke 11:20: "But if it is by the Spirit of God ('finger of God' in Luke) that I cast out demons, then the kingdom of God has come upon you." Whether the original phrase was "Spirit of God" or "finger of God," the clear import is that Jesus understands his exorcisms as coming from the power of God. This saying suggests several things about Jesus' self-understanding: "Here coming to clear expression is Jesus' consciousness of spiritual power, the visible evidence of the power of God flowing through him to overcome other superhuman power, evil power, to restore and make whole."[17] Further, this exorcism ministry is evidence that the longed-for kingdom of God has already come upon his hearers. The last days are already present. Whatever may be the source of the power of exorcism in other Jews (presumably it is divine), the force at work in Jesus is distinct in that it is the eschatological Spirit of God.[18]

In Mark's version of Jesus' response to the scribes' charge that he casts out demons by Beelzebul, Jesus answers in what Mark calls parables (3:23–27)—the images of the house divided, the kingdom divided, Satan divided, and the strong man overcome by the stronger one. There is no doubt that Jesus understands his exorcisms as moments in a battle against the power of Satan. The "Q" version of this account in Matthew and Luke reinforces this perception: "If Satan is divided against himself, how will his kingdom stand?" (Lk. 11:18; par. Mt. 12:26). The reign of God, which Jesus preaches and acts out (with healing and exorcism), is an invasion of far more than a vacuum; it confronts nothing less than another reign.

2. Jesus' perspective in this matter is also that of the Synoptic evangelists.

From beginning to end, Mark presents the story of Jesus as a confrontation with the satanic and demonic. After John the Baptist announces Jesus as the one who will baptize in the Holy Spirit *(en pneumati hagiō*—1:8), the Spirit comes upon Jesus at the Jordan (1:10). The same Spirit then drives him into the desert to be tested *(peirazomenos)* by Satan. Ten verses later, we see Jesus confronted by a man with an unclean spirit *(en pneumati akathartō*—1:23; cf. parallel phrase, *en pneumati hagiō*, in 1:8). This sample of healing (1:21–34) also ends with the driving out of demons.

A one-line summary of a Galilean preaching tour emphasizes his exorcism ministry: "And he went throughout all Galilee, preaching in their synagogues and casting out demons" (1:39). This is underscored in the summary of 3:11f. When the evangelist tells of the choosing of the Twelve, he describes the purpose as "to be with him [Jesus] and to be sent out to preach and have authority to cast out demons" (3:14f). The first extended speech of Jesus in Mark consists in the parables describing his exorcisms as a victory over Satan's rule (3:23–30). The parable of the sower which follows receives, at 4:15, the interpretation that Satan is the first threat to the sown word. The narrative of the stilling of the storm (4:35–41) is told in exorcism language echoing 1:23–28. There follows the extended account of the exorcism of the Gerasene demoniac (5:1–20). The missionary charge to the Twelve underscores their power over unclean spirits (6:7, 13). Two more exorcism narratives ensue as the Gospel unfolds—the cure at a distance of the Syro-Phoenician woman's demonized daughter (7:24–39) and the deliverance of the boy with a dumb spirit (9:14–29). In 9:38–40, this ministry is even extended to include an exorcist who does not follow the Twelve, inasmuch as "he who is not against us is with us." When Peter balks at the note of suffering which Jesus attaches to his messiahship, the Lord rebukes him for joining forces with the enemy, "Get behind me, Satan!" (8:33).

As the second half of the Gospel unfolds, the scribes' and Pharisees' mounting opposition to Jesus is described with the word first used of Satan's testing of Jesus in the desert *(peira-*

zein, to test or tempt, used at 8:11, 10:2, and 12:15). This battle climaxes at the cross, in the midst of demonic mockery, darkness, and dereliction.[19]

To remove the thread of the exorcism ministries of Jesus and the disciples would be to destroy the fabric of Mark's account. Moreover, it would not be linguistically or exegetically honest to take literally language of the New Testament about a Holy Spirit *(pneuma hagion)* and to psychologize the language referring to an unclean spirit *(pneuma akatharta)*.

Matthew transmits intact this aspect of Mark's account. As in Mark, two summaries of Jesus' ministry mention exorcism (Mt. 4:24, par. Mk. 1:39; Mt. 8:16, par. Mk. 1:32), and the sending of the Twelve twice mentions exorcism along with healing (Mt. 10:1, 8). Matthew heightens the satanic nature of Simon Peter's resistance to messianic suffering by introducing the parallel command, "Begone, Satan" into his account of the testing in the desert (4:10). If he omits the story of the demoniac in Capernaum and the demonic confessions of Mk. 1:34 and 3:11, he twice introduces a Q tradition about the exorcism of a dumb demoniac (9:32; 12:22). Further, Matthew's version of the Lord's Prayer contains, at 6:13, the petition, "but deliver us *apo tou ponērou,* " which, taken as a neuter form, is translated "from evil," and, as a masculine form, "from the evil one." Matthew's use of the word elsewhere favors the translation "from the evil one."[20]

Luke, too, passes on the Markan picture of the exorcism/ deliverance ministries of Jesus and the disciples. Indeed, his version heightens that demonic element in some striking ways. Luke's setting of the Great Discourse (6:17ff) involves healing and demonic deliverance. His summary of Jesus' activity introducing the Lord's response to the question of the Baptist's embassy (7:21) refers to exorcisms in a way that seems to allude to the freeing of captives announced at 4:18 (Is. 61). The women of Jesus' entourage are described, at 8:2, as persons "who had been cured of evil spirits and maladies," including Mary Magdalene, "from whom seven demons had gone out." In response to the Pharisees' warning that Herod wants to kill him, Jesus'

own word summarizes his ministry in this way: "Go tell that
fox, 'Today and tomorrow I cast out demons and perform
cures and on the third day my purpose is accomplished' "
(13:32). Finally, the understanding that the passion of the Lord
is a climactic expression of this confrontation surfaces at 22:53,
". . . this is your hour and the power of darkness (*hē exousia tou
skototus*)."

In some respects, Luke's way of describing the ministries
of Jesus and the Church as a confrontation with Satan is even
broader than Mark's. For example, whereas Jesus' charge to
the seventy-two is phrased entirely in terms of healing (10:9),
their report of success and Jesus' response to that report is entirely in terms of exorcism, the fall of Satan, and their authority
over the "power of the enemy" (10:17–20).

This broad portrayal of Jesus and his people vs. Satan is
even more pronounced in two key texts in Luke's second volume, the Book of Acts. The summary of Jesus' healing ministry
in Peter's speech at 10:38 describes this activity as "healing all
who were oppressed by the devil." Again, the words in Paul's
speech before Agrippa describe the process of Christian conversion as turning from the power of Satan (*apo . . . tēs exousias
tou Satana*) to God" (Acts 26:18).

3. When we look to the Bible for a mandate to extend Jesus' exorcism/deliverance ministry, perhaps the strongest support is to be found in the very structure of the narrative in
Luke/Acts. For one of the purposes of the author in writing
this two-volume work seems to have been to demonstrate how
the story of the Church is in continuity with the story of Jesus.
What God the Father began in the power of the Spirit through
the ministry of Jesus, he continues through the same Spirit in
the name of Jesus through the ministry of the Church. That
this understanding of the Church's ministry includes an extension of Jesus' direct confrontation of the demonic is asserted,
sparsely but firmly, in Luke 9:1 and 10:18–20, and in Acts 5:16,
8:7, 19:12, and 26:18.

4. In the Fourth Gospel, as we saw earlier, John chooses to
focus the whole confrontation with "the ruler of this world" in

the "hour" of Jesus' death/resurrection. No exorcism narrative, nor even a summary reference thereto, occurs in this Gospel. Judas' betrayal is underscored as collusion with the devil at 6:70 and 13:2, 27. And for rejecting him, Jesus' enemies are called children of the devil—a "murderer from the beginning" and "the father of lies." As Jesus' "hour" approaches, the "ruler of this world shall now be cast out" (12:31), "is coming" (14:30), and "is judged" (16:11). At 17:15, Jesus prays that his Father will keep his disciples "from the evil one." This Johannine understanding of the whole "Christ event" as victorious over Satan is caught in a single verse in 1 John 3:8: "The Son of God revealed himself to destroy the devil's works." That the final skirmishes of that victory are not over is evident in 1 John 5:19, ". . . the whole world is in the power of the evil one." Raymond Brown's comment on this is worth quoting: "Perhaps we can say that the victorious hour of Jesus constitutes a victory over Satan in principle; yet the working out of this victory in time and place is the gradual work of believing Christians."[21] Therefore, although the fourth evangelist fails to mention an exorcism/deliverance ministry as one of the means for working out the victory of Christ, it is clear that he sees Christian life as worked out in tension with "the evil one" and his "world." And since elaborating upon the details of ministry is clearly not one of the intents of the Fourth Gospel, we may presume that its vision is open to a variety of means for implementing that victory of the risen Lord.

5. As for the New Testament literature known as the Pauline corpus, we noted in the first section that Paul nowhere shows himself preoccupied with demonic powers or an exorcism/deliverance ministry. But we must still take seriously what he presumes and celebrates regarding the victory of God in Christ over all the evil forces in the cosmos. These "principalities and powers" appear to belong to that apocalyptic tradition, mentioned in Part I, of the corrupted guardian angels of the nations. While Paul does not expatiate upon the origins of these powers, they are clearly very real components of reality for him. Among them we must include, Caird suggests, the

"rulers of this age" mentioned in 1 Corinthians 2:6–8 (cf. 15:24):

> Behind Pilate, Herod and Caiaphas, behind the Roman and Jewish religions of which these men were earthly representatives, Paul discerned the existence of angelic rulers who shared with their human agents the responsibility for the crucifixion. . . . Paul's principalities and powers included the powers of state; though we shall find that he greatly enlarged the conception of the powers so as to include the Jewish religion, and indeed the whole natural order, under the demonic reign which the Jews had seen at work in the Gentile world.[22]

At the parousia, the Lord will destroy these enemies (1 Cor. 15:24).

In Colossians, the principalities are said to be under Christ (2:10), for they were among the things created through and for him (1:16). But, what is more important, they were totally disarmed at the crucifixion by the triumph of God in the person of Christ (2:15).

In Ephesians, as in the Fourth Gospel, we hear of a victory definitively won, yet not fully implemented. The risen Lord has been seated high above every principality, power, virtue, and domination and every name that can be given in this age or the next (1:21). Yet the author, five verses later, can speak of the devil as "the prince of the air, that spirit who is even now at work among the rebellious" (2:2). This tension is expressed most vividly in the famous verse, 6:12: "Our battle is not against blood and flesh but against the principalities and powers, the rulers of this world of darkness, the evil spirits in the regions above." The battle against these forces is quite real. The weapons, as we noted in Part I, are the undramatic ones of faithfully and lovingly living out our relationships within the Christian community (Eph. 4:1–6:9). What, then, does Ephesians say to support the contemporary deliverance ministry? Simply that the superhuman forces of evil are still very real and that the battle is not yet over.

Paul seems to have the same thing in mind when in Gala-
tians 4:3, 9 and Colossians 2:8, 20, he speaks of the "elemental
[spirits] of the world" (*stoicheia tou kosmou*).[23] It appears to be
a handy piece of contemporary jargon for Paul to use to refer
to both the demonic forces of Jewish legalism and cosmic
forces behind the pagan astrological fatalism.[24]

Perhaps the best text to illustrate Paul's view of these realities is Romans 8:38f:

> For I am certain that neither death nor life, neither angels
> nor principalities, neither the present nor the future, nor
> powers, neither height nor depth [*hypsōma* and *bathos* are
> astronomical technical terms for the space above and the
> space below the horizon] nor any other creature will be able
> to separate us from the love of God that comes to us in
> Christ Jesus, our Lord.

There is, then, no threatening reality in the universe (biological, spiritual, chronological, spatial) of which Jesus Christ is not
Lord. The definitive deliverance has been won. The continued
defense against their threat is, according to Romans, walking
in the Spirit and living the life of the body of Christ. And what
is the implication regarding the contemporary deliverance? To
the extent that any such practice seems warranted, we are to
see it simply as the implementation of a victory already won.
As G. B. Caird observes,

> . . . the concept of world powers reaches into every depart-
> ment of Paul's theology and . . . it cannot be dismissed as a
> survival of primitive superstition. Paul is using mythological
> language, but his language has a rational content of thought;
> he is working with ideas which have had a long history, but
> he is describing spiritual realities with which he and his fel-
> low Christians have personal acquaintance.

And if the "classic" deliverance passages of 1 Peter 5 and
Ephesians 6 are not in fact specifically about deliverance but
about Christian life, they do picture that ordinary Christian existence as pitched against evil forces which are more than hu-

man, and they surely can be applied to those occasions when the experience of the demonic seems to be encountered directly and appears to call for a direct confrontation in the name of Jesus.

6. As for the cultural fact that first-century Palestine attributed to the demonic many pathologies that medical science would today diagnose otherwise, two observations should be made.

First, although, as we saw in Part I, many New Testament passages treat healing and exorcism as the same thing, a good number of other passages clearly distinguish between persons who are demonized and those who are sick in other ways. For example, Mark shows Jesus heal one deaf and mute man with an imposition of hands, spittle and a command (7:33ff) and another deaf and mute person with exorcism.[25] This distinction also surfaces in some of the summary lists (e.g., Mk. 1:32, 34, 39; Mt. 4:24; 8:16; 10:1, 8; Lk. 6:18; 13:32; Acts 5:16; 8:7).

Second, it must be acknowledged that our own late twentieth-century world view regarding man's place in nature no more deserves canonization than that of first-century Palestine. We hear staff members of psychiatric hospitals admit that few of their patients are being cured. On the other hand, many persons in the healing prayer and deliverance ministries are finding often that persons whom conventional psychotherapy has not helped are returned to mental health through prayer for inner healing and deliverance. Some have been led to observe that perhaps many cases which modern medicine diagnoses as purely psychological are in fact at least partially demonic. (This is not even to mention the third possibility suggested by the work of English psychiatrist Dr. Kenneth McCall—ancestral bondage.) It may well be, as Fr. Francis Martin suggested in a 1977 talk at Steubenville, that our anthropology is sadly out of joint. It is not impossible that the world view shared by the educated of the North Atlantic community is less developed than that of first-century Palestine, or, for that matter, twentieth-century Nigeria.[26]

7. The fact that New Testament angelology, demonology, and diabology are taken over from the highly imaginative, var-

iegated and exotic literature of Jewish apocalyptic need not, in itself, deter us from ascribing reality to the powers of evil thus named. To do this would be to yield to what in the discipline of history is called the genetic fallacy—to look to its earliest stages for the truth of a concept.[27] The fact that some of the Hebrew psalms are discovered to be reworked Canaanite hymns does not detract from their value for Jewish or Christian prayer. Neither should the exotic origins of Christian names and notions for the powers of evil discourage us from acknowledging the realities and experiences they label.

CONCLUSIONS

Theories of the origin and structure of the demonic world do not exist in the canonical Christian Scriptures. The existence and activity of the devil and his demons is, however, presupposed. What the New Testament writers stoutly affirm is the victory of the crucified and risen Lord Jesus over all these forces.

The closest we come to biblical support for the contemporary ministry of deliverance is the Synoptic portrayal of Jesus commissioning the disciples to carry on his work of preaching, healing and exorcising. This is presented most forcefully in Luke/Acts, where the story of the Church is clearly meant to be an extension of the story of Jesus.

The New Testament failure to distinguish between exorcism and deliverance need be no more disconcerting than the New Testament failure to distinguish between overseers and elders.

Whatever the reality of Satan and the demonic, the overwhelming teaching of the New Testament epistles (even Ephesians 6 and 1 Peter 5) is that the ordinary way of battling the demonic is by walking in the Spirit, showing forgiveness, serving one another—in short, by living the Christian life. This fact provides a healthy warning to keep deliverance in its subsidiary role.[28]

Finally, to end with a new thought, the Book of Revelation, with its identification of the demonic with idolized social structures, might prompt us to ask what kind of social deliverance might be appropriate with regard to the structures of militarism and greed, which in our day seem to have taken on a life of their own.[29]

NOTES

1. For this discussion of the Old Testament material, I am especially indebted to G. B. Caird, *Principalities and Powers* (Oxford: Clarendon, 1956); Theodore H. Gaster, the articles "Demon, Demonolgy" and "Satan," in *The Interpreter's Dictionary of the Bible* (New York: Abingdon Press, 1962–76), Vols. 1–4, and supplementary volume; D. S. Russell, *The Method and Message of Jewish Apocalyptic* (Philadelphia: Westminster Press, 1964), pp. 235–62; and Jeffrey B. Russell, *The Devil: Perceptions of Evil from Antiquity to Primitive Christianity* (New York: New American Library, 1977), pp. 174–260.

2. For the evolution or devolution of this celestial courtier into the prince of demons and his identification with the serpent of Eden we must wait for the later developments of intertestamental Jewish apocalyptic literature.

3. The most convenient English language edition of these writings is still that of R. H. Charles, *The Apocrypha and Pseudepigrapha of the Old Testament in English: Vol. II, Pseudepigrapha* (Oxford: Clarendon Press, 1913).

4. In ch. 69, one of the fallen, Penemue, is accused in this manner: ". . . he instructed mankind in writing with ink and paper, and thereby many sinned from eternity to eternity and until this day. For men were not created for such a purpose, to give confirmation to their good faith with pen and ink."

5. Bruce Vawter, *On Genesis: A New Reading* (Garden City, New York: Doubleday and Co., 1977), p. 111. Vawter also thinks that, in the mind of the tenth-century author, the judgment of God may well be aimed at the current practice of ritual marriage or sacred prostitution (p. 112).

6. A. Y. Collins, *The Combat Myth in the Book of Revelation* (Missoula, Mont.: Scholars Press, 1976), pp. 81ff. For a representative scholarly commentary on this passage in Isaiah, see Otto Kaiser, *Isaiah 13–39* (Philadelphia: Westminster Press, 1974), pp. 38–41.

7. Charles himself provides a convenient summary of similarities between the New Testament and Jubilees on p. 10 and between the New Testament and 1 Enoch on p. 185.

8. Markus Barth, *Ephesians: Translation and Commentary; Anchor Bible* (Garden City, New York: Doubleday & Co., 1974), p. 786.

9. C. K. Barrett, *The Holy Spirit and the Gospel Tradition* (London: SPCK, 1947, 1970), pp. 64f.

10. Ernst Haenchen, *The Acts of the Apostles: A Commentary* (Philadelphia: Westminster Press, 1971), p. 475. Haenchen also observes: "The story shows the reader two things: first, that the truth of the Gospel has been confirmed also by the supernation acknowledgement of the spirit-world, and second, that Paul through the exorcism in the name of Jesus is plainly superior to the spirits" (p. 502).

11. Caird, p. 75.

12. Adela Y. Collins, "The Political Perspectives of the Revelation to John," *Journal of Biblical Literature*, 92 (1977), pp. 241–56.

13. For two representative interpretations of Revelation, one quite simple and popular and the other a more technical study, see John Randall, *The Book of Revelation: What Does It Really Say?* (Locust Valley, N.Y.: Living Flame Press, 1976) and A. Y. Collins, *The Combat Myth in the Book of Revelation* (Missoula, Montana: Scholars Press, 1976).

14. See, for example, the discussion of this in J. Jeremias, *New Testament Theology: The Proclamation of Jesus* (New York: Charles Scribner's Sons, 1971), pp. 93f. See, too, S.V. McCashland, *By the Finger of God* (New York: Macmillan Co., 1951).

15. James D. G. Dunn, *Jesus and the Spirit* (Philadelphia: Westminster Press, 1975), p. 94.

16. "It seems far more likely that Luke altered 'Spirit' to 'finger' to fit his new Exodus theme than it does that Matthew changes 'finger' to 'Spirit,' inasmuch as he seems bent on curbing pneumatic enthusiasts in his community and also would appreciate how the 'finger of God' reference would reinforce his New Moses theme" (Dunn, pp. 44f).

17. Dunn, p. 47.

18. "The logic here is not that the endtime is here because he is here (although later Christians will surely understand it that way) but that the eschatological kingdom was present for Jesus only because the eschatological Spirit was present in and through him" (Dunn, p. 48).

19. Frederick W. Danker, "The Demonic Secret in Mark: A Re-

examination of the Cry of Dereliction (15:34)," *Zeitschrift für die neutestamentliche Wissenschaft,* 61 (1970), pp. 48–69.

20. John Reumann, *Jesus in the Church's Gospels* (Philadelphia: Fortress Press, 1968), p. 96.

21. R. Brown, *The Gospel According to John: Anchor Bible* (Garden City, New York: Doubleday & Co.), p. 477.

22. Caird, pp. 16f.

23. See Eduard Lohse, *Colossians and Philemon* (Philadelphia: Fortress, 1971), pp. 96ff for a good discussion of the background of this phrase.

24. Caird, pp. 47ff.

25. Adolf Rodewyk notes this in *Possessed by Satan* (Garden City, New York: Doubleday & Co., 1975), pp. 26f.

26. See Francis MacNutt, O.P., "Report from Nigeria," *New Covenant* (May 1975), pp. 8–12.

27. J. B. Russell, *The Devil,* p. 174.

28. Matthew 7:21f should be a salutary reminder of this fact.

29. Much of the recent work of Daniel Berrigan has gone in this direction. See, too, William Stringfellow, *An Ethic for Christians and Other Aliens in a Strange Land* (Waco, Texas: Word Books, 1973).

3
Deliverance From Evil: Private Exorcism

by Robert Faricy, S.J.

When talk in a group of priests turns, as it does once in a great while, to the devil or to matters diabolical, I find myself edified by the innocence of those priests who no longer give credence to the devil's existence, holding him and all evil spirits to be holdovers from medieval times, mere popular symbols of evil in the world. Priests who have had so little experience of evil do edify me; in their goodness and in the tranquillity of their calm ecclesial lives they have surely met sin and evil, but not to the extent of recognizing a personal evil force at the heart of the mystery of iniquity. I thank God for goodness.

On the other hand, the naiveté of priests and other pastoral workers who ignore the action of the devil can be dangerous. They go to battle unarmed and not knowing even the existence of the enemy. They can get hurt, and those around them whom they should protect can get hurt too. "We are not contending against flesh and blood, but against the principalities, against the powers, against the world rulers of this present darkness, against the spiritual hosts of wickedness."[1] So let us, following Paul's advice, "put on the whole armor of God" that we "may be able to stand against the wiles of the devil."[2]

This armor consists of faith, hope, love, truth and righteousness, the Gospel of peace, and the word of God. It consists also of the common-sense pastoral practice of the Roman Catholic tradition. An important element of that tradition, one we have almost lost sight of, is private simple exorcism. As a standard pastoral tool, it has no substitute. Since many pastoral workers seem unfamiliar with it, it seems a good idea to describe it enough so that people can use it more.

EVIL SPIRITS EXIST

Theology, and therefore seminary training, has notoriously neglected the significance—the meaning for us today—of the exorcisms in the New Testament. Because the Holy Spirit is with Jesus in power, he casts out evil spirits, and his many exorcisms herald the presence of the kingdom of God. "But if it is through the Spirit of God that I cast devils out, then know that the kingdom of God has overtaken you."[3] Moreover, Jesus teaches his disciples to exorcise demons.

If theology has neglected the existence of Satan, of evil spirits, of personalized forces of evil in the world, even in the face of overwhelming biblical data, Church teaching, on the other hand, has regularly referred to the existence of the devil and of devils.[4] In 1972, Pope Paul VI spoke clearly: "Evil is not merely a lack of something, but an effective agent, a living spiritual being, perverted and perverting, a terrible reality, mysterious and frightening. . . . We know that this dark and disturbing spirit really exists and that he still acts with treacherous cunning; he is the secret enemy that sows errors and misfortunes in human history. . . . It is not a question of one devil but of many. . . . This question of the devil and the influence he can exert on individual persons as well as on communities, whole societies, and events is a very important chapter of Catholic doctrine."[5]

Evil spirits, then, have an important if obscure role in the world. The "prince of this world" exercises what power he has chiefly through his action on individual persons. "He is the tempter, the seducer, the perfidious counselor, the agitator of evil enterprises; he fools, he blinds, he corrupts . . . murder, hatred, and lies are his works; he is 'the father' of assassins and of those who do not love their brothers and sisters."[6]

With regard to diabolical influence on individual persons, theologians distinguish between possession, oppression, and temptation.[7] The signs of possible possession are given by the Roman Ritual in the section on exorcisms: the ability to speak or understand a previously unlearned language, to see future or distant things, extraordinarily great strength—especially when these signs are found together.[8] Cases of possession seem extremely rare. Father de Tonquédec, S.J., official exorcist for the Paris archdiocese, said after twenty years of practice that he had never encountered even one.[9]

Oppression occurs when a demon or demons exercise some control over a person, torment him, sometimes provide him with extraordinary powers, but do not deprive him entirely or almost entirely of free choice. Grave cases of oppression, which are rare, can seem almost like posession. Less serious oppression, which is common enough, can account for the apparently compulsive element in some cases of habitual sin such as hatred or anger or resentment or gluttony or lust. Oppression is also at least a partial explanation sometimes, though certainly not always or most often, of habitual fear, sadness, irrational guilt feelings, anguish, and scrupulosity. When temptations are sudden, strong, persistent, and hard to account for by natural means, we can conclude that there is a special intervention on the part of the devil; in such cases, we call this intervention "oppression."[10]

Temptations can come from the world, the flesh, or the devil (i.e., from evil spirits). Temptations that derive wholly or partly from the action of evil spirits can come and go in a transitory way, or they can persist in an aggravating and continuous manner in a way that can hardly be distinguished from oppression. Often one can identify or at least guess at the diabolical origin (total or partial) of a temptation by a certain manifest compulsion coupled with a certain strangeness of irrationality or even weirdness.

But, after all, has not the modern science of psychology and psychiatry shown us the psychological origins of much behavior that used to be considered diabolical in origin? Even granted the existence of the devil, and if we grant that he can influence human behavior, how do you know what comes from mental illness or neurotic tendencies and what comes from demonic influence? Do we not risk diagnosing mental illness as, say, diabolical oppression, and thus doing more harm than good?

Mental illness and the influence of evil spirits are two different things, and we want to avoid reducing all diabolical influence to mental illness, or reducing mental illness to the work of the devil. And, in practice, it is difficult and sometimes impossible to know the exact origins of such problems. The pastoral response is, of course, to try whatever seems appropriate under the circumstances, and to follow up whatever approach seems to be working. This applies to psychological therapy, to psychiatric treatment, and to exorcism.

AUTHORITY OVER EVIL SPIRITS

The fact that the devil and his minions exist should be seen in the light of the victory of Jesus' resurrection. Christ's triumph over evil, not only during his public ministry but especially in his resurrection, helps us to avoid any kind of Manichaean dualism regarding God and the devil. God wins. The devil has been beaten. As Christians, we share in Christ's victory over the powers of darkness, and because we are his, members of his body, sharing through grace in his victory, we have authority over evil spirits.

Jesus has given us this authority to use. And this authority over the devil and over all evil spirits, the authority that Jesus has given to his Church and to every Christian, holds its power from him who has given it. So it is not necessary to somehow embellish the authority of Jesus—which he gives to us—with shouting or with efforts to converse in some way with evil spirits. This authority is powerful enough to stand on its own, to be used calmly and quietly and briefly.

In the Protestant Pentecostal tradition, Christian authority over evil spirits is often used dramatically and sometimes in a way that seems theatrical. Some of this style can still be found here and there in neo-pentecostalism and even in the Catholic charismatic renewal. In pagan religions, particularly in animist religions, the drama takes on great theatricality. I have witnessed an attempted exorcism by a Ugandan witch doctor, complete with chants, shouts, and the beating of drums; the idea, I believe, was to frighten the evil spirits away. The Catholic tradition, on the other hand, has always observed a certain moderation of style which derives not from some sense of good taste but from faith, buttressed by experience, in the power of the name of Jesus. There is no need to embellish the authority Jesus gives us, but only to use it firmly and with faith in him.

REBUKING THE DEVIL

The most common way that evil spirits attack human beings is by temptation. Not all temptations, obviously, come from the devil, but some do. In getting rid of temptations that seem to or that might at least partly come from the devil, we can use the advice of Ignatius Loyola in his "Rules for the Discernment of Spirits" in his manual of *Spiritual Exercises.*

Throughout the *Exercises,* Ignatius refers to the devil as "the enemy of human nature." He clearly had no illusions about the devil and his minions, and we know that his "rules" for dealing with evil spirits find their basis in Ignatius' own experience as well as in the Church's pastoral tradition. That he did, in fact, perform exorcisms is commemorated in an old painting hanging in the hall just outside his rooms in the Jesuit theologate in Rome; it shows Ignatius exorcising a person from whose mouth issue three or four tiny black stick figures, going up into the air. The ingenuous quality of the painting contrasts with Ignatius' own hard-headed realism in dealing with the devil.

The "enemy of human nature," Ignatius teaches, acts like a military chief: "He prowls around and explores on all sides all our virtues, theological, cardinal, and moral, and where he finds us weakest . . . there he makes his attack, and strives to take us by storm."[11] We might expect to be tempted at our weak points.

Again, writes Ignatius, the devil "acts like a false lover, inasmuch as he wishes to remain hidden and undiscovered; for as this false man . . . paying court to the daughter of some honest father or the wife of some honest man, wishes his conversations and insinuations to be kept secret," so the devil "is very displeased when they [his wiles and deceits] are discovered to a good confessor or some other spiritual person who knows his frauds and malice."[12]

Most importantly for our purpose here, Ignatius describes the devil as acting "like a woman, inasmuch as he is weak in spite of himself, but strong in will." Just as a woman backs down when quarreling with a man if the man shows himself firm and strong, but acts ferociously if the man behaves in a weak way, so too the devil runs when we face him fearlessly and becomes ferocious if we act fearfully.[13] Whatever one thinks of Ignatius' evaluation of a quarreling woman, he did understand the devil, and his advice is practical.

The traditional Catholic practice of "rebuking the devil" holds today as valid and as useful as ever. One prays briefly, asking the Lord or his mother for help, and one simply addresses a command to whatever evil spirit or spirits might be present—for example: "Leave me immediately in Jesus' name," or "Spirit of fear, leave me immediately in Jesus' name," or "Spirit of anger (or of lust, or whatever), go now in Jesus' name and never come back," or a similar formula.

The Lord has given Christians authority over evil spirits. It works. We should take that authority and use it to defend ourselves against temptations that come from the devil.

Let me give one example. A businessman asked my advice; he had been falling into serious sins of a perverted sexual nature, and felt very weak as well as ashamed of himself. He asked how he could avoid these sins. The element of compulsion as well as a certain strangeness about the sins, together with the fact that the man had lost so much self-esteem and hated himself (always a goal of the devil), led me to suggest that perhaps he was tempted by the devil. I suggested that the next time he felt tempted he should take authority and command the devil to leave him in Jesus' name. He did, and he had no more trouble from that time on.

SOLEMN EXORCISM

Catholic theology, at least from the time of St. Alphonsus Liguori and probably before, distinguishes between exorcism that is solemn and exorcism that is private. Moral theology manuals right down to recent times formulate this distinction clearly because of its pastoral implications.[14]

The term "solemn" refers to the fact that a solemn exorcism follows a specific liturgical rite and is an official, and therefore in some sense "public," act of the Church, performed by officially delegated ministers of the Church, in the name of the Church.

Solemn exorcism can be performed only by priests who have explicit jurisdiction from the bishop of the particular locality. It is to be used for cases of possession.[15]

PRIVATE EXORCISM

What is a private exorcism?[16] When is it used? Who can do it? How do you do it?

1. What is it? The word "private" means that there is no liturgical rite or particular formula to follow, and that the minister acts in his own name, not in the name of the Church nor with a specific and official delegation or mission from Church authorities.

A private exorcism, then, is an informal act which consists essentially of a command given in the name of Jesus to any evil spirit or evil spirits to leave in the name of Jesus. "Rebuking the devil" can be understood as a kind of private exorcism that one does for oneself.

2. When is it used? In cases of temptation and oppression—that is, whenever one has reason to suspect the activity of evil spirits, and where the activity falls short of possession.

3. Who can perform a private exorcism? Anyone—lay persons as well as priests. In the Appendix, Rev. James McManus, C.Ss.R., quotes the various dogmatic theologians who have stated through the centuries that private exorcism is the minis-

try of all the faithful, both men and women, and can be prayed without special permission of the bishop. A priest, however, all other things equal, would seem to have greater authority, in virtue of his orders, than an unordained person. Also, there exists a charism of exorcism; this charism consists in a greater than usual authority over evil spirits, and it appears not restricted to the clergy. Some priests seem to have this charism to various degrees, as do some lay persons.

4. How does one perform a private exorcism? It depends on the situation. In any case, the exorcism itself is not a prayer but a command directed to any evil spirit in Jesus' name. The command might be one such as, "Evil spirit, leave in the name of Jesus," or something similar. This command should be preceded by a prayer of praise and by a prayer for protection from harm, and followed by a prayer for grace for the person freed. Thus the basic formula is:

(a) Prayer of praise and prayer for protection.

(b) Command addressed to any evil spirit or spirits to leave in Jesus' name.

(c) Prayer to the Holy Spirit for grace for the person being prayed for.

Two very important points:

(a) Ordinarily *the exorcism is done silently.* In almost every case, a minor or informal exorcism should take place without a word being said aloud. The person being prayed for, then, usually will not know that an exorcism has taken place.

(b) It is much better *not to speak of the probable presence of evil spirits,* except sometimes in those cases where the person himself brings it up. That is, if the person feels and talks about some diabolical presence, and if it seems that there is truth in what he feels and says, then one might ask a few questions and make the command of exorcism aloud. Otherwise, silence seems much better.

The most common situation, then, is this: I find myself praying, alone or with others, with someone who has asked for prayers. The presence of one or more evil spirits seems to me probable; I have some reason to think that the devil is acting as the cause, or a partial cause, of this person's problems. Without saying anything to anyone, I pray silently praising God, I pray for the protection from any evil spirits for all present, I command all evil spirits to leave in Jesus' name—silently and with authority—and I pray that the person be filled anew with the Spirit of Jesus—all in silence.

It can be upsetting and even harmful to tell people that they have, or might have, evil spirits, or that they might somehow be under some kind of diabolical influence. To suggest this seems to me highly irresponsible.

On the other hand, if such persons *say* they think they are acting to some degree under the influence of the devil, then the matter might be talked about briefly and with great reserve. However, some who suspect the presence of demons in their lives are mistaken completely, so considerable discernment should be used.

5. The sacrament of penance is a privileged situation for silent private exorcism. From St. Alphonsus Liguori down to recent manuals of moral theology, the practice is recommended to confessors who suspect the presence of some demonic activity.[17]

For example, if a penitent remains completely unrepentant, or seems very hard of heart, the confessor can perform an informal exorcism silently, without saying anything about it to the penitent. Or, if the penitent appears to be acting sinfully with a notable degree of compulsion, this could be one sign of the devil's activity. Also, sometimes, a confessor might find reason to suppose the presence of a spirit of scrupulosity, or of anger, or of fear, or of false guilt feelings, or of lust, or of pride, or of depression; if so, he can command that spirit and any others in Jesus' name, silently. These problems do not always or even often indicate diabolical influence, but sometimes that influence plays at least a partial role.

6. It can happen that some bond must be broken before any exorcism can be efficacious. Let me give three typical kinds of negative bonding that impede efforts to restrain the devil's influence.

(a) Contact with astrologers or seers or other kinds of occultists such as certain kinds of "healers," or with some religions (e.g., Hare Krishna), can cause a kind of negative bond, an impediment to exorcism. This can be easily broken, in Jesus' name, either aloud or silently, depending on what seems best. It is a good idea, and sometimes necessary, to have the person explicitly renounce any occult activity he has in any way engaged in.

(b) Another kind of negative bond is a curse. I have found this kind of thing in parts of Italy and in Africa. There are, I suppose, many curses made that have no effect whatsoever, but some do seem to have some deleterious effects. Usually the person cursed will know about it or suspect it, and so bring it up. It can be easily broken by saying: "I take authority in Jesus' name to break any curse," or "I dissolve any curse in the name of Jesus."

(c) A third kind of bond can be the result of some morbid or violent association, as in cases of rape or of grave and habitual sins with another person. If the matter is delicate, it is better to dissolve any such bond silently.

7. Is it not necessary to know the kinds or names of the spirits one is dealing with? No. On the other hand, the gift of the discernment of spirits can help not only to ascertain the activity of demons but also to determine what kind of demon is acting. Someone with this charism can command the spirits by name, i.e., by category ("spirit of anger," "spirit of fear," and so on).

8. What I have been calling private exorcism is called in the Catholic charismatic renewal, as well as generally in the whole pentecostal tradition, "deliverance."[18] If the charismatic renewal in the Catholic Church has depended, in matters regarding exorcism, much more on the pentecostal tradition than on the Catholic tradition regarding both vocabulary and style, this is understandable in view of recent Catholic neglect of the Church's traditional pastoral teaching and practice. The term "deliverance," on the other hand, can be useful, and it does not carry the sinister and even esoteric overtones of the word "exorcism."

The practice in charismatic renewal prayer groups and communities of praying for a person's deliverance in a group—

sometimes two or three people praying together, sometimes a larger group—is acceptable, it seems to me, if discretion, prudence, and moderation are used, and if the style avoids the dramatic, the theatrical, and any attempted conversations with demons. A brief, simple, matter-of-fact prayer seems to me best:

(a) Prayer for protection.

(b) Prayer of praise.

(c) Perhaps, on the part of the person being prayed with, forgiveness of those who have hurt him, with an act of repentance for and renunciation of sins.

(d) On the part of the person leading the prayer, a command to any evil spirits to leave in the name of Jesus.

(e) Prayer for a new outpouring of the Holy Spirit, that the person will be filled anew with the Lord's grace.

9. Sometimes, before a private exorcism or deliverance can effectively take place, or in order to facilitate the exorcism, the person prayed with should renounce all sin connected with whatever kind of spirit or spirits are involved. For example, if someone has spoken to me of very strong temptations and sins of lust, I might suggest that he pray aloud, telling the Lord that he renounces all lust, or I might ask him to say after me the words of a simple prayer renouncing lust. Then I can silently command the spirit of lust to leave in Jesus' name.

EXORCISM AND THE LORDSHIP OF JESUS

Any exorcism, whether solemn or private, whether aloud or silent, is a deliverance not only from evil but to God. Exorcism has as its purpose not just to drive away evil, but to bring into a distorted situation, through ministry, "the grace of our Lord Jesus Christ, the love of God, and the fellowship of the Holy Spirit." Exorcism takes seriously the absolute lordship of Jesus Christ over all that troubles us and banishes evil in his name so that we may walk more freely in his Spirit.[19]

NOTES

1. Eph. 6:11.
2. Eph. 6:10.
3. Mt. 12:28.
4. For example, the Fourth Lateran Council (1215): "The devil and other evil spirits were indeed created by God good by nature, but they became evil by themselves" (DS 800); the Council of Florence (1442): "It is firmly believed, professed, and taught that no one conceived from man and woman was ever free from domination by the devil, unless through the faith of our Lord Jesus Christ" (DS 1347); the Second Vatican Council (1965): see *Gaudium et spes* (n. 13), *Sacrosanctum concilium* (n. 6) and *Ad gentes* (nn. 3 and 9).
5. General Audience, November 15, 1972, quoted in *L'Osservatore Romano,* English language edition, November 23, 1972, p. 3.
6. J. de Tonquédec, "Quelques aspects de l'action de Satan en ce monde," *Satan* (Paris: Desclée de Brouwer, 1948), p. 495.
7. Some theologians in the past have distingushed between possession, obsession, oppression, and temptation. The term "obsession," however, does not seem useful, can be confused with psychological obsession, and might possibly have its origin in the Latin word used in the Roman Ritual and in the Code of Canon Law for "possessed": *obsessos;* see note 15. Many theologians today prefer to call everything between possession and ordinary temptations "oppression."
8. Roman Ritual, ed. P. Weller (Milwaukee: Bruce, 1964), p. 641.
9. See G. Maloney, "How To Know and Evaluate the Occult," *Crux* (21 March 1977), 3–4; F. MacNutt, *Healing,* pp. 208–231.
10. See A. Tanquerey, *The Spiritual Life,* tr. H. Branderis (Tournai: Desclée, 1932), p. 719; Tanquerey, however, has his own special vocabulary, calling "obsession" what I call here "oppression."
11. *The Spiritual Exercises of Saint Ignatius,* tr. J. Morris (Westminster, Md.: Newman, 1943), p. 111.
12. *Ibid.,* pp. 110–111.
13. *Ibid.,* pp. 109–110.
14. Ferreres-Mondria distinguishes "solemn" and "private" exorcisms (J. Ferreres and A. Mondria, *Compendium theologiae moralis* (Subirana: Barcinone, 1949), pp. 282–283), as do J. Aertnys and C. A. Damen, *Theologica moralis,* Vol. I (Turin: Marietti, 1950), pp. 398–399); L. Wouters (*Manuale theologiae moralis,* Vol. I (Bruges:, Beyaert, 1932), p. 476; D. Prümmer (*Manuale theologiae moralis,* Vol.

II (Friburg: Herder, 1936), p. 384; J. McHugh and C. Callan (*Moral Theology,* Vol. II, revised and enlarged by Edward P. Farrell (New York: Wagner, 1958), p. 365; C. Marc and X. Gestermann, *Institutiones morales Alphonsiane* (Lyons-Paris: Vitte, 1933), p. 409, and others. Noldin distinguishes "solemn" and "simple," referring to the kind of exorcism (expelling demons who strongly control the person, or getting rid of their influence on the person), and also "public" and "private," referring to whether the exorcism is done in the name of the Church or on one's own authority (H. Noldin, *De sacramentis,* Vol. III, ed. 15 and 16 (New York: Pustet, 1923), pp. 58–59; H. Noldin and A. Schmitt, *De sacramentis* (New York: Pustet, 1929), pp. 51–53.

15. All the authors in note 14 point this out. Canon 1151 states: "1. No one possessed of the power of exorcising can lawfully perform exorcisms over those who are possessed [*obsessos*] unless he has obtained special and express permission from his ordinary. 2. This permission shall be granted by the ordinary only to a priest marked by piety, prudence, and integrity; and the latter shall not proceed to the performance of the exorcisms unless it shall have been established by a thorough and a prudent investigation that the person to be exorcised is really under the possession [*obsessum*] of the devil." Some commentators in the English language, unfortunately, translate the words *obsessos* and *obsessum* as "obsessed"; see, for example, J. Abbo and J. Hannan, *The Sacred Canons,* Vol. II (St. Louis: Herder, 1960), p. 424; T. Bouscaren and A. Ellis, *Canon Law* (Milwaukee: Bruce, 1957), p. 633. These words are forms of the past participle of *obsideo,* which means "to remain in," "to inhabit," "to *possess.*" A Tanquerey, *op. cit.,* on the other hand, uses the term "obsession" to mean what I am calling "oppression," except in the translation of the Roman Ritual, where it means "possession." This deplorable confusion in terminology helps explain the confusion some have regarding diabolical activity and the countermeasures to be taken.

16. On private exorcism, see especially Marc (*op. cit.*), McHugh and Callan (*op. cit.*), Wouters (*op. cit.*), Prümmer (*op. cit.*), Noldin (*op. cit.,* pp. 60–61), and Tanquerey (*op. cit.,* pp. 720 and 725).

17. See, for example, McHugh and Callan (*op. cit.,* p. 365): "It is recommended that priests frequently use private exorcisms, at least secretly, for persons who are vexed by temptations or scruples, and for which they may use the form, 'In the name of Jesus Christ, unholy spirit, I command you to depart from this creature of God.' "

18. See the excellent and well-balanced treatment of deliverance

in Francis MacNutt, O.P., *Healing* (Notre Dame: Ave Maria Press, 1974), pp. 208–231.

19. See John Richards, *Exorcism, Deliverance and Healing* (Bramcote-Notts: Grove, 1976), p. 18; see also his book *But Deliver Us from Evil* (London: Darton, Longman and Todd, 1974).

4
The Tradition for Charismatic Deliverance Prayer

by Rev. John B. Healey, S.T.L.

There would probably be little or no problem among Catholics today about deliverance were it not for the widespread experience of those involved in the charismatic renewal. What they are encountering regularly and everywhere simply does not fit into current religious theory and belief concerning the existence, nature and influence of evil spirits. It is my own contention, however, that much, perhaps most, of the experience of the renewal with deliverance does find its adequate explanation and justification in the traditional understanding, teaching and practice of the Church with reference to evil spirits.

I: FAITH AND EXPERIENCE

Acceptance of the validity of deliverance from evil spirits is primarily a matter of faith. It presupposes (minimally) one's acceptance of the lordship of Jesus Christ and his victory over Satan, sin and death, that his power of victory over Satan is available to Christians, and that there exist intelligent, free spirits who are permitted by God to adversely affect human beings.

However, unlike other areas of Christian belief which do not need to be concretized in experience to guarantee their acceptance in faith, the question of deliverance from evil spirits is very much a matter of a particular kind of religious experience related to faith. It contends to be dealing with the actual presence of (frequently identifiable) hostile, spiritual entities in particular persons and with the expulsion of these entities by the power of Jesus Christ working through the ministry of Christian believers. Deliverance, like some other areas of Christian healing, is therefore something that is open to verification, to "failure" or "success," etc. That is to say, it is open to investigation on other levels of human life than that of faith-acceptance.

Further, since the practice of deliverance entails not only Christian faith but also a particular kind of experience, by its very nature it (1) requires verifiable evidence for its acceptance, (2) is open to error, deceit, exaggeration and manipulation, and consequently (3) is rightly an area of special concern for Church authority.

Two Ways to Approach the Question

It is of great importance regarding deliverance whether one approaches the question out of the experience of praying for deliverance, or solely from one's speculative convictions about it. Further, this will be a truly theological discussion to the extent that it proceeds on at least some minimal data of revelation that are accepted commonly in faith. Otherwise it will not be a theological discussion, whatever else it may be and however valuable. For it is the function of theology to relate religious experience to the data of revelation accepted in faith.

Deliverance must be approached from experience and faith combined. For while the experiential group may sometimes be tied into a "contra factum non est argumentum" position that closes them to legitimate ideological (psychological, theological, philosophical, etc.) challenge, so also those who are speculatively determined in their viewpoint may, in turn, be so closed to the reasonable claims of others that, rather than examine these claims, they may be forced to assume that there is always "another explanation" which fits into their own tenets. To sum it up: in this matter speculation without experience is at best inadequate, while experience without an adequate ideological (psychological, theological, philosophical, etc.) basis, and, for a Catholic at least, legitimate magisterial control, is dangerous.

"Bone of Contention"

Deliverance, it seems, is sometimes the single "bone of contention" in the faith of Christians who agree about almost everything else. While both sides may present good reasons for their respective positions, problems with deliverance regularly seem to appear larger than the facts warrant. They are easily taken out of context because of the fascination many have for anything connected with evil spirits. By one who believes that Satan is an infernal nuisance, this distortion is readily attributed to the "father of lies."

Division of This Article

This article will attempt to clarify and reflect upon (1) current attitudes and beliefs about evil spirits, (2) the experience of deliverance in the charismatic renewal, and (3) the teaching of Holy Scripture and the Church about evil spirits, their influence upon us and the practice of commanding them to depart by the power of Jesus Christ; (4) finally, it will offer some reflections by way of summary and conclusion. In this way we hope that we shall have provided an acceptable skeletal framework for further investigation and reflection by those who are especially qualified to do so by their scriptural, theological, psychological, etc., expertise, as well as by those who have a great deal to offer because of their experience in praying for deliverance.

CURRENT ATTITUDES AND BELIEFS ABOUT EVIL SPIRITS IN GENERAL

Growth of Catholic interest in and devotion to the Holy Spirit since Vatican II has been paralleled by a widespread fascination, preoccupation and involvement with the world of spirits and with the "supernatural" in society generally. Popular literature and the mass media present a conglomeration of imaginative, bizarre, weird, shock-oriented beliefs and entities that defy rational and theological inquiry. Along with this, millions here and abroad delve into every sort of satanism, witchcraft, spiritism, occultism, etc. Use of a daily horoscope is virtually universal. Catholics engage in all of this, about as much as any others.

In the midst of all of this, however, contemporary man maintains a curiously contradictory stance toward the world of spirits: he at one and the same time is both fascinated and intrigued by their power and influence upon us, while ideologically denying that they exist at all.

Catholics

Among Catholics, and not least so among theologians, there is currently every shade of belief, unbelief, disbelief and denial concerning evil spirits and their relationship to human beings. Since most Catholics understandably have little precise knowledge of theology, they have few exact ideas about spirits and find it most difficult to articulate what they do have. As with other matters of faith, they are usually ready to accept whatever the Church teaches about spirits. Today, however, they receive very little clear, definite and consistent teaching about spirits on the popular level. In practice they engage in all sorts of superstitious activities with vague understanding of what they are engaged in but with great "faith" expectancy.

Catholic Denial of Personal Nature of Evil Spirits

An increasing number of Catholics deny the personal (intelligent and free) nature of evil spirits, reducing them, most often, to destructive social forces such as poverty, racial hatred, violence, etc. Some go further and deny all personal evil as well. This was exemplified recently when the awesome immensity of the events at Jonestown, Guyana, brought into the public forum the question of possible diabolic influence in it. The suggestion was generally ridiculed as a throwback to medievalism. However, *Time* magazine (Dec. 18, 1978) quoted John Giles Milhaven, a Catholic theologian of Brown University: "I think that what happens with people like Hitler and Jones is simple psychological sickness. The only response to Guyana, it seems to me, is pity, not moral horror. Psychological illnesses that keep people from being good, sociological causes that compel people to turn to Jones or to Hitler—that's what one should be concerned with." The *Time* article added that theologians Gregory Baum of Toronto University and Margaret Farley of Yale also defend the modern de-emphasis on personal evil.

Traditional Catholic Teaching

There are many Catholics who know and accept the traditional teaching of Scripture and the Church about evil spirits and their influence in human life. They accept it in faith because it is Catholic doctrine. Some of these, perhaps most, hesitate to engage in or to interpret matters connected with deliverance without clear-cut approval by the Church's teaching authority. Since, in the current state of affairs, this is not available to them, their faith remains abstract.

Others, like myself and many involved in the charismatic renewal, accept traditional teaching of the Church and find that it is generally validated in their experience of praying for deliverance. I believe that, were it not for this experience, and knowing my theological beliefs and tendencies before involvement in the renewal, I would now most likely be among those who deny the personal nature of evil spirits.

Attitude of Teaching Authority

On the part of those who have teaching authority in the Church, there is today, generally, an official prudence based, it seems to me, more on fear than on the needs of people and on

the recognition of the abundant "fruits of the Spirit" that are clearly manifest in many who have been prayed with for deliverance. Concern for false doctrine and for the misuse of gifts, legitimate in itself and often enough justifiable, should not prevail over widespread and urgent spiritual need.

II: THE EXPERIENCE OF DELIVERANCE IN THE CHARISMATIC RENEWAL

That certain individuals have need for deliverance from evil spirits is a fact recognized and acknowledged throughout the world today. To call it a fact is not to "beg the question" since those who have first-hand experience with the phenomenon have no doubt about (1) a lack of freedom in certain individuals who do not improve therein by continued prayer for healing and/or the regular use of the sacraments, (2) the experienced and ascertainable presence of alien, hostile, intelligent entities within many who are being prayed with for deliverance, (3) the verifiable change for the better and recognizable "fruits of the Spirit" that are often effected through the expulsion of these entities and the subsequent "infilling" by the Holy Spirit, and (4) the fact that this procedure is not inconsistent with Catholic doctrine and practice with regard to evil spirits and their influence upon us.

Not an Incontrovertible Fact

To assert that deliverance is a fact of experience is not to deny (1) that sometimes, perhaps often, what seems to be deliverance is not really such, (2) that the practice of praying for deliverance lends itself readily to abuse, is a ministry that attracts aggressive individuals, leads to bizarre activities and sometimes causes great harm to those who are subjected to a misplaced ministry, (3) that those who have first-hand experience with deliverance do not always agree about its lasting effectiveness, the need for it in particular instances, or perhaps at all among Christians, or about the presence of evil spirits generally within persons, and (4) that there is urgent need today for solid teaching and guidance in this matter. It is ironic that some who are the most qualified to provide teaching and guidance about deliverance are the least disposed to do so because of their attitude toward the whole question.

Insights Gained From Experience of the Charismatic Renewal

The experience of deliverance in the renewal provides many valuable practical insights that might well be shared with other Christians generally, examined for their consistency with acceptable Christian doctrine and for their effectiveness and fruitfulness in the Spirit, and, let us prayerfully hope, be considered by Church liturgists in their updating of the liturgical books, called for by Vatican II, which, to my knowledge at least, has not as yet been implemented in the area of dealing with evil spirits.

No Ideal Way

There is no ideal way to approach deliverance, which is true whenever we pray for healing in any of its various aspects. Shared experience reveals, however, what is often effective and what is not. What is offered here is not intended to be either complete or to constitute a norm of procedure for anyone else. It is offered as the fruit of limited experience and reflection.

The Ministry of Deliverance

Very few are called to a ministry of deliverance. It requires, besides the call itself, a high degree of personal and religious maturity. It calls for (1) an ongoing, secure and confident personal relationship with Jesus Christ which is fostered, among other ways, by daily commitment to prayer, (2) a compassionate, Christian love and concern for those being prayed for, which is always ready to be called upon and tested by serious inconvenience, loss of sleep, willingness to fast, etc., and (3) a conscious, strong and manifest reliance on the "once-and-for-all" victory of Jesus Christ over sin and Satan that eliminates any suggestion that deliverance is a struggle between two equal powers, God and Satan.

Headship, Community, Church Authority

More perhaps than any other requirement, involvement in this ministry calls for willingness to submit to headship and discernment in one's community, and to the authority of one's bishop and his representatives. "Going into business for oneself" with any Christian ministry is usually self-serving, manipulative and ultimately destructive. A fortiori, engagement in this ministry when separated from community (wherein alone does a Christian find the variety of gifts of the Spirit, the personal encouragement and prayerful support that are essential for spiritual warfare) leads inevitably to greater harm than good.

Discernment

There is indispensable need for the use of the gift of discernment in determining who might need prayer for deliverance. Such discernment must be entered into prayerfully, patiently, prudently and in union with others in community. It is a process that calls for knowledge of the person—the background, family relationships and personal problems. It demands ability to recognize and properly interpret external signs of possible demonic presence. The Roman Ritual in its "General Rules" enumerates a few external factors as possible signs of possession, adding that there are also "various other indications which, when taken together as a whole, build up the evidence." Among these latter, we might add from the experience of the charismatic renewal, are a manner of speaking, looking, and acting, emotional signs, attitudes and moods, physical illnesses of various kinds, enslaving habits and compulsions, and fanaticisms (not least of all, religious fanaticism).

Medical Disciplines and Discernment

Discernment in this area demands not only that one be sensitive to the guidance of the Holy Spirit through one's own gifts, the gifts of others and the use of Scripture, but that, wherever possible, the disciplines of psychology, psychotherapy and counseling be made use of. Some consider this last a "sine qua non" before praying for deliverance.

Inner Healing and "Follow-Up"

Anyone in need of deliverance is never without need also for inner healing. Ongoing prayer for inner healing is especially necessary afterward, together with continued community and individual support and spiritual direction. Without definite assurance of such "follow-up," some will refuse, or at least will be reluctant, to pray for deliverance.

How Evil Spirits Gain Entrance

There are many ways in which evil spirits may gain entrance into persons. The experience of the renewal has indicated that their influence may go back to birth and even before birth, sometimes for generations in a family. The power of family ties can be adversely influential during infancy and early childhood in an especially deep way, just as it can be enormously beneficial at that time. The entrance of evil spirits is in our time greatly facilitated by the persons themselves through their curiosity, fascination and especially involvement in any of the countless forms of popular occult practices and superstitions that prevail and are so readily accepted. Drug use and/or sinful habits are often avenues of access for the evil one.

Spiritual Warfare

"Praying for deliverance" is, in its essential approach, not prayer at all, although it must be supported with prayer. Deliverance is spiritual warfare, requiring the "whole armor of God that you may be able to stand against the wiles of the devil" (Eph. 6:11). It seems important: to have only one person at a time in charge of this confrontation; to have great prayer support, especially praise of God, and sometimes to fast; to exclude the merely curious; to invoke and to use every protection, even beforehand, for the one being prayed for, for oneself, for all those present and for the place itself; that the one in command elicit from the person being prayed with a profession of faith in Jesus Christ and an expression of repentance for all past sins, also making use of the sacrament of reconciliation where this is judged necessary; to ask for an expression of forgiveness of all who have in any way sinned against the person throughout life; that the one in command deport oneself with authority and confidence in manner and voice and not dialogue with evil spirits, but command them in the name of Jesus; that there be a command made to have the spirits identify themselves by name; and, finally, that the spirits be commanded to depart in the name of Jesus Christ and to go directly to him to be disposed of.

Developing Teams

Since praying for deliverance among Catholics is presently engaged in mostly by "charismatics," it would seem that deliverance teams are the proper concern of liaisons of bishops for the charismatic renewal. In the diocese of Brooklyn, for example, we are now in the process of completing guidelines for about a dozen "deliverance teams." Our procedure has been to ask the leaders of some mature prayer groups to affirm those from their healing teams who felt called to this ministry and were willing to volunteer. Without such affirmation of local leaders they were not accepted.

A layman experienced in deliverance and I conducted for these volunteers a series of full-day sessions (prayer, teachings, discussions, discernment, liturgy, commitment) with a view to forming teams. They would be subject to definite guidelines as to reference of persons to be considered for deliverance, discernment, etc. The diocesan pastoral team, of which I am chairman, is attempting presently to finalize these guidelines. Admittedly, the more we study and discuss them and pray about them, the more difficult seems the task of producing something satisfactory. The teams and the guidelines have not been sufficiently tested up to this point. There are many problems. We do not anticipate that things will go smoothly. Some question the wisdom of the way we are proceeding. Only time will tell us what value it all has. Our ordinary is aware of our efforts.

Admonition by Cardinal Suenens

Cardinal Suenens in his recent *Ecumenism and Charismatic Renewal* (Malines Document #2) warns against a "trick of the evil one that would draw our attention away from Jesus and his paschal mystery and toward himself." This he calls "demonomania." He advises that "only those of spiritual maturity, pastoral experience and proper training should practice deliverance. Moreover they are always under the authority of the bishops." He adds that authorities of the Church should provide "definite and sound teaching" in this area and that "every Catholic should strive to see what is the *mind of the Church* as expressed in the living magisterium."

While indeed these admonitions are wise and helpful, most of them have relevance only to what is exceptional among Catholics concerned with deliverance, and what is therefore not the ordinary situation. For (1) the vast majority of these make every possible effort to keep the paschal mystery of Jesus central when addressing themselves to deliverance; (2) with rare exceptions they desire to learn the *mind of the Church* therein and to follow the living magisterium; (3) wherever deliverance is engaged in, in any ongoing way, there is concern that those involved have "spiritual maturity and pastoral experience." As for "proper training," this can be acquired, it seems to me, only by actually praying for deliverance, unless by "training" is here meant speculative understanding.

Jesus Acting Today in Real Situations

However, need for deliverance arises out of concrete, painful situations, and not merely from our understanding of it or our preparedness to deal with it. People everywhere today need to be freed from the power of evil spirits by the power of Jesus Christ. Sometimes Jesus frees them directly without other human ministration. Often this happens where the power of the Holy Spirit is strong amid great praise of God, sometimes quietly, at other times not so. And we cannot doubt that Jesus frees many others from evil spirits in ways about which we know nothing.

Need for Deliverance Not Always Responded To

Frequently, however, it is discerned by the person involved and/or by others that deliverance is called for. Catholics generally and rightly look to their priests who are ordained and commissioned to pastor them, but receive very little help from them. They then look elsewhere. Sometimes they are fortunate enough to find prayerful, dedicated Christian brothers and sisters, and occasionally a priest, to pray with them for deliverance. Sometimes in their distress they simply submit themselves to any who seem to promise help. These may be sincere, prayerful Christians. They may be mercenary charlatans at whose hands one can become worse than before.

Urgent Need for "Definite and Sound Teaching"

Cardinal Suenens rightly suggests that the appropriate basic remedy for our confused current situation with deliverance is "definite and sound teaching." This teaching is all the more urgently needed because, as we said, those Catholics most competent to do so are not providing it. And so, many Catholics who are interested and/or involved in deliverance turn for information and guidance to sources that are very often not supported by solid scriptural and theological scholarship.

The teaching that Catholics need today cannot be entirely deductive, without reference to the rich experience of those who are presently engaged in deliverance. (As we noted before, theology is, in the first instance, reflection on religious experience.) Nevertheless, "definite and sound teaching" in the matter of deliverance from evil spirits is to be sought first and foremost, as the cardinal reminds us, in the living magisterium of the Church, based upon Holy Scripture and the traditional doctrine and understanding of the Church. We now turn to that.

III: THE TEACHING OF THE CHURCH ON EVIL SPIRITS AND DELIVERANCE

The question of evil spirits and deliverance is related to the more general "problem of evil" in human life and to the questions of God's providence, the paschal mystery of Jesus, human free will, etc. These will be referred to only where they have relevance.

Skepticism about and denial of the personal nature of evil spirits among Christians is the result of a number of concurrent modern ways of thinking, including especially rationalism and scientism. Many today believe that only that exists which can be measured and/or analyzed, that education (understanding) is the fundamental premise for solving all human problems, and that God and spirits, if they exist at all, do not "interfere" in human life.

Sources of Christian Doctrine

The principal sources of Christian doctrine ("loci theologici") are Church councils, Sacred Scripture, the Fathers of the

Church, the liturgical books (in our case especially the Roman Ritual), dogmatic, moral and ascetical theologians and guides, and the general understanding and practice of believers (*sensus fidelium*).

Holy Scripture

Since the New Testament is basically an expression of the early Christian community's (the Church's) consciousness of its own belief and of its remembrance of Jesus Christ, it constitutes a part of that Church's teaching and is (still) subject to the Church for its proper interpretation and understanding. It is clear from Scripture (1) that Jesus Christ in his public life frequently cast out evil spirits from individual persons and from groups of persons, (2) that on several occasions he transferred this power of his to his disciples, and (3) that his disciples used this power to cast out evil spirits.

Nature of Evil Spirits in Scripture

Jesus saw the spirits he cast out as personal (intelligent and free), evil, hostile to humans, and powerful. He did not dialogue with them. He expelled them with a command. From many texts, especially Revelation 12:7–12, we see that the devil is a fallen angel, cast out from heaven down to earth, that he is filled with rage because he knows his time is short, that he has knowledge, a will, and power over death, and that he can perform miracles, can test humans, can enter humans and control them. His two principal powers are to accuse us and to deceive us.

Dispensationalism

Although many Catholics believe that the power of Christians to cast out evil spirits and their other "extraordinary" gifts mentioned in Scripture, such as prophecy, healing and speaking in tongues were intended by God to be limited in their use to (approximately) the apostolic age, there is no basis for this belief in Scripture nor in the practice of the Church down the centuries.

All Christians Share Power of Jesus to Expel Spirits

The power of believers (Christians) over evil spirits belongs to all the baptized, not merely to a certain few. This power is, of course, not magical. It is not to be used in an arbitrary and indiscriminate way. To say this is not to say that any Christian cannot and ought not to make use of it when necessity demands. The fact that it lends itself to abuse, sensationalism, etc., does not negate its rightful and necessary place in Christian life and practice. We must not therefore deny that it exists nor forbid its proper use by all believers. To do so would, in effect, be to "throw out the baby with the bath water."

Need for a Balanced Approach

In the whole question of evil spirits and their influence upon us a balanced approach is called for: one that gives them neither too much attention nor too little. Too much attention generates unnecessary fears in believers, gives a distorted, minimizing view of the complete victory of Jesus over sin and Satan, lessens in this way the confidence Christians should have in this victory and, in effect, denies the lordship of Jesus Christ in certain areas of human life. On the other hand too little attention to evil spirits, or a denial of their existence or influence completely in human life, makes useless a God-given, necessary power that resides in every Christian.

Teaching of Two Councils of the Church

The Fourth Lateran Council states: "In their nature the devil and other demons were created good by God, but they became evil by their own choice" (Denz. 428). Vatican Council II states in its *Constitution on the Church in the Modern World:* "Although he was made by God in a state of grace, from the dawn of history man has abused his liberty at the urging of personified evil. . . . All of human life shows itself to be a dramatic struggle between good and evil. . . . Man finds that by himself he is incapable of battling the assaults of evil successfully so that everyone feels that he is bound by chains" (n. 13). "For a monumental struggle against the powers of darkness pervades the whole history of man. The battle was joined from the very origins of the world and will continue until the last day, as the Lord has attested. Caught in this conflict, man is obliged to wrestle constantly if he is to cling to what is good. Nor can he achieve his own integrity without valiant efforts and the help of God's grace" (n. 37).

These Council declarations give the central points of the Church's perennial teaching about man, the devil, the struggle against evil and the need of grace to succeed in it. These doctrines are, of course, related to other teachings, namely, the paschal victory of Jesus, since he came among us and lived and died "in order to destroy the works of the devil" (1 Jn. 3:8), and original sin. The Church also teaches that the devil cannot affect man's will directly, that he influences us only to the extent that God permits it, that since man was created good, his tendency to sin did not come originally from within himself, that evil spirits retain their angelic powers, and that God permits the devil to influence us ultimately for our own good. He brings good out of evil.

Theological Speculation

The Fathers of the Church speculated that envy and jealousy, springing from pride, are the cause of the devil's opposition to man. They attributed this envy variously to the fact that a bodily creature is created in God's image, that man has dominion over the physical world, and that men are destined to take the place of fallen angels. Some modern theologians conjecture that the devil's pride induced him to take a stand against God's uniting himself personally with human nature, so lessening his own glory.

The Roman Ritual

The Roman Ritual is a major "locus theologicus" for Catholics, since it is both a reflection and crystallization of the universal Church's prayer experience and, conversely, the official liturgical directive of that worship. "Ecclesia orans, Ecclesia docens" ("The way in which the Church worships itself teaches the Church") is a traditional way of summing up this truth.

In the matter of evil spirits, the teaching and guidance of the Ritual are entirely in accord with Church doctrine. In its section on "Exorcism" it provides instructions, cautions, and official prayers and rites for the Church at large to deal with these spirits. It proceeds on the unstated assumptions that they exist, that they act adversely in human life, that the Church has received from Jesus the mandate to deal with this effectively, and that Christians are expected to do so in accord with Church teaching and direction.

The Roman Ritual also teaches implicitly that the harmful influence of the evil one touches all creation, since throughout its pages it provides prayers and rites for exorcism not only of persons but also of places and things. For example, the blessings of water and oil for daily use by the faithful include prayers for the exorcism of evil spirits. In the Rite of Baptism of infants and of adults there are prayers for exorcism of evil spirits.

General Rules in Roman Ritual

Among its "General Rules" for exorcism the Roman Ritual recommends discernment of spirits and warns against the "arts and subterfuges that the evil spirits are wont to use in deceiving the exorcist" and states: "At times the evil spirits place whatever obstacles they can in the way so that the patient may not submit to the exorcism."

Terminology: "Possession," "Obsession,"
"Infestation" and "Deliverance"

As a result of the experience of deliverance in the charismatic renewal we realize that there is a lesser degree of demonic influence, recently labeled "infestation," that is neither total possession nor mere temptation. It involves in the person affected some lack of freedom, or "bondage." It is from this that all Christians have the power to pray for what is called "deliverance."

The Roman Ritual uses the word "possession" for a more serious attack by the evil one, and the word "obsession" for anything less. It does not use the word "deliverance" except in a general way. Today those who pray for "deliverance" take "possession" to mean complete, voluntary submission to the influence of the evil one. They understand also and accept that in such instances exorcism requires the bishop's permission, the leadership of a priest appointed by him, and the use of the official rites and prayers of the Roman Ritual for exorcism.

Moral and Ascetical Tradition of the Church

The teaching of moral and spiritual theology in standard texts maintains consistently (1) that evil spirits exist, (2) that we need to exorcise them regularly in order to grow as Christians, (3) and that demonic possession and attack should not be regarded lightly. Moral theologians distinguish "private" or "simple" exorcism (when one acts in one's own name) from "solemn" or "public" exorcism (performed by a minister of the Church in the name of and with the authority of the Church). St. Alphonsus Liguori writes: "Private exorcism is permissible to all Christians; solemn exorcism is permissible only to ministers who are appointed to it, and then only with the express permission of the bishop."

In traditional texts of moral theology confessors are consistently urged to make use of "private" exorcism whenever it seems needed, and even without the penitent's knowledge of it. As to the use of "private" exorcism by lay persons, nowhere in traditional texts is it forbidden. Rather, it is encouraged, together with the use by lay persons of holy water and blessed oil, for the expulsion of evil spirits.

The Statement of Pope Paul VI

In order to counteract current loss of belief among Catholics concerning evil spirits, and their power and influence over us, Pope Paul VI in 1972 issued a strong statement reaffirming the traditional teaching of the Church. It was published in *L'Osservatore Romano* on November 15, 1972. In it Pope Paul stated: "Evil is not merely a deficiency; it is the act of a live, spiritual, perverted and perverting being . . . a terrible, mysterious and fearful reality. Those who refuse to recognize his existence . . . or who present him as a pseudo-reality, a fabrication of the mind serving to personify the unknown causes of our evils, are departing from the teaching of the Bible and of the Church. Christ defines him as the one who was determined to murder man from the start . . . the 'father of lies.' He insidiously threatens man's moral equilibrium. . . . It is evident that not every sin can be directly attributed to the action of the devil. But it is nonetheless true that he who does not keep a strict watch on himself is exposed to the influence of the 'mystery of impiety' of which St. Paul speaks (2 Thess. 2:3–12) and is risking the salvation of his soul."

IV: SUMMARY AND CONCLUSION

It is difficult to get a handle on the problem of deliverance. At whatever point it is approached, it seems to present itself in the form of a dilemma: something good, but also something dangerous and potentially destructive; something to be pursued, but then again better left alone; a means of great spiritual good, but possibly making people worse. From the nature of the problem it is easy enough to conclude that this continuous divisiveness is the work of the evil one, but then again it may not be so. And so it goes.

As I have indicated before, the question of deliverance tends to draw Christians themselves into opposite camps. This in itself is perhaps the most destructive aspect of the whole problem, and the one about which we ought to be most concerned: on the one hand, denial and/or unwillingness to become involved with it, and, on the other hand, compassionate Christian concern and involvement because of an evident need in our suffering brothers and sisters, which can be alleviated by a power that Jesus Christ himself has given to us.

On the evidence it seems to me that there ought to be no question in the minds of Catholic pastors and teachers that the basic decision is not whether or not we should deal with deliverance, but simply how we should go about doing so. It seems to me that the key question for each of us personally is whether or not we accept deliverance as a fact of experience, at least in some instances. If we do not, then we must ask ourselves whether we are a priori excluding its possibility.

I contend that those without experience in this area, and who work therefore out of an exclusively intellectual position, are not dealing with the real problem, no matter how sincere they may be. As with the incarnation itself, the reality comes first and then our understanding of it, not vice versa. Deliverance is but one aspect of the fact of the incarnation and the paschal mystery of Jesus Christ. Ultimately, however, as I have said, acceptance of deliverance is a matter of faith.

The inclination of most Catholics is to have nothing to do with deliverance. Fear of the spirits themselves, lack of belief in their existence and/or influence, and fear of the reaction of Church authority if they become involved all contribute to this attitude. For us pastors and teachers to turn our back on the problem of deliverance, however, because of its dangers and difficulties, would be to go against the whole thrust of Church teaching, of Scripture, and of Christian practice, as well as against the validated experience of many who do pray for deliverance with abundant "fruits of the Spirit." Most importantly, we would leave in the grip of the evil one many of our suffering brothers and sisters who today are turning to us for comfort, strength and guidance. Our neglect of this pastoral duty would be to surrender them inevitably into the hands of the misguided and the mercenary.

Section Two

The Present Practice
of Deliverance Prayer

Introduction

For many groups the present practice of deliverance prayer has undergone an evolution from dramatic battles to quiet, peaceful prayer. Rev. William Sneck, professor of clinical psychology at Georgetown University, has participated in the charismatic renewal for ten years and researched this evolution within a community. His article reveals how early deliverances occurred with dramatic physical manifestations reinforced by the group expecting the dramatic. But after the leaders endorsed a quiet form of deliverance, the dramatic manifestations largely ceased. The focus of deliverance became not a colorful battle sometimes leaving psychic scars but a prayerful removal of obstacles that left spiritual fruit. More peaceful ways are possible where expected.

Expectations can also produce a devilmania finding demons where there is only a psychological problem. Professor Sneck believes in the spirit world but equally sees the need to have psychology's skepticism so that all psychological skills are used to treat a person. He proposes that more attention be given to third force psychologists such as Laing and Jung who can offer wisdom for dealing with the spirit dimension of the psyche. In turn he proposes that Christians can also help psychologists who might totally deny the demonic realm.

This article raises many questions. How much of the evolution is due to group expectation rather than other factors such as more maturity and power in prayer? What can we learn from the experience of those who have found a quiet, mature form of deliverance with spiritual fruit?[1] How can we further the dialogue between psychology and those practicing deliverance? What is the interplay between demonic and psychological factors? The articles in this section will attempt to illustrate the mature practice of deliverance, while Section Three will address the psychological issues.

NOTE

1. The experience of another mature community is offered in Michael Scanlan, T.O.R. and Randall Cirner, *Deliverance From Evil Spirits* (Ann Arbor: Servants, 1980).

5
Evil and the Psychological Dynamics of the Human Person

by William J. Sneck, S.J., Ph.D.

Psychology is one of God's more complicated gifts to the modern world. Like any of his gifts, this one can be used in the service of building up his people, or it can be idolized and inappropriately exalted into metaphysics or a neo-religion whose devotees promote psychology's and psychiatry's hierophants to the positions of high priests and prophets of a post-Christian era. Before elaborating upon some of psychology's more insightful contributions to the questions facing us, we might inspect the theoretical foundations upon which the majority of contemporary therapists and researchers establish their procedures and practice. Dom Edward McCorkell, the abbot of Holy Cross Monastery in Berryville, Virginia, muses that "there are many who dismiss the evil spirit as unreal," and among those legions the American psychological and psychiatric establishments must list many of their members. In pastoral situations, we are often hard pressed to find a counselor for someone requesting a "Christian therapist." Who of us has not experienced difficulty in discovering a mental health professional who will refrain from ridiculing a client's/patient's religious experience, much less understand and value it? Religiously committed therapists must struggle both to heal the hurt and doubt inflicted by skeptical colleagues in the lives of their counselees, and to square our own faith stance with our professional training. For it is not merely the evil spirit who is dismissed as unreal but any spiritual dimension of life. It is ironic that psychology, the study of the *psyche,* and psychiatry, the healing of the *psyche,* attract practitioners who are made distinctly uncomfortable with even the mention of *psyche,* soul, spirit, free will. Why is this state of affairs so?

Behaviorism and Freudianism, the two dominant currents in American psychological thinking, both base themselves on materialistic presuppositions. Whether attempting to analyze observed behavior "from the outside," as a response to environmental stimuli (the behaviorists), or "from the inside," as a series of processes governed largely by instinctual needs (the Freudians), most psychologists agree to turn man into an *object* of study with the methods inherited from the natural sciences. Even a very cursory familiarity with the history of science acquaints one with the tremendous progress in human knowledge achieved since scientists adopted a stance of *methodological* materialism and freed themselves from having to account for the intervention of divine factors in explaining nature. Methodological materialism enables natural scientists to pursue their researches in biology, chemistry, and physics, and to embrace whatever ontology they choose—*philosophical materialism,* idealism, hylemorphism, etc.

In the social sciences, blind acceptance of the methods of the natural sciences has not always led to such benign outcomes. Since the opening of the first psychological laboratory by Wilhelm Wundt at the University of Leipzig in 1879, psychologists have claimed that their work has been untrammeled by philosophical and religious ties, and they have indeed shed much light on the human condition. Yet unexamined biases are the most dangerous because they produce unexpected effects. In the case of psychology, *methodological* materialism has shifted subtly over into *philosophical* materialism with the result that man is quite often regarded as little more than a highly complex animal, with a very large cerebral cortex, to be sure, but whose behavior can be explained *in an ultimate sense* by the same laws which describe the material universe. While it would have been possible for social scientists, like natural scientists, to keep their methodologies and metaphysics separate, in actuality the most frequently heard voices in the psychological fraternity/sorority speak with a materialistic accent. Hence the moral relativism endorsed with the sincerest good will; hence the "nothing-but" attitude of many to the question of "something more" in the realm of spirit; hence the view of religion as an illusion (Sigmund Freud, *The Future of an Illusion*) and human freedom as a delusion (B. F. Skinner, *Beyond Freedom and Dignity*). And so, not only are there many who dismiss the evil spirit as unreal, but any talk of spirit/Spirit, human or divine, is frequently disregarded as pre-scientific at best, and oppressively anti-human at worst.

Such a viewpoint is usually communicated as scientific objectivity not only in learned books, papers and conventions among fellow professionals, but also to the psychological neophytes, the many untutored youngsters (philosophically speaking) who flock to our lecture halls and continue to make psychology one of the most popular majors in American colleges and universities. I have been unable to locate a beginners' textbook in Abnormal Psychology or in General Psychology whose introductory chapters on method and the history of the discipline fail to glorify the scientific method as the favored way to truth. Typically, such texts contain references to exorcism as an outmoded medieval remedy for psychopathology, and to the tortures of the Inquisition and witch-burning as logical outgrowths of unhealthy belief in the power of evil spirits. Students' horror is further elicited by pictures of skulls with holes bored in them by trephining, a procedure supposedly resorted to by primitive men to allow evil spirits to escape. Occasionally, authors will also provide an illustration from the 1487 manual by Johann Sprenger and Heinrich Kraemer, *Malleus Maleficarum* (*The Hammer of Witches*), a treatise on the "diagnosis" and "treatment" of witchcraft. What is the result of such instruction? Students experience relief that such outmoded practices and beliefs have been discarded in the dustbins of history, but come away with a deepened skepticism for claims about the spiritual dimension of reality.

I say a "deepened" skeptcism about the spiritual because,

in fairness to my colleagues, I cannot blame them entirely for an attitude or mind-set which seems to pervade our culture. Theologically speaking, such a world view might be called an anti-interventionist notion of the deity. A study conducted with my colleague, Dr. David A. Kopplin, on a random sample of University of Michigan students illustrates and supports this claim. Our questionnaire explored which forces students felt controlled their lives (i.e., self, powerful others, chance and/or God). A fairly normal distribution of responses occurred for self, chance and powerful others (most students agreed or disagreed a little; fewer disagreed or agreed strongly). However, there was a strong disagreement that God controlled their lives. Forty-eight percent disagreed or disagreed strongly that "My life is controlled by God's purposes" or "If the plans I make work out, it is because they fit into God's plan." This does not imply that Michigan students are atheists, because sixty-one percent reported belief in God or some power greater than themselves, with only fifty-three students (seven percent) choosing atheism.

This can be correlated with other indices to see whether, for example, people who believe strongly in the influence of fate have similar attitudes and behavioral patterns. Here are two striking intercorrelations within the scale itself: the chance and powerful-others scales correlate .54. This means that students tend to answer items about both variables similarly (e.g., "When I get what I want, it's usually because I'm lucky," and "Getting what I want requires pleasing those people above me"). On the other hand, students who reported agreement with "God control" items tended to disagree with "self-control" items and vice versa (correlation: .27). Students tended to give opposite answers to "best way to protect my personal interests is by trusting in the Lord" and "I can pretty much determine what will happen in my life."

Students who disagreed that God controlled their lives also tended to reject items (5:1) which measured an extrinsic orientation to religious faith (people who use their religious faith to gain peace, security, friendships, and social position). At the same time students who saw God as intervening in human affairs also rejected extrinsic items (3:1) but did endorse intrinsic or committed items ("I try hard to carry my religion over into my other dealings in life"). Yet the God worshiped by most of the students seems to have little influence or power to make their interpersonal and public lives any better or worse.

At the beginning of this article it was claimed that psychology could be used in building up God's people. At this point, remembering Nathanael's quip, "Can any good come out of Nazareth?" (Jn. 1:46), some readers may be paraphrasing and wondering, "Can any good come out of such a mentality, such a psychology?" Without adhering to either of the two dominant American psychological schools myself, I wanted nevertheless to state their positions as strongly as possible and demonstrate why the proponents of a spiritual dimension in human reality are cautious before and even suspicious of the reigning psychological consensus. Yet even in this materialistic ideology, much good can be discerned, and Abbot McCorkell suggests why:

> I find a good number of people too readily attributing to the evil spirit situations that could be the result of other factors, e.g., psychological disorders or even physical conditions. . . . There are also a good number who are quick to jump on a sort of "bandwagon" that is branded diabolical.

Without condoning the metaphysical denial of a spiritual realm preached by modern psychology, I do find that Christians, especially charismatic Christians, need much more healthy skepticism regarding the supposed presence and power of the demonic. We can learn such skepticism readily from psychologists who would rarely be tempted to fall into the error just described by the abbot. Psychologists are swayed by training and temperament to search out natural causes and apply this-worldly remedies to interpersonal "evil" behavior and events as caused by the impersonal laws of nature: physical, biological, sociological, psychological, all on a continuum. Intrapersonal and interpersonal evil can be healed through providing a more reinforcing environment by means of educational programs, behavioral modification therapies like token economies, etc. While the Freudians focus much more directly on the individual than on society at large, they prescribe careful childhood nurturance (especially before the age of five) and psychotherapies for adults needing help as aids for bettering the human environment. Such a focus of theory, effort and professional resources, to speak modestly, has done incalculable good for individuals and institutions and must not be gainsaid because of ultimate disagreement over metaphysical presuppositions. Psychology spurns devil mania wherever it is found in the culture: whether in the increasing popularity of astrology, demon worship, consultation of fortune tellers, and horror movies like "The Exorcist" and "The Omen" or in hysterical exorcism ceremonies conducted in fundamentalist branches of Christianity. The popularity of invoking demonic explanation for humanly caused ills is interpreted as a failure in responsibility, like that of the drunkard in his alcoholic haze who quotes the inscription on the bar tray, "The devil made me do it." Psychologists see their task as educating the public against the temptation of societal regression to a modality of behavior and theory both superstitious and dangerous.

An example of such group regression is provided by the following account about deliverance from members of a Catholic charismatic community whom I interviewed as part of my doctoral research. To my knowledge, this community was the earliest in the renewal to buy into the ideology and practices of the more fundamentalist churches/sects. A good dose of psychologists' skepticism might have prevented some of the bizarre behaviors from emerging. (It is important to add that most of the members of this group were middle class, college educated persons, adherents of Catholic and mainline Protestant denominations who had never been schooled to pay much attention to demons.)

The interviewee's first words were that deliverance "came out of nowhere," but that since then there had been growth and development. This statement is, of course, not quite accurate because the pentecostal churches are the source of most of the practices and techniques of deliverance. It all started on a Monday in March 1970, known ever after as "Deliverance Monday." Two preachers from Florida had come to town and were "amazed that Catholics were getting baptized in the Spirit." At supper with the leaders, they shared about deliverance and prayed for the gift. In those days, prayer meetings were held on Mondays, and the ministers came to explain about delivering people "from the work of Satan in their lives."

After the prayer meeting, they held a deliverance session. The research subject goes on:

> People were told to denounce the spirits that might be operative in their lives. The ministers were into certain kinds of cultural, Protestant fundamental things. They're into jumping up and down, screaming when you pray. They feel there should be a dramatic physical manifestation of spirits leaving like rolling on the floor, drooling, vomiting. It caused quite a stir.
>
> The ministers wandered around the room. People were in various states of disrepair on the floor screaming. They were acting out the departure. People were coughing, hacking, wheezing.
>
> The police came. Someone explained and the police went away: they were used to weird things in those days!
>
> People thought this was a real breakthrough. They all had stuff in their lives they couldn't come up against. The ministers prayed for people, laid hands on them violently, moved people about.
>
> For six or eight months thereafter there were two big opinions: first, it's the greatest thing that ever happened; secondly, it's crazy—let me out!

The speaker himself believed that it was a good thing, but he wasn't sure the approach was best. People got "too hung up on blaming evil spirits instead of working things out in other ways." One couple wound up with opposite opinions. At the house where he lived, there began to occur basement deliverances day and night. "People foamed, shrieked in the cellar all hours of the day and night." And then, when he himself got delivered, he related:

> I felt absolutely obliged to do something. The best I could work up was coughing. For certain Fundamental groups, you can't be baptized in the Spirit without praying in tongues; can't be delivered without physical manifestations. There was an unconscious social pressure. Yet I saw people I respected go flying out of their chairs: they were literally thrown from their chairs. It struck me as odd but real. Their experience was that they were being acted on. Things happened I couldn't explain.
>
> I prayed gently one time, and the guy was thrown to the floor, was drooling. We were in shock: nobody knew what to do next. I thought it was something genuine, but was the work of evil spirits. I knew from the Gospel it could happen. The fine distinction between possession and oppression was not yet worked out. Because we didn't know much about it, possession was the most common thing from the New Testament.

This man spontaneously explains many of these phenomena as being due to social pressure. The distinction referred to comes from the Catholic exorcism ritual where "possession" means the taking over by demon(s) of someone's personality whereas "oppression" or "obsession" means forms of violent physical harassment of people and places by the evil spirits.[1]

After half a year, the next major phase occurred, namely, talking to the spirits, sometimes for hours on end. People kept in touch with the ministers and began reading "old Catholic works." People were told to say aloud what the evil spirit had in mind to say. The deliverers were getting beaten up. "Unuseful," foul talk was heard like that in "The Exorcist." People's characters were assaulted; sin in their lives was revealed. Though they were told that they didn't need to give vent to violence, blasphemy, and indecency, some people had been "pretty messed up and into the occult."

> I remember being called over to a cellar. A brother and I got our heads bashed. A woman had said, "We need strong men around." This young guy had been around but not in the community. He had been into drugs and the occult. He asked for deliverance one Thursday night. When we got there, the guy couldn't sit still anymore. He was on the floor screaming with people holding him down. The leaders wanted it to be gotten over with. All of us were praying; the main person would address spirits, command them to leave. There would be conversation with the spirits as needed. It was supposed to be useful to find out how spirits got in and how they worked in people's lives. We got back-talk. I really experienced something more than normal going on. He's not a particularly strong guy. We got smashed together, my friend and I.
>
> It went on for a long time, a long night of needless talking. People from all over would come in in the evening and pray till "dawn's early light." It had good effects because the guy seems to be doing much better.

Not all deliverances "work." The subject narrates such a case:

> This guy was into drugs and having flashbacks from hallucinogens. When we prayed with him he got physically violent: one guy took on the dozen of us! We prayed and he did too. The leaders would address him, "Spirit of such and such, I cast you out in the name of the Lord Jesus." When they started this, he became extremely violent; he became so powerful. We couldn't hold onto him, the dozen of us. The leader said it would be better to take care of the doors and windows and let Willy do his thing. Some people got pounded. He made his escape out a door, went to a dorm, smashed Michael in the mouth and went on his way. People have kept up with him. He's into Hare Krishna, has been back a few times. He's such a hurt person; he needed lots of repair work to get his act together.

Deliverance is not without its occasional humorous moments too: "One nice older lady came. We prayed all night. She was into verbal violence. A funny thing happened; at 4 A.M. we had a tea and chocolate chip cookie break!"

In the next and final phase described by this subject, deliverance becomes much more acceptable in a middle class ethos.

> One of the community's leaders developed a new approach. There was a change away from colorfulness to deal with things in one's life in a more constructive kind of way. He would explain that things were obstacles in your life. Together they would pray; if they prayed they were delivered. We moved on from there: it's not a cure-all. It became more quiet and peaceful. We don't blame the devil. People would discern things. . . .
>
> Deliverance was like the Catholic confessional experience, but now they don't mention their vices anymore. People don't even mind having it happen in their basements! The whole thing was a learning experience: we went from a cultural thing to a more quiet way of helping people deal with difficulties in their lives. It's like a rite of passage now—from what people were, into what they choose now.

The genius of this community's leaders is revealed in this passage. Seeking to use this gift of deliverance, yet make it less spooky and violent, they took the spectacular element out of it (talking with evil spirits) while reaffirming the basic belief in demonic influence. In this way, the community has tamed and institutionalized a practice inherited from the classical tradition of pentecostalism. The subject interviewed recapitulates the phases by giving a quick summary of them as they affected his life:

> When I first joined the renewal in 1969, I was demythologizing, wasn't believing in a personal Satan. The Lord gave me an experience; I met a practicing witch who worshiped the old Druid gods. He told me things about myself, read Tarot cards. I saw personal evil operate in a concrete kind of way in someone's life.

In the second phase, I witnessed physical violence. They would yell at deliverers, reveal sin in people's lives. It was a distraction while praying. They didn't need to say everything, nor do things which weren't nice or were blasphemous. I had some people say things about me which no one knew.

The signs of a successful deliverance are the fruit in people's lives. They are able to cope better, make progress in the spiritual life. There are a lot of concrete changes. Now it's a calm, everyday sort of thing.

How might we react to such a narrative? We are immediately reminded of Dom McCorkell's "bandwagon" upon which members of this particular community jumped so eagerly for a number of months until the leadership endorsed a less bizarre method of exorcism. The folklore of the renewal contains many tales of individual and group reactions similarly hysterical in nature. With the aid of good pastoral guidance and experience in the ways of spirits, many communities seem to have come through such interactions relatively unscathed, yet a psychologist can't help but be concerned about the potential damage unleashed by such primitive displays of emotionality, and of course skeptical about attribution to demonic influences. The research subject, himself untrained in psychology, wondered out loud about group expectations causing the outbursts of strange phenomena. Many psychologists would simply write off the behaviors as interesting but predictable effects of social learning, social control and suggestibility. Under the strong and respected training of the Florida ministers, this community's members quickly learned to behave as expected, and to reinforce each other's responses such as physical contortions, speaking in altered speech patterns about unmentionable subjects, and blaming it all on the devil. Psychologists of the Freudian persuasion would speculate further about the unleashed forces of the id arising out of the murky depths of the unconscious in uninhibited expressions of sexual and aggressive instinctual urges. Lest the psychologists' skepticism be too hastily written off as unnecessarily reductionistic due to their materialistic metaphysics, we might note that their attitude is recommended by no less an authority than the Roman Ritual. In the third of the General Rules guiding priest exorcists, the manual sanely advises:

> Especially, he should *not believe too readily* that a person is possessed by an evil spirit; but he ought to ascertain the signs by which a person possessed can be distinguished from one who is suffering from some illness, especially one of a psychological nature.[2]

Psychology, therefore, can teach us a healthy skepticism before irrational claims of the intensity of demonic powers at work. Yet the Christian can rightly accuse the psychological community of naiveté and remind us in the words of St. Paul that "our battle is not against human forces but against the principalities and powers, the rulers of this world of darkness, the evil spirits in regions above" (Eph. 6:12). Caution and skepticism is one thing, but a total denial of the demonic realm constitutes as ineffective a response as possible to an enemy by pretending he isn't there.

Fortunately, there exists within European and American psychology an admittedly minority tradition, the humanistic or "third force" position[3] which bases itself on a broader metaphysics than the philosophical materialism of most behaviorists and Freudians. This group includes a wide range of thinkers like Abraham Maslow, Carl Rogers, Rollo May, Gordon Allport, Kurt Godstein, Thomas Szasz and many others who are united in their dissatisfaction with a psychology that turns man into an object and often fails to respect the specifically human and subjective sides of human experience and personality. Often but not always, they conduct research within the existential phenomenological tradition and are concerned with such topics as self-actualization, creativity, love, meaning, higher values, and religious experience. It is to thinkers in this tradition that we now turn for further clarity about the dynamics of evil operating in the human person. These writers are not embarrassed about discussing the spiritual; rather, they integrate this dimension as a central factor in understanding and interpreting human life. Because these authors do not rule the demonic out of existence, and at the same time do reflect profoundly on the specifically human aspects involved, they steer safely between the two extremes charted by Abbot McCorkell.

Ronald D. Laing, a British psychiatrist who has spent his life developing a revolutionary and successful treatment of the most dreaded and most common of mental disorders, schizophrenia, argues passionately in *The Politics of Experience* and *Reason and Violence* that the positivistic methods employed by the behavioral sciences denigrate human dignity by reducing man to a mere object of study. Positivism, with its emphasis on objective measurement of quantifiable data, does not really study "data" but rather "capta," that is facts ripped from their matrix of happenings and experience. Positivism is a force for demoralization, for splitting subjective inner experience from outer behavior which alone deserves the accolade of "objective" and "scientific."[4] His writing style is trenchant and concrete, and his criticisms are aimed not only at the psychological profession, but at the entire modern materialistic *Weltanschauung:*

> Many people used to believe that the "seat" of the soul was somewhere in the brain. Since brains began to be opened up frequently, no one has seen "the soul." As a result of this and like revelations, many people do not now believe in the soul.
>
> Who could suppose that angels move the stars, or be so superstitious as to suppose that because one cannot see one's soul at the end of a microscope it does not exist?[5]

Laing's harsh critique is positively balanced, however, by a call for nothing less than a total reunification and reintegration of all aspects of human experience with a new respect for the inner life of fantasy and dreams, a respect for the avid exploration of the inner space and time of consciousness (to match our eager exploration of outer space), and a respect, finally, for mystical and transcendental experiences. His controversial treatment of psychosis—without psychotropic drugs, but with much interpersonal support—represents an effort to help his patients face their own inner demons and become "delivered" from demonic power. Laing interprets psychosis as the effort of a mind struggling to achieve mastery over the cruel absurdities of existence. He salutes the reality of realms of being beneath the level of observable behavior in the following passage whose original context makes it clear that he is not employing "mere" metaphor:

> In this journey, there are many occasions to lose one's way, for confusion, partial failure, even final shipwreck; many terrors, spirits, demons to be encountered that may or may not be overcome.[6]

Thus Laing employs a secular form of healing which recognizes and encounters forces of the intrapsychic spiritual realms, while insisting meanwhile that the remainder of "sane" humanity face squarely its insane denial of that dimension of reality in the name of scientific objectivity.

Carl Gustav Jung is perhaps the psychological theorist most deeply versed in the history of religions, philosophy, and mythology. Accordingly, his writings articulate a broadly humanistic vision whose sweep includes a cross-cultural and interdisciplinary perspective unmatched by other representatives of the field. Like Laing, Jung worked with schizophrenics, and also like Laing, he refused to write off their puzzling verbalizations as "nonsense" and "crazy," but struggled to interpret their implicit meaning. Jung discovered resemblances among the tortured utterances of the schizophrenic, the dream images of "normal" people, and the myths and symbols of cultures widely separated by time and geography. He postulated a "collective unconscious," or storehouse of racial memories and impressions inherited by each individual, for only in this way could he explain these demonstrated resemblances. If, for example, an uneducated psychotic spoke about a fantasy whose features exactly reproduced a symbol from a medieval text on alchemy, Jung would argue that the material in both cases had arisen from the collective unconscious. The images in the collective unconscious are shaped by structural conditions, pre-dispositions called "archetypes," inherited potentialities for molding contemporary experience in ways similar to the modes of our ancestors. One of these archetypes, the "shadow," forges symbols of demons, devils and evil ones. Into this archetype are poured all of one's own repressed and unacceptable motives, tendencies and desires, the "dark half" of one's personality, which are then psychologically fused with the racially inherited memories of evil events, situations and persons. Jung employs the shadow archetype to explain deeply irrational human hatreds and behaviors as demonstrated, for example, in the Nazi persecution of the Jews: a whole people projected its shadow onto another race and violently reacted against what was despised in itself. It was through this religio-psychological borderline concept of the archetypes that Jung was able to study the psychological aspects of the interchanges between man, God, and the spiritual realms.

Limitations of space allow only a brief mention of the work of two other psychologists concerning the problem of evil. My colleague at Georgetown University, Juan B. Cortes, a scholar trained both in Biblical Theology and psychology, argues forcefully in *The Case Against Possessions and Exorcisms*[7] that although evil spirits exist and can harass and oppress mankind, no good scriptural or psychological evidence supports the popular belief in actual demonic possession. His pastoral conclusion is that the ritual of exorcism should never be used.

Finally, David G. Myers, professor of psychology at Hope College, delivered the Finch Lectures at Fuller Theological Seminary in January 1979 and reflected on "Our Human Condition" with specific reference to the problem of evil.

In the writings of Laing, Jung, Cortes and Myers we see psychologists navigating between the shoals of metaphysical materialism's denial of the spiritual and hyperenthusiasm for demonic influences. Perhaps future studies can further elucidate and elaborate on the implications of their work as it affects theoretical explanation and pastoral practice.

NOTES

1. Philip T. Weller, *The Roman Ritual* (Milwaukee: Bruce, 1964), pp. 636–644.

2. *Ibid.*, p. 641; italics mine.

3. The most recent brief overview of the third force tradition in psychology is provided by John B. P. Shaffer's *Humanistic Psychology* (Englewood Cliffs, N.J.: Prentice-Hall, Inc., 1978).

4. Ronald D. Laing, *The Politics of Experience* (New York: Ballantine, 1967), pp. 60–62.

5. *Ibid.*, pp. 21–22.

6. *Ibid.*, p. 126.

7. Juan B. Cortes and Florence M. Gatti, *The Case Against Possessions and Exorcisms* (New York: Vantage, 1975).

6
The Imperative Need for the Church's Involvement in a Deliverance Ministry

by Francis MacNutt

Editors' Note: *Throughout the centuries Christians have prayed for deliverance from evil spirits. But with present progress in the sciences of medicine and psychology is there still a need for such prayer? An affirmative answer comes from Francis MacNutt who was one of the first Catholics in the charismatic renewal to teach on deliverance through his book* Healing *(1974). His article shares how he did not want to do deliverance prayer but was drawn into it because the need was so great both in suffering individuals and in cultures throughout the world.*

He too raises questions: Is the Church failing to evangelize the world because it is not preaching Jesus Christ's personal love through his actions of healing and deliverance? Are the suffering turning to other churches and even to the occult because the Catholic Church has ignored the need for deliverance? When deliverance prayer is necessary, why do chanceries so often ignore the reality of evil spirits or simply send the person to a psychiatrist who may not know how to treat the spiritual bondage? While we need to work with psychiatrists, are there not many people who have tried psychiatry and received inadequate help until prayed with for deliverance?

Just recently we gave a five-day retreat to one hundred priests who were facing some of these real questions. The

teaching on praying for deliverance was given by a very com-
petent psychiatrist who took off five days from his practice be-
cause he wanted to tell the priests that he needed them to help
his patients through confession, through prayer for healing of
memories, and especially through loving deliverance when
needed. This same psychiatrist three years ago stated that he
never saw a need to pray for deliverance. Why did he change
his mind? Deliverance prayer and therapy had brought heal-
ing to several of his patients hurt by the occult. Now he often
works with a priest and was calling for more collaboration. He
was asking Francis MacNutt's question: "Is the Church going
to help those suffering from evil spirits or just keep sending
them to others?"

I. HOW IT ALL HAPPENED IN MY LIFE: A PARABLE

Like most of those I know who have gotten actively involved in praying for deliverance, my involvement came
through experience, not through theory, and, in the beginning, I was reluctant. The desire to help people who were suffering was what motivated me to push beyond the bounds of
what was theologically respectable. At that point, the only
practical instructions I knew came from Protestants; almost all
of my teaching came from them and from my own trial-and-
error learning through experience. Inevitably I made mistakes, and have learned through some of them. Of all the
prayer ministry I have been engaged in, I can honestly say I
know of thousands being healed and can remember only a few
who were harmed through the healing ministry. But of my
ministry in deliverance, so closely connected with healing, I do
know of persons I have tried to help who were (at least temporarily) harmed through my ignorance—mostly because I did
not have time to follow through, or because I attacked the negative, the demonic element, at times when positive building
up or inner healing was needed.

We are all aware, I think, of the danger of deliverance
ministry; it is the most dangerous I know (not for the exorcist,

as Malachi Martin claims in *Hostage to the Devil,* but for the sufferer who is being prayed for). But the answer to this danger is to learn how best to pray for deliverance (at a time when little teaching is available) so that we won't make harmful mistakes. The other solution—closing down on deliverance (as now seems to be happening in Europe)—is far worse, for it leaves multitudes of the afflicted to suffer for the rest of their lives, or even to commit suicide in despair of ever receiving help from the Church.

My own need to learn something and get involved began almost as soon as I became active in a healing ministry. For instance, I would be praying in a quiet way, with people coming forward to ask for physical healing, when suddenly, with no outward provocation, a person's face would contort and he or she would shout something like "We hate you"; upon occasion persons would even try to strangle me, or their hands would go to their own throats. A number of bizarre occurrences like this took place. They were only occasional, to be sure, but almost always one or two bizarre episodes would take place if we prayed for enough people on any given evening. I could have passed them off as simply psychotic episodes, except that there were puzzling factors, such as:

(a) The persons were ordinarily very normal in behavior. At times, this was the first time something like this had ever happened to them.

(b) The atmosphere was usually not highly charged emotionally, but was quiet, characterized by an atmosphere of love and prayer. What, then, could be the cause of such hysterical manifestations?

(c) Often the voices spoke in the plural: "We will kill you."

What was the best thing to do when these episodes happened? Those times when I continued praying (often just praying in tongues, without structuring the prayer), the person would sometimes fall to the ground with a great amount of struggling and shouting. (Some critics describe this as hysteria generated by an over-emotional prayer group, but I believe the hysteria is usually in the person, not in the group, although the natural reaction of my group is to respond by shouting or praying an equally loud way.) I would then try to get the person alone, or with a small team in a private room; often after a period of prayer (say, an hour) commanding the spirits to leave, they would appear to leave (often through coughing or such external manifestations), and afterward the person would almost always know that, whatever it was, it was all gone (this certainty was another unusual thing; my experience is that prayer for healing is almost always a process, and the sense of "It's all over" is more common in deliverance). The person would then be at peace and was often radiantly transformed. The team would be exhausted, but the freed person usually felt exhilarated and joyful. Another unusual thing was that the person often couldn't remember anything that went on from the time he or she came forward in line until the process was over and he or she was freed; it was as if the demonic had taken over for a time, like a temporary possession, and the spirits had spoken through the person. These scenes reminded me of the Gerasene demoniac story in the Gospels, where the Legion spoke through the man until at last he sat rested, in his right senses.

Most of my ministry in the early days was ad hoc. What do you do when you are praying with people for healing, and a person starts screaming? How do you help such persons? Just send them home, as they came?

Basically, I tried to stay clear of all this and only emphasize the positive elements of the love of Jesus in any healing service we had, because I didn't think I knew enough to avoid mistakes. (A voice from one of the first persons who asked me for deliverance taunted me, when I started praying, by jeering, "You can't drive us out; you *don't have enough experience*.")

But in 1972 a case was thrust upon me that embodied a great amoung of teaching. It concerned a young married woman (we will call her Roberta) with a history of mental illness who had spent much time in hospitals. I had previously met her on a day of renewal and prayed for inner healing with her, but no evident healing happened; she wanted my help, but she didn't want the prayer. There were some strange things about her; aside from her beautiful, haunted face, there were rows of patterned burn marks on her arms, like a tattoo, caused by her sticking a lighted cigarette to her flesh. She said it hadn't hurt, and I ascribed all her scars to self-hatred or other psychological causes.

Then in the summer of 1972 some friends brought her to see me again at an ecumenical retreat in Iowa, and I began to suspect that maybe I was dealing with something more than a psychological problem. Every time she got near me, she ran. When her friends finally corralled her, she told me that she had been consecrated to an evil spirit as a young girl in Brazil; she had become a priestess of Satan, but now that she was in the United States she was trying to live a normal life.

Realizing that I was over my head in this case, I called for a Protestant who had much experience with deliverance and introduced her to him. I told her that I would start the prayer, but that I wasn't prepared to pray for her, and that the Protestant would have to do whatever casting out was to be done, because I didn't have enough knowledge or experience. She pleaded with me to direct the prayer, but I felt incompetent (besides, I realized that it might require the rite of exorcism and the permission of the bishop). Therefore the Protestant started the prayer of deliverance; he prayed for several hours, and the spirits were speaking through her, but nothing positive seemed to happen. Finally, at two in the morning I left the deliverance scene to go to bed. (I was to speak at the retreat the next morning, and I was already exhausted.)

Before dawn there was a knock at the door and a man told me to come quickly, for Roberta had tried cutting her wrists. I was irritated. Why come to me? But they brought Roberta over because she had asked to talk to me. And so we sat down on the doorstep as the sun came up, and she told me that she was leaving to go home and maybe end it all. My thought was: "She's playing games, using guilt to get me to talk to her." She said, "You are the only one in this camp with the power to free me. I came to you, and you turned me over to somebody who can't do it." This hit me very deep. Suppose she were right? On the other hand, if it were the devil, what better way to wipe me out as a speaker than to get me trapped the way the minister was last night?

I finally decided that I had better try to help her, provided that she did everything possible to help me. She agreed. She also told me that she had been consecrated to a particular demon mentioned in the Bible, and that a Scripture verse had been pinned to her when she was consecrated to Satan. She didn't know the Bible, but she asked if there was a book named "Jop." I told her that maybe she meant "Job," and she said, "That's it."

The next morning she came. She had found the verse, Job 18:14: "He is torn from the shelter of his tent, and dragged before the King of Terrors." " 'King of Terrors' is the one I was dedicated to," she said.

For the next hour I led her through repentance (the sacrament) and had her renounce all her involvement in the satanic ritual. Then I prayed to break the curse and cast out the King of Terrors. After that she consecrated her life to Jesus, was baptized in the Spirit, prayed in tongues and interpreted her own tongue: "Just as Satan has been using you for his purposes, I will now use you for My glory."

This entire prayer was very quiet, yet at the end she looked very different. In addition (what I didn't know at the time) she was addicted to various drugs and her addiction was broken through that prayer. She was also to begin a new life with her husband and children. (Her original motivation in coming to me was because one of her daughters had asked her if she was a witch.)

This story is, I think, a parable of what is happening to the Church in a whole variety of ways. I shall now try to show how Roberta's case spoke to me then, and what it says to the Church now.

The Human Need

The first teaching from Roberta's history is that I was forced to take action simply because I was confronted by immediate, deep human need—a case of life and death—and no one else was there who seemed able to do anything. Ignorant as I was, I could not "stand by watching a suffering humanity with folded arms." I didn't know much, but the basic question was: Did I have an obligation to try to help, even though I didn't know much? This seems to be the way most priests get involved in praying for deliverance. Knowing that they know little, they finally decide that they have to do something.

In this connection it is well here to turn to the results of a small survey I made. In the summer of 1978 we held a seminar on deliverance for priests and bishops at Mt. Augustine Retreat House in Staten Island, N.Y. A good number—one hundred and thirty-two (including two bishops)—came. A few laymen with experience in deliverance came by special permission, but almost all were priests. Afterward, some fifty-eight (fifty-four of them priests) responded to a questionnaire. To the question "How did you learn about the need for this ministry?" the largest number (twenty-six) learned through their experience: "It just happened at retreats" ... "Through conducting healing services" ... "When confronted by one in confession" ... "A psychiatrist sent them to me" ... "Demonic problems began to appear in our prayer groups, so we started inquiries." Another five said that people just started coming to them for help. Two more said that they discovered it in their parishes as a need. Another three priests admitted that their own personal need for deliverance opened them to the need for this ministry!

So, like me, most of them were not conditioned by teaching; they just found that there was an imperative need to help a person who seemed to be suffering from demonic oppression. These dramatic experiences were what motivated them to learn more about the subject (although nineteen originally learned about the subject through reading or hearing tapes, and another nine learned through hearing about it from friends).

For many priests, then, exorcism began, not just as an intellectual question about the causes of evil, but as a vital pastoral problem of what to do when faced with a desperate, suffering person asking for help.

Since then I have seen that this pastoral need is far larger than this or that afflicted individual; it is a pastoral problem affecting the well-being of the Church as a whole in several major areas—notably:

(a) The lack of deliverance ministry in the Church forces Catholics to look for help from the *wrong sources.*

(b) We need deliverance as an integral part of *evangelization.*

II. FORCING CATHOLICS TO SEEK HELP FROM THE WRONG SOURCES

Just as I tried to turn Roberta over to someone else who I thought could do better for her (an action that seemed prudent at the time), I think that most of us have been trained to look for help for these difficult cases in anyone but ourselves. My experience is that, by and large, people who seem to need deliverance come first to the priest. He then refers them to the psychiatrist. If the problem is emotional the psychiatrist may be able to help, but if the problem is demonic, the person will probably not be helped, but may end up institutionalized, out of harm's way, for the rest of his or her life; meanwhile, priests and ministers rest, contentedly assured that they have done the best they could. I am convinced that priests (or, sometimes, Christian laypersons) could help or heal many of these patients, and they are responsible for helping them. Moreover, most counselors and psychiatrists do not believe in the demonic, nor can they recognize its presence even when it is there.

I certainly believe that we should refer people to counselors or psychiatrists, but I also believe that there are many patients, including those in mental hospitals, who could be cured by Christians who understand how to pray for inner healing or deliverance. Admittedly, this is a proposition impossible to prove; I just present it as a heartfelt belief on my part. (Among other instances, I once prayed for a twenty-six-year-old woman who had been in a mental hospital for twelve years, suffering from a schizoid condition. I talked to her and prayed with her for repentance, inner healing and deliverance. At the end of two hours the glazed look in her eyes had changed and she was able to converse in a normal way. Several weeks later, the doctors recognized the change and she was released from the hospital.)

But, far more serious, we leave many people, especially in other cultures, no other choice (or so it seems to them) but to go to some other church or even to an occult source for help. In Nigeria about half the Christians belong to "Aladura" churches, which are independent Pentecostal churches that feature exorcism and healing. When I was in Nigeria in 1974 it was estimated that nearly half the Catholics when sick went to Aladura churches to pray for healing or exorcism. In Latin America many Catholics go to the "curanderos" or "spiritistas" when they are sick. Last year in Venezuela, the missionaries who were our hosts estimated that eighty percent of the Venezuelans go to a witch doctor or to a curandero upon occasion. The same phenomenon holds true in New York, Miami (among the Cubanos), New Orleans and many other United States cities with large Hispanic populations. In the July 1978 issue of *U.S. Catholic,* an article "Saturday Night Voodoo; Sunday Morning Mass" points out how Caribbean Catholics in Brooklyn are as much at home at a voodoo service as they are at a Mass. The main effort at these services is to hex some people and to heal others. "When Haitians become sick, they believe that their priests can invoke spirits to cure diseases caused by magic. When they are hospitalized in Brooklyn's Kings County Hospital and are not getting well, they are often advised by fellow Haitians, including medical doctors, "Go back to your country. . . . See a special *houngan* or *mambo* as only they can cure you of your illness" (p. 36). This article suggests that voodoo is no more a problem than are leprechauns for the Irish; this cultural prejudice which sees voodoo as a harmless superstition reflects the cultural bias of most educated Catholics. The pastoral advice given by priests usually seems to regard these practices as superstitious but not to be taken seriously. However, the common people sense that there is real power in spiritualistic sources (witness the fascination in movies on the occult), and they continue to go to non-Catholic sources for healing or deliverance. Regrettably, not only do many priests and ministers avoid the deliverance ministry to which they have been called, but many of them don't even believe in it.

A fascinating research article, " 'El Duende' and Other Incubi," mentions the disbelief of priests and bishops that causes the "possessed" to seek help from non-Christian sources (*Arch. Gen. Psychiatry,* Vol. 32, Feb. 1975, pp. 155–162). El Duende is a particular form of familiar spirit that is believed in some Latin American countries to haunt certain young girls and their families. The author, Carlos A. León, M.D., investigated and interviewed twelve families who reported cases of obsession with El Duende to the hospital where he worked in Colombia. What concerned Dr. León was that psychiatry did not seem to help these patients. Nor did *traditional religious practices.* The only real help that they received was from occult healers. Of the twelve cases, six found sessions with the "spiritistas" effective, while only four found them ineffective.

This is in contrast to "blessings by a priest" which none found effective and eight found ineffective, "common prayers" which none found effective and twelve found ineffective, and "crucifixes and religious objects" which two found effective and ten found ineffective.

To me the evidence indicates that psychiatry is not the appropriate remedy for what could well be demonic activity; on the other hand, occult healers, since they deal with these demonic forces, can heal, but they put the person under deeper spiritual bondage. The appropriate remedy is Christian prayer, but Dr. León's case histories indicate that there was real unbelief on the part of Church officials; like the sons of Sceva in Acts, their skepticism rendered them ineffective. For example, Dr. León remarks, "Requests for exorcism were formulated in several instances, but never granted; the present position of the local clergy concerning these cases seems to be one of extreme caution if not outright skepticism. When priests came to help, they only offered some blessings and prayers. On the other hand spiritualists were anything but reluctant or hesitant" (p. 158).

One of the cases was that of Ursulina; her family believed that El Duende wanted to take possession of Ursulina and carry her to his realm, and so her family sought help to protect her from this fate.

> The family first approached the parish priest right after Ursulina had been troubled by the duende at Mass. He advised them to go to the bishop and ask him to appoint an exorcist for the case. The bishop sent two nuns to investigate the case and make a report. During their visit the duende displayed frantic activity: whistling, scratching, and hitting Ursulina; singing obscene songs; passing flatus; and making profane remarks about the visitors who, in spite of not seeing or hearing him, were terrified by all the gesticulations and wild activity exhibited by the girl.

The family then tried the spiritualists who, at that point, were not helpful, so "her family decided that Ursulina had to go to confession and Communion. Then, all hell broke loose: the duende dragged Ursulina by the hair through the house. . . . The girl was in such a state the following morning that the priest refused to confess her and ordered her relatives to take her to the psychiatric hospital" (p. 160). In short, Ursulina got the run-around: priest to bishop; bishop to nuns; nuns drop out; back the family goes to the priest, who sends them to the psychiatrist.

After she was discharged by the hospital uncured, Ursulina was taken to a group of spiritualists where she was taught to communicate with spirits; she later became a gifted medium and the center of a cult. This is a good example of a more general situation; just as I tried to pass off Roberta to someone else, Ursulina's pastor referred her to the psychiatrists. When they were not able to help sufficiently, her family had only one recourse left—to go the occult route.

(An interesting addendum is that a woman came to my

friend, Mrs. Barbara Shlemon, for ministry. Although the woman was not acquainted with the tradition of the duende, she described being oppressed by an unusual looking apparition, who corresponded exactly to the description of El Duende—a little pot-bellied apparition with dark complexion and large white teeth who usually dresses in red or black and always wears a large tall hat and pointed boots.)

Another area where priests are called to help but often cannot, or will not, is on behalf of those who have entered into satanic groups and want to get out. They are often afraid to make the break, because of their fear of retaliation from Satan or the coven, if they try to make the break. In desperation they approach a priest who may not believe them or know how to set them free. In this regard, a fascinating private interview was given to me by a psychologist who was instrumental in helping a witch of the third degree break loose from her bondage in a coven which had been desecrating churches and using blood sacrifices in their rites. She approached several priests asking for help, and they weren't sure whether to believe her. Her reaction was to retaliate against one of them in various ways. Part of the interview goes as follows:

Q. You told me earlier that one of the reasons why you were engaged in that incident was because you were angry against the Church?
A. Any church.

Q. Where did this anger originate?
A. From their not believing it was real.

Q. And your anger was first directed against St. _____ parish?
A. Yes.

Q. And the prayer group there?
A. I wanted to split them up and cause division.

Q. That was three years ago?
A. Yes, and I did.

Q. How did you cause division?
A. Put thoughts in people's minds ... like "This stuff isn't for real; what's in it for me?" Gossip about each other—not being secretive about each other when they should.... I directed my anger also at a priest. I just started putting crazy ideas into his head, about men and relationships with men, getting him to wonder if he was cut out to be a priest. I was trying to disillusion him, and I wanted him to leave here very badly ... and he did....

Q. What would you say if someone said that you were crazy?
A. I would say, maybe so, but I know what I'm talking about. If they say that, they had better back off, because they are in line of fire. I know what is real and what isn't. I know what I've been into, and they don't know what they are talking about. If they had seen and felt the power that I have, they wouldn't be saying that.

Q. What power do you have?
A. I'd rather not have it.

Q. What power is it?
A. The power of destruction and the power to help.

Q. The power to help?
A. The power to help is white magic; the power to destruct is black magic....

Q. Some people say that magic is only superstition.
A. Then they don't know what they are talking about; they are going by what someone else has said. I know for one that it is not superstition, that it is real. I have seen what it can do; it can hurt real bad sometimes. (Here she describes an instance of human sacrifice.) That was before they believed me, but now that they believe me I have hope.

Q. So now you want the Catholic Church to get involved?
A. I don't care how they get it. I want help. I can't do it by myself. If there were not people helping me the past

couple of weeks, I would not be here talking. I would already be dead.

So, just as Roberta was saying to me, "Don't you believe in who you are?" this former witch, and countless other people, are asking the Church—and priests, in particular—"Why can't you help us? Don't you believe in what you were called to do?"

III. THE POWER OF EVANGELIZATION

This brings us to a major point: the Gospel is not only teaching doctrine; it includes a *power* to free, to save, to heal, to deliver. In my experiences preaching in thirty countries, I have seen that peoples of every culture are waiting to hear the message of Christ's salvation; when we preach about God's love, about his sending his Son, Jesus, to free the human race from the evil they experience—some now, some in the next life—the people respond eagerly. When I taught homiletics I thought that the problem was to figure out how to make the Gospel relevant to the needs of contemporary people and how to translate it into other cultures. I now see that the Gospel is in itself relevant, that it does appeal, but I was not fully preaching it because I did not understand the need for the power to heal and free people from evil spirits. I conceived of myself basically as a teacher and did not experience the power with which Jesus commissioned his followers when he sent them out to preach: "He called the Twelve together and gave them power and authority over all devils and to cure diseases, and he sent them out to proclaim the kingdom of God and to heal" (Lk. 9:1–2).

In every culture except the European (and those influenced by the European, such as ourselves), I have found that ordinary people have a lively appreciation of spiritual bondage and the reality of demonic forces. They are waiting for the good news that they can be freed by the power of God, and when they hear that news, they come in droves (in Bombay, India in November 1978, some twenty thousand people came to a healing service; remarkably, many of the testimonies of healing were from Hindus).

In our contemporary understanding of Christianity I believe that we impose a heavy cultural overlay of rationalism. While we may think that we are bringing these other "less enlightened" cultures into Christian truth, what we are really doing is bringing them a Western (that is, Western-since-Descartes) view of humanity and the world, which is basically prejudiced against a number of spiritual practices that we label as "superstitious." To us, superstition and a magical view of the universe include God's "interfering" in creation through healing and the lively belief that many of these peoples hold about the presence and activity of evil spirits.

The people of every culture I have visited, except the European, say that they know that they experience the reality of a spiritual world that oppresses them and they don't understand why many Christian missionaries seem to have less belief in it than the ordinary, uneducated people do.

Meantime, the missionaries are trying to educate the people, to enlighten them, so that they will no longer fear this dark world of "spirits" and superstition. The missionaries seem to believe that once the people are educated they will no longer be bothered by these primitive fears, just as we are not in Europe and the United States.

I believe that one of the reasons why we have not succeeded in bringing the Gospel to many cultures is simply that we do not understand fully what Christianity has come to bring. We have turned it from good news into good advice.

For example, in Nigeria, my invitation to come in 1974 came from the Dominicans there. One contributing factor was that they had decided that the native seminarians were somewhat superstitious and should be enlightened. For instance, the black seminarians were afraid of witch doctors putting curses on them and various things like that. And so the seminary brought in a black psychologist from the local university to tell the students that they shouldn't worry over things like that and that there were psychological explanations for what was going on. The students simply told the psychologist that he had been working with white people too long. All they knew was that if somebody back in their village got angry with one of them and had a curse put on, he would wake up in the morning sick—without anyone having told the seminarian anything. Therefore, it wasn't just suggestion. (I know that parapsychology offers explanations for incidents like this; I'm only saying that our culture pretty well rules out the demonic as any possible explanation.) And so the psychologist left, having failed to convince the young black Dominicans.

Or, to take another common instance, we would be praying with a group of Nigerians and suddenly one would go into some of the manifestations that indicate the possibility of demonic activity. The Nigerians understood what was going on immediately, and if the person started going through some of the unpleasant and violent manifestations sometimes associated with deliverance, say, of coughing, the Nigerians would stand and applaud until it was over. Meanwhile the Irish missionaries would be headed toward the door, shaking their heads at what they regarded as a throwback to a primitive religion out of which they were trying to educate the people.

As I mentioned earlier, many of these Nigerian Catholics attend the "Aladura" (Pentecostal) churches to get the help they need in healing and deliverance. Within two miles of the Dominican seminary in Ibadan were some seventy-two Aladura churches!

While the missionaries tend to look at the Nigerians as prone to superstition (and there may well be many elements of superstition in their popular beliefs), still it seemed to me that the Nigerians were more in touch with some basic spiritual realities than we are—that they are basically healthier and more in touch with a biblical cosmology than are Europeans and Americans. It is only a kind of blindness that enables us to think we are bringing them Christian enlightenment, when actually we have mixed our Christianity with a heavy cultural bias. In recent years we have become sensitive to the fact that our missionaries were importing too much European architecture, etc., to the missions and not respecting the culture to which they were sent. But the possibility exists that we are still involved in the deepest kind of intellectual bias and look down on other cultures as basically ignorant simply because they believe in such concepts as demonic activity and possession. Like the witch in the earlier example, these peoples know the reality of the power to destruct and the power to help. Unless missionaries exhibit a greater power, the Nigerians will remain subject to witchcraft or will feel a need to attend an Aladura church.

Lest it be said that only pre-literate cultures are affected by beliefs in ju-ju or the fear of demonic activity, I might here point out that most people in the Orient also believe in such activity. (In fact, everywhere around the world there seems to be a *common natural religion* and a *common experience* of the activity of *evil spirits,* which *everywhere manifest themselves in much the same way,* although the names of these forces are, of course, different.)

In Japan, for instance, although traditional Shinto and Buddhist religions today seem more to be part of cultural background than something to be practiced, there is still a lively belief in the need for exorcism. In the *Japan Times* of July 30, 1978, there is an account of how Shinto priests were called in to conduct rites to drive evil spirits out of a vast public housing complex in Tokyo, where thirty-two persons, in a six-year period, had committed suicide by jumping from the heights of the apartments. The American reporter in the *Times* suggests that perhaps psychologists should be called in, or that the apartments should be made more hospitable; but the important thing to observe is that the Japanese themselves believed that evil spirits could be operative in the high suicide rate.

Another unusual aspect of Japanese life, not realized by most of us in the United States, is that there is an extraordinary growth in the so-called "new religions." Whereas only one percent of the Japanese are Christian, some fifteen percent of the Japanese now belong to these new religions. These religions are centered on God, but are not Christian; most of them have been formed since World War II. It appears, then, that the fastest growing religious interest in Japan centers on the new religions, and they, in turn, all center on healing and deliverance. I think this indicates the great need of people for healing and that the *basic pre-evangelism of Christianity* is meant to be *healing and deliverance.* In default of our believing actively in a healing and deliverance emphasis, the field has been left open to anyone who offers to supply this basic need.

To personally investigate one of these new religions I went to a center of the group known as Mahikari No Waza ("The Art of Spiritual Purification") and was ushered into a large room where various members of their group were praying, one on one, for people who needed healing or deliverance.

The literature I was given opens with the statement, "What do you think if you are told that your life is partly controlled by some invisible force?" In twenty years some 300,000 Japanese have converted to this group founded by Kotama Okada, whose initial conception of his mission is quaintly described as follows (misspellings and wrong grammar included):

> At five o'clock in the morning, February 27, 1959, Great Saint Kotama Okada, A Japanese, was revelated by God, the Creator; Rise up, name yourself Kotama (literally, Jem of Light). Hold your hand up and purify the world. The world will become more and more bitter and severe for the human beings." Great Saint Kotama Okada started holding his hand over people soon after the revelation, and he found a dying man come to life again, the paralysed started to walk, and the blind began to see, just like Sakyamuni or Jesus Christ performed miracles, God ordered the Saint; "Go and save the human beings, distributing the Light of God, and give the power of Makikari No Waza to everybody who wishes to obtain it."

In this pamphlet there are several descriptions of adherents of the sect being freed from spirits of the dead, together with a picture of a young woman minister praying for a possessed man whose body is jumping off the ground with a "movement which is impossible to make normally." *Modern*

Japanese Religions (by C. B. Offner and H. Van Straelen, S.V.D., printed in 1963 at the Salesian Technical School, Tokyo) points out, "If sickness is considered as the representative 'evil' and healing as the representative 'salvation,' the main elements in the entire teaching and practice of these religions will be clarified" (p. 20).

In a private interview with the archbishop of Tokyo, he observed that perhaps we Catholics had made a mistake in the past hundred years of evangelization by primarily aiming at the intellectuals, guided by the idea that, if we could reach them, we could reach the nation. He said that we had only reached a few intellectuals in that prolonged time, and the few who were reached were not zealous in spreading the Gospel. This is in marked contrast to the rapid spread of the three hundred new religions which all emphasize healing and fill their halls and churches, while Christians ponder in the locker room, as it were, about the lack of success or their own game plan.

The need for deliverance in healing is clearly seen by many priests in other countries. In India, for instance, Fr. Rufus Pereira, a graduate of the Pontifical Biblical Institute in Rome, has performed some five hundred deliverances in the past two years—most of them for people who seemed to be possessed by Hindu gods. He taped an interview for us in which he evaluates the need for deliverance as part of the Church's evangelization in India. I also have a paper written by Archbishop E. Milengo, of Lusaka in Zambia, concerning the imperative need for understanding and practicing deliverances in Africa. Unfortunately, there isn't time to go into all this in this brief article. I just want to give enough evidence to intimate that one of the basic problems of the Church in evangelizing is that we are so closed into a Western, rational thought system that we are unable to understand and put into action that part of the Gospel that includes the power to save, to free and to heal. I see this as a major pastoral opportunity and responsibility: to sort out and restore a balanced deliverance ministry to the Church.

IV. DELIVERANCE MINISTRY IN THE CHURCH: SOME PROBLEMS

1. Problems with the Chancery

Unfortunately (and it is understandable why) most chancery officials don't seem to want to get involved in deliverance. They, as are most educated clergymen, are embarrassed by the whole idea of possession as somehow scientifically disreputable. Furthermore, they have been burned badly by adverse publicity in several notorious cases that became famous worldwide. For instance, I have before me an article entitled "A Fatal Possession" which describes a wretched case in Germany in 1976 where two priests were brought to trial for trying to exorcise a woman who ended up starving to death without proper medical assistance. The general reaction of some Church authorities to such cases seems to be, "Let's close it all out. It represents the last gasp of an outdated practice that should have died with the Middle Ages." (In Europe this seems to be a common reaction.)

A more traditional view would hold that we should not shut exorcism down altogether, but we must proceed with great caution, and all cases of deliverance must pass through the proper Church authorities, namely the bishop's office. This makes a great deal of sense until you actually try to do it.

Roberta is a case in point. Like most situations I have met, I had to make some kind of immediate decision. I had tried to avoid getting mixed up in her case, but here it was dawn, and she was threatening to go home and commit suicide. Moreover, I had no real possibility of checking it out with the chancery by a telephone call. It was either play it safe (for *me*) by doing nothing, or try to help her, even at some personal risk. For her it was life or death, and I couldn't justify myself not acting.

These questions have a Catch 22 aspect, and we need to discuss these factors *honestly* and *realistically* if we are ever going to be able to sort out the ministry of deliverance in the Church.

Catch 22: The theory states: "Keep your hands off unless you check first at the chancery." The problem in practice, though, is the same one that Dr. León describes as common in Colombia. The people go to the chancery; the chancery has little or no experience in exorcism and refers the person to a psychiatrist, and the entire deliverance dimension (if there is one) is left out precisely because a reference to the chancery is almost the same as a reference to a psychiatrist. In one instance where a priest friend of mine referred a person to the chancery and an exorcist was appointed, it turned out that the exorcist did not himself believe in the personal existence of Satan.

In the seminar at Mt. Augustine only four of the fifty-eight respondents knew if there was a formal exorcist appointed in their dioceses, and only two were in communication with him. I think we really need to be honest about this; when we do turn to the local chancery, we find that they, like us, have received virtually no training in these matters, and they don't really know what to do. Until they learn, there may be real harm done by omission, in that a spiritual problem may be handled on a purely medical level.

2. Problems with the Teaching Magisterium

"Let us turn to the living magisterium of the Church and her wisdom." Again, who could be against this? But what does it really mean?

I think there is a great deal in the tradition of the Church on the subject of deliverance, and I would like to get back to it and learn more from these sources. For instance, there is a fascinating *Manual of Exorcism,* translated from a Spanish manuscript of about 1720 (Hispanic Society of America, 1975, distributed by Interbook Inc., 545 8th Ave., New York, N.Y. 10018). The present contemporary Catholic teaching on this subject however is almost nil; in my own excellent, seven-year training in the seminary, only three minutes, in passing, were devoted to the subject of exorcism. The present situation is simply one of benign neglect. The few traditional resources such as Tanquerey ignore the number of people who are devoted Catholics and regular communicants, but who all still seem to be tormented (often at the point of receiving Communion), and who need to be freed in order to receive the sacraments in peace. This I'm sure is a point we need to discuss. I know a number of people who have been freed just by going to confession or receiving Communion, or who were freed when there was a great atmosphere of prayer in some meeting, but a certain number of people are not freed through those positive means alone (Roberta, for example, was a practicing Catholic). Most surprising of all to me has been my discovery of the number of priests and sisters who have benefited by deliverance. On one retreat in Santiago, Chile, in 1972, there were seventy-five participants; almost all of them were priests and sisters, and seven of them received deliverance during the retreat or during the week immediately after. The emphasis on the retreat was not deliverance, nor were these easily suggestible people; they were missionaries, hardened by years of suffering. This may sound exaggerated to some, I know, but we need to discuss how common the need for deliverance is and whether the need can exist in regular communicants. (I cannot remember this ever being discussed in the "living magisterium.")

Teaching from the living magisterium would come largely from books, so it is relevant that of the fifty-eight respondents at Mt. Augustine, most learned about deliverance from their own experience or from hearing about it from friends. To the question "What books have been most helpful to you?" twenty-three got the most help from *Deliver Us From Evil* by Don Basham (a Pentecostal), eighteen from the chapter on deliverance in my book *Healing,* seven from *Pigs in the Parlor* by Frank Hammond (a Protestant) and four from *But Deliver Us From Evil* by John Richards (an Anglican), while three each mention the Linn brothers, Fr. Michael Scanlan and Malachi Martin as sources of teaching. Considering that most of the respondents (fifty-four) were priests, it is notable that their sources of teaching are almost all Protestant or Catholic charismatic authors. So, if we are told to turn to the living magisterium, we have a natural question to ask: "All right—can you tell us what books to read that offer help?"

3. Problems with Terms

Another major source of confusion that we must begin to work out here is that of finding the right words to clarify what we mean. Almost always, when you talk about deliverance with people who have had no experience with it, they think you are talking about freeing someone who is *possessed*. Their natural response is, "But that is very rare and you need a specialist for it. Turn it over to the chancery." I think we would all agree that possession is rare, and that, when it occurs, we had best turn it over to the chancery office.

Yet, the other traditional words, "oppression" and "obsession," indicating spirit harassment from outside the person, do not adequately reflect what we discover in a certain number of cases. What we discover is that, seemingly, demonic forces or familial spirits are harming the person *from within*, not from without (by temptations and oppression). We might use the word "infestation" to denominate this fourth state to go along with the three terms traditionally used: "possession," "oppression" and "temptation."

Why is it important to add this fourth? Because we need it to clarify our experience, for people will often describe the spirits as being within them and will sense the spirits leaving as you pray. It is more than their being harassed from outside, where a simple prayer should be enough to free the person. The condition is different and the kind of prayer needed to cast out the spirits is also different.

Also—and this may seem strange to those who have not had the experience of praying for deliverance—many people who are not possessed, but who go into a state that seems *like a temporary possession* when you pray for them, find that their speech takes a form as if spirits are speaking through them, and their actions are as if controlled by an outside force. Usually, it is very easy to get back in touch with the real person, who, incidentally, is aware of the difference between what he is saying or doing and what the spirits are saying or doing through using his body. (Admittedly, this kind of phenomenon allows of a purely psychological explanation, but I think the ultimate explanation in many cases is that there are spirits present.)

As I understand it, the Greek used in the New Testament usually does not refer to persons being possessed but rather to their "having a demon" or being "demonized." Perhaps to say that a person "has a demon" may be one way of getting out of the bind of talking about possession (total control from within) or oppression (attack from without) as if there were no middle ground.

This possession bind creates a further problem, because if you refer a person to a chancery the officials usually start looking for the marks of true possession which are very rare; they then decide the person doesn't need an exorcist but a psychiatrist. By and large, we are not sending them possessed persons, nor are we asking for permission to do the rite of formal exorcism. Within the traditional framework of requesting permission for formal exorcism we are wasting the chancery's time; we cannot prove the case of need! Again, it is Catch 22.

Of the fifty-eight respondents at Mt. Augustine, it is highly significant that some fifty-one prayed for people for deliverance, but only one priest and one layman had been involved in formal exorcism! And yet fifty-one had had experience in deliverance: twenty-six had prayed for between one and five deliverances, nine had prayed for between five and ten, six had prayed for between ten and twenty, and ten had prayed for more than twenty. From this it seems clear that there is a need for a clarification of (a) what to call this state that lies between "possession" and "obsession," and (b) whether "deliverance" is a term that can be used to characterize the ministry of freeing people from this state, or whether we should use some other term such as "simple exorcism" (cf. the articles by Fathers Faricy and McManus).

4. Problems with Priests' Lack of Experience

Another source of confusion is that priests who have never experienced actual cases of deliverance are almost bound to consider that the descriptions of them sound excessive, if not hysterical, and they consider it ridiculous to say that the need for deliverance is common when they themselves have seldom, or never, run into such phenomena in a lifetime of pastoral experience. For the first ten years of my own pastoral experience I never ran into any person that I thought needed exorcism or deliverance. (In retrospect, I believe now that deliverance would have helped some of the people I was counseling ten years ago; often they were trying to tell me something which I didn't believe and I wrote it off as a purely psychological problem.)

This difference in priests' experience comes about in part because the phenomenon of deliverance seems to occur commonly only where there is a power of prayer sufficient to drive the spirits out. Then they seem to surface. Sometimes they leave; at other times they erupt and try to disrupt or halt the meeting. This happens often in Africa and South America, and, at times, in the United States. Again, this is my own interpretation, and someone could readily claim that these eruptions come from persons who are hysterically inclined, and the emotionally charged atmosphere of a pentecostal gathering triggers their wild reactions. This may be true in some cases, but my own experience inclines me to believe that most of our religious practices do not disturb most evil spirits; they are not worried, as it were, by routine prayers; they only erupt when they really feel threatened by the power of the Spirit. Roberta was comfortable as long as I just talked to her the first time we met; the one thing she feared was prayer for her deliverance.

At any rate, there must be a reason why exorcism and deliverance are coming to the fore again in the Catholic Church almost solely through the agency of charismatic groups. Three possible reasons are:

(a) The emotional component in charismatic gatherings engenders emotional explosions among the unstable.

(b) Charismatic groups have learned to think of demonic activity as a facile explanation of sickness and tend to find spirits where there are none.

(c) The power of the Spirit is re-emphasized among pentecostal Catholics, and this provokes a counter-reaction on the part of the evil spirits.

I believe that all these explanations are partly true, but that the last explanation is the deeper truth for what is happening in the Church today.

V. COLLABORATION BETWEEN THE CHURCH AND PSYCHIATRY

The last problem in discussing this whole phenomenon of demonic activity is simply: "How do you know?" All the weird phenomena we see in the deliverance ministry are ambiguous; spirits seem to speak through the person and shout out, "We will kill you!" How can we be sure that this isn't just the person's subconscious erupting? Usually we can't judge this with any certainty by any rational process. We need to rely more on intuition, but intuition of its nature is not susceptible to logical proof. That's why trying to prove a case to the local chancery seems to be such a fruitless expenditure of time; by and large you can marshal evidence, yet never prove anything. In many ways it is like the difficulty at Lourdes of trying to prove medically that a supernatural cure has taken place. Thousands of healings take place every year; yet only one in every four years is certified by the Medical Bureau as clearly beyond natural powers.

Here is where the "gift of discernment" can play such a vital part. There are persons who have this gift, who can tell whether the afflicted person's problem is purely on the natural, psychological level or whether there are evil spirits involved. I myself tend to work on the basis of intuition, aware that I may be wrong at times and that my judgments are often based on past experience—e.g., this woman has a peculiar look on her face, and she is saying these vicious things in an unusual tone of voice that reminds me of a number of other people who have responded to prayer for deliverance; therefore, she probably needs that kind of prayer, too. But there are people who *know* what they are dealing with; it is a real gift, and most priests I know who are involved in the deliverance ministry either have this gift themselves, or have discovered someone who does have the gift who can help them (as have the Linns and Fr. McAlear). The ideal would be if every diocese had an official exorcist who had the gift of spiritual discernment (or who worked with someone who did) and who also worked in collaboration with a Christian psychiatrist who believed in deliverance himself.

Happily we are beginning to see such collaboration take place. In a group such as the Association of Christian Therapists, priests, counselors and psychiatrists are now openly discussing the deliverance ministry and learning from each other. At a time when the Church is opening up to a renewed understanding of the influence of evil spirits upon people's lives, some counselors and psychiatrists are also discovering the same thing in their practices. No longer is it true to think that all of what we used to call "possession" is simply mental illness and that the psychiatrist is the only one competent to deal with a psychotic.

In evidence of this, there are a number of counselors and a few psychiatrists who now pray with their patients for inner healing and, upon occasion, for deliverance. Dr. Conrad Baars describes one such experience:

Some years ago I became the "victim" of such a spirit in one of my patients, a woman religious with severe obsessive-compulsive neurosis and deprivation neurosis. In our therapy sessions this woman developed an uncanny ability to arouse my anger. This, of course, is not too uncommon, but what concerned me was my inability to control it. This had never happened before, or since, but in this case session after session ended with a loud exchange of angry remarks and the patient storming out of the room in tears.

Finally, after weeks of my wondering what was happening, and why I could not handle my anger in a calm, professional manner, the sister expressed her own concern with this development in what was once a consistently pleasant, friendly physician-patient relationship. She told me she liked and respected me greatly and had no reason to be angry with me, but she knew exactly what to do or say that would make me lose my temper. It seemed, she added, that there was something in her that made her do or say these things.

With her permission, I consulted Fr. Francis MacNutt, O.P., who happened to visit me around the time. On his recommendation we prayed over my patient for deliverance. She was indeed delivered of several spirits that left her quietly and without much objection. None of them identified themselves, nor were they instructed to do so, but if one of them had, I am certain it would have used the word "anger." There was a dramatic change in the patient's behavior and appearance from then on. Never again did her words or facial expression reveal any feeling of anger or hate toward me (*Feeling and Healing Your Emotions,* Logos International, Plainfield, N.J., 1979, pp. 204–205).

Dr. Baars has also pointed out to me a remarkable case in the *Archives of Sexual Behavior* (Vol. 6, No. 5, 1977), written up by David H. Barlow, Ph.D., Gene G. Abel, M.D., and Edward B. Blanchard, entitled "Gender Identity Change in a Transsexual." These authors describe the remarkable change of a transsexual (whom they name John) through exorcism; the remarkable part of this case was that John suffered from a psychological disorder that resists all treatment through psychotherapy. They had thoroughly tested John and finally decided that the best thing was to encourage him in his determination to have a sex-change operation. In preparation for surgery John had changed his name to Judy, his facial hair had been removed through electrolysis, and enlargement of his breasts had been produced through estrogen. The date of the operation had been set, but on the insistence of a Christian friend of his, John visited another doctor who told him that his real problem was "possession by evil spirits." John consented to a three-hour exorcism session at which twenty-two evil spirits purportedly left him.

After this session John felt affirmed in his masculine identity and discarded his female clothing. At a subsequent prayer session the enlargement in John's breasts almost immediately subsided.

The doctors tested John afterward for two-and-a-half years and were amazed that he showed a clear reversal of gender identity—something they had never seen in their own practice or heard about in psychological literature. They concluded their report by stating, "What cannot be denied, however, is that a patient who was very clearly a transsexual by the most conservative criteria assumed a long-lasting masculine gender identity in a remarkably short period of time following an apparent exorcism."

So here we have the paradox where psychiatrists are saying that, from their perspective as medical men, there is evidence that exorcism is necessary, while spiritual authorities in the Church question or even deny the validity of such a ministry:

> A priest-professor on the campus where the forthcoming suspense thriller "The Exorcist" was filmed says that the ancient ritual of casting out demons is worse than useless and should be abolished by the Roman Catholic Church. Not only are there no such things as "demons" for exorcists to cast out, says the Rev. Juan B. Cortes of Georgetown University, but the lengthy and harrowing rites performed on the "possessed" are potentially dangerous to the emotional stability of the disturbed person they are intended to benefit. . . .
>
> Finally Father Cortes remarks that almost anyone opting to undergo the ritual of exorcism will live to regret it (*St. Louis Post-Dispatch*).

Where is the living magisterium of the Church? Almost all the books written recently by non-charismatic Catholic authors (except Malachi Martin's *Hostage to the Devil*) reflect a systematic doubt about the value of exorcism. Since the presence or non-presence of evil spirits cannot be proven scientifically, it is imperative that we rediscover the proper criteria for discerning whether or not evil spirits are present. The statement of the legendary official exorcist of Paris who never in twenty years discovered a person who was possessed is not in itself an impressive testimony. I would suspect that his mental set may have caused him to interpret all evidence on a psychological plane.

Here is a person brought to him who claims to be afflicted by evil spirits. The man is schizophrenic, so the official exorcist has him checked out by a psychiatrist, who says "Yes, your suspicions are correct. The man is not possessed; he is schizoid." But this is illogical. To say that he is schizoid says nothing at all about whether or not he is not also possessed. Is it more likely for a psychologically healthy person or a psychologically wounded person to be victimized by spirits? In my experience there is more demonic activity in the emotionally troubled, and the traditional test of checking out possibly possessed persons at the psychiatrist's office to rule out the possibility of their having an emotional illness is not valid in determining whether or not they are possessed. (Such a test would, of course, be valuable in determining how best to treat the psychological problem on its own level, but, of its nature, it cannot determine whether or not evil spirits are also operative.)

In short, there is evidence that the whole system at present employed by the Church in determining whether or not exorcism is to be performed needs to be thoroughly reassessed.

A new—and traditional—point of view is that much of what we call mental illness is, in fact, the result of demonic activity. Perhaps we are narrower in our view than any other culture or any other age in that we do not admit of the possibility of a real spiritual world of angels and demons. In consequence, we label any infestation or possession that does take place as neurotic or psychotic. In this way, we abdicate and allow the psychiatrist to become the priest of our contemporary world.

A Case Exemplifying All That Has Been Said

The following excerpts from two letters illustrate the difficulties of suffering persons trying to receive help from the Church. Happily, the results of this woman's search were eventually successful.

July 16, 1979

Dear Father,

Never before have I written to someone I knew only from reading his book. . . . I pray that you may be able to give me the advice I need. Only in the last five weeks have I put a "tag" on my trouble, and I still have a problem using the names which sound so out of the Dark Ages and which go against my educational background.

About three years ago I began to reach for a closer relationship with God. At the same time I became chronically depressed and actually suicidal. I didn't understand and talked with my priest and told him I needed help. I am 37 years old, well educated and analytical. I majored in psychology and hated to admit it but something was wrong with me and a Mental Health Center seemed the answer. I began psychotherapy, worked hard and did all the right things but still felt no better—nothing changed inside me. . . . I was being driven. . . . My doctor couldn't understand why we couldn't change things. There is a voice in my head (we called it a parent-tape then) that said I couldn't live. Two years ago I tried twice in one week to kill myself. I went from intensive care to the psychiatric unit of the hospital. I told my doctor and Father that it wasn't me—I didn't want to feel that way; I sounded crazy so I stopped saying it.

I got permission to go to Mass daily and I prayed and prayed . . . but I felt even worse.

At this time God sent Sister _____ into my life; she is an intelligent, well-read, down-to-earth woman. . . . She said that perhaps I should have prayer for deliverance. . . . Finally, to please her I agreed. . . . We went to see a Catholic couple. While there I realized for the first time in my life the evil I am dealing with. I was asked to renounce all my occult activities. It sounded simple; I had long ago relegated them to the level of the unnecessary, but I found them extremely difficult to renounce. I have had a voice in my head since I was about three years old. It was in *my* head, so I assumed it was me, even if I did know it wasn't. It told me what to do and how—I felt it took care of me. It told me how to make things happen and how to read the future or see the past. . . . I told fortunes when I was older, but people were frightened because I could tell so much. I am what Sybil Leak calls a born witch. . . . After these people prayed with me it was quiet, but I could feel its presence, and I knew it wasn't gone.

The next week was awful; this thing no longer pretended to be my voice or me. It attacked me almost continually. I was desperate, so we went back again to pray with the couple. This time it was very hard. I could not talk and they physically restrained me. The voice kept saying, "Make the 'connection'; let me do it. They can't hold you if you do; they don't know how." I was so afraid someone would be hurt that I didn't let go, and we didn't expel it.

This brings me to my problem. I am trying to be rational in the light of my twentieth-century upbringing, but I *know* this is a very powerful demon that is tormenting me. I want to be free; I want to give my whole will to God. . . . I will try deliverance again, but only if I feel that the people with me—and me—are protected. I don't want to be part of an exhibition which leaves me the same way afterward. . . . I feel like a battleground. I have talked to my priest and he is sympathetic; he tells me to go to confession, but it is not enough. I need help. Can you give me any advice or aid?

What do we do with people like this from other cities? I did the best I could and referred her to a priest I knew who was fifty miles from her home. But here we have what I have come to see as a common pastoral case: an intelligent person who has already turned to the Church and to psychiatry but has gotten no help from very fine, well-intentioned priests and doctors. So desperate was she that she telephoned me several times to see if I could see her, but I just wasn't able to. Then she wrote again.

July 30, 1979

Dear Father,

As soon as I mailed my letter to you the demon began
to push and torment me harder than ever. My friends took
me to the emergency room because I had overdosed. Sister
_____, the head of the psychiatric unit . . . asked me
if I was trying to kill myself or separate myself from the
voice. I felt the only way I could separate from it was to die.
Dr. S_____ came and told me I had to be admitted.
I refused. I knew I could not get the help I needed in a hospital.

When I met Fr._____ I liked him at once. He is
intelligent, well-read and very pleasant. I talked with him
and was open and honest. He seemed to avoid the subject of
the voice and the demon. . . . After talking and talking Father said, in essence, that I was a nice, confused lady who
needed a psychiatrist. That hurt, not because I hadn't heard
it before, but because I had come all the way to a distant
city to hear it. I then asked him point-blank about the
voice. . . . He was very distressed but said he thought the
voice was mine. I cannot describe to you in words how I felt;
I felt God was being very cruel. I had bitter tears running
down, and I told Father I didn't know what to say except
that I *knew* the voice wasn't me. "How do you know?"

She then goes on to describe how she roamed around in
desperation that night until she ended in a retreat house
where she went to see another nun she knew.

I wasn't sure if she thought I was sane or not, but she
was nice. . . . I must have looked as if I was about to leave,
because she asked me to stay while she got her Bible. . . .
She sat still, looking at the book for a moment; then she
looked at me and said, "The Lord wants me to pray with
you." I wasn't surprised; after all she is a nun. . . . First we
prayed together; then she read Mark 9:14–29 and said, "I
believe that's how it is with you." I agreed and she said,
"Let's pray." She began praying that God would be with us
and guide us; then I was startled to realize that she was

praying for deliverance. Her voice was very low and she didn't look at me. She took authority, bound the spirit, and commanded it to leave and never return. I felt the spirit, but that little room was full of God. Sister was open and God was pouring through her. I was not afraid; I let go completely and the demon left. God held me very gently. I told Sister it was gone. She looked at me and her eyes were full of tears. She said, "Let's go to the chapel and thank God and praise him." . . .

The Sister who is my friend commented that I looked different.

"It is gone."

"When did that happen?"

"Just now. Sister prayed for deliverance."

"I didn't know she could do that."

I don't know if she had ever done that before; I didn't ask, but I think she is beautiful to let the Lord use her in such a special way.

It feels strange but good to be just me. The voice and the connection in my head is gone. Thank you for helping me—God used you, too.

All this is to God's glory.

Peace!

7

Deliverance:
A Perspective From Experience

by Richard McAlear, O.M.I.
and Mrs. Elizabeth Brennan

Editors' Note: *We first met Fr. Richard McAlear, O.M.I. while he was helping unload 6,600 dozen English muffins. He was lifting a muffin rack with the "muffin man" Ralph who had been disabled when crushed by a 2,000 pound machine but healed when Fr. McAlear's group prayed for his crushed back. In gratitude for the Lord's healing, for the past four years Ralph has donated all his time to Fr. McAlear's group as they collect food and furniture for the poor. The English muffins as well as the other food and furniture often are donated by people grateful for healings they have received through the group's prayer for healing and deliverance. Perhaps one reason the Lord blesses Fr. McAlear's group with such a powerful healing and deliverance ministry is that they have such a deep love for his poor and for fighting the evil one not just in suffering individuals but also in the social dimension (Is. 58:6–12).*

Another reason the Lord can work so powerfully in Fr. McAlear's healing and deliverance ministry is because he usually tries to work with a team. Generally he teams with Mrs. Elizabeth Brennan, a compassionate mother with three children. One of the first times I prayed with Fr. McAlear and Mrs. Brennan was in a setting where they prayed with about one hundred Christian therapists. Before Mrs. Brennan began praying, she told me that she sensed there was a bearded man with a green coat somewhere in the room who was calling on other spiritual powers. I looked around until I could spot such a person and then asked him to come forward. After he came forward, Mrs. Brennan asked him to renounce TM and seven or eight other occult practices. Though Mrs. Brennan had never met the man before, he admitted his involvement and then renounced each practice. After doing some inner healing regarding the emotional wounds that led to these occult involvements, Fr. McAlear then commanded the spirits to leave.

During the next hours as therapists came forward, Mrs. Brennan would discern if an evil spirit was present and what kind of inner healing was needed. Fr. McAlear, or a member of the team, would then do the inner healing and command the spirit to leave. Most of their prayer time was spent not in commanding spirits to leave but in doing the inner healing so as to build Jesus' life within so that the spirits would have to leave easily and wouldn't return.

Because the experience was such a positive one for the therapists, some of the therapists have invited Fr. McAlear and Mrs. Brennan to pray with their clients. One therapist, the director of a clinic in Connecticut, wrote the following after thirty-two of his clients received prayer ministry from Mrs. Brennan:

> Regarding the people Mrs. Brennan prayed with, we found interesting results. I had been seeing all thirty-two of these in therapy and sensed something blocking their full freedom. So I selected these for Mrs. Brennan to pray over. Twenty-eight of the thirty-two did have evil spirits holding them in bondage and the other four had deep woundedness that still needed inner healing. Mrs. Brennan discerned the spirits, and the aspects of each spirit fit exactly the psychological patterns I knew from my counseling of them. For example, a spirit of rejection would have aspects of fear, anxiety, turmoil, confusion, deceit, despair, and detachment that fit the psychological path of the person's broken life and what had happened—even to the order in which it happened. This has exciting possibilities for therapy and the

*process of inner healing. All the patients moved more freely
and more easily after the deliverance to new growth—even
within a few weeks—and this really freed me to do binding
up and deliverance whenever I encountered blocks.*

Though this testimony deals with only thirty-two people
who "move more freely and more easily after the deliverance," Fr. McAlear and Mrs. Brennan have ministered to over
two thousand people (three hundred of these in great depth)
over the past four years without any known casualties. They
find that ninety percent of those having evil spirits have an
open door due to deep hurts in life making it difficult to get
close to Jesus. Often they counsel those seeking deliverance to
first attend the Eucharist daily for a month and after the Eucharist to spend a half hour adoring Jesus. This weeds out those
coming only for relief and unwilling to make a deep commitment to Jesus. They also find that those returning are often
free of all spirits because they have grown closer to Jesus.
Those who still need ministry primarily need inner healing
prayer touching the deep pains of hurting memories and disordered emotions with the love of Jesus. The evil one will leave
easily and for good only when all wounds inviting him back are
healed. Thus they counsel those who come not to be so concerned about whether or not they have an evil spirit but rather
whether they are growing closer to Jesus Christ. When a person is growing closer to Jesus Christ, then the evil spirit is
pushed out by Jesus' new life. In the following article Fr. McA-
lear and Mrs. Brennan share their approach to inner healing,
binding spirits, breaking occult bondage, and using Mary as
the model in order that deliverance may take place peacefully
and with deep healing.

* * *

"Blessed be the Lord, God of Israel, because he has come
to his people to set them free" (Lk 1:68).

We live in a world tainted by evil. Although God created

the world good and perfect, sin entered the world and evil
pervaded God's work, destroying its beauty. On all sides we
witness this bondage and its effects. It touches every level of
creation from nature itself to an individual's personal torment:
poverty, war, disease, famine, social injustice, addiction and
violence of man and nature. Selfishness, sin and man's corrupt
nature are to blame for much of this evil. On a deeper level
there is a personal force of evil, the devil, Satan, who bears a
certain weight of responsibility. That there is such a personal
and very real entity or power is the teaching of the Church. It
is a fact of experience that individuals suffer torment and are
bound and unfree because of such a reality. It is also a fact that
a certain number of people have entered into the service of
this reality called Satan and to them this power of hell is very
real indeed. A whole spectrum of human experience is centered on Satanic reality, from Satanic worship to witchcraft
and various forms of the occult. There is a personal reality in
the world of evil that causes much of the disorder and chaos
that we encounter in the world.

It is to such a tainted and tormented world that Jesus
comes. He comes to set captives free. Even with all our resources, technology and ingenuity, men find it impossible to
deal with the forces and powers of evil. Such forces and powers
stand beyond any human attempt to control. Only God in Jesus
has provided a way to victory over what threatens constantly
to destroy us, both individually and collectively. In Jesus, by his
cross and resurrection, the power of evil is broken and the
kingdom of darkness is overthrown. Jesus is raised higher than
any power, force, dominion or kingdom and now shares with
his Church his power and authority (cf. Eph. 1:20–23).

The Church is well aware of its responsibility to minister
the authority of Jesus and to stand against the forces of evil
that torment and bind people. The rite of official exorcism and
prayers for simple and private exorcism have been part of the
Church's unbroken tradition. Although spotty and uneven,
that tradition exists.

Within the charismatic renewal there has been a rediscov-

ery of the reality of evil and evil spirits. This was not the result
of a conscious search, but rather a new awareness that
emerged from experience. That this experience should
emerge from the charismatic renewal is not surprising. First,
the explicit proclamation of the Lordship of Jesus coupled with
authentic praise is sufficient to rouse infernal powers of opposition. Second, the charismatic renewal leads people to a radical
openness to the Spirit. The Holy Spirit of Jesus is not the only
spirit encountered or experienced, as all leaders in the renewal
are well aware. Third, the healing ministry specifically has consistently touched on reality that can only be understood as demonic. Through experience those in the healing ministry have
come to accept that there is such a bondage and torment in
people that can only be dealt with through the power of Jesus
Christ.

Experience, reflection, a return to Scripture, tradition and
the wisdom of others have brought about the development of
the ministry known as deliverance. This ministry has not been
without problems and mistakes. However, there is a solid basis
of consistent experience that has something to offer the
Church. The positive thrust is more important than the unfortunate lapses and errors. The truth may be marred but not ne-
gated. That there should be problems and mistakes is
inevitable. First, in an area where the current lived tradition is
presently weak and spotty, little wisdom is available to draw
on. Growth has come mainly from trial and error—learning
through experience. Second, the deliverance ministry tends to
attract a type of person overly fascinated with the demonic or
the type that is authoritative and/or seeks simplistic solutions
to complex problems. Third, the nature of what the ministry
deals with—demonic reality whose essence is deceit and hatred—is bound to exact its toll. Many are not prepared to deal
with the difficulties encountered in deliverance.

Those who oppose the work of deliverance are very often
reacting to mistakes, imbalance or simplistic approaches. The
proper thing would be to respond calmly, sifting out errors and
gleaning the treasures of wisdom and kernels of truth.

DELIVERANCE AND HEALING

One of the very first principles to be grasped is that deliverance makes sense only in the context of healing. Deliverance, outside the context of healing, runs the risk of becoming a monster. The fact is that there is in truth no such thing as a "deliverance ministry"—only a healing ministry in which deliverance plays a role. The goal (*causa finalis*) of healing is wholeness in Christ, an integrated person in relationship to God and others.

The goal of deliverance on the other hand is freedom. In and of itself, freedom is not wholeness but a necessary pre-condition. Along with freedom there must be a responsible use of freedom, resulting in progress and growth along the path of salvation. He sets us free—"free to worship him without fear, in holiness and justice before him all our days" (Lk. 1:74).

The corollary to this is that the end result (*terminus ad quem*) is more important than that situation of bondage or torment from which we start (*terminus a quo*). The all-important fact that can never be lost is that the wounded and broken people are to be made whole. We work with persons before we work with spirits and demons; the human reality always overrides the demonic reality.

This said, the truth is that some people cannot achieve the wholeness they seek and which the Lord desires for them unless they first are freed from the bondages by which they are held captive. It pleases God that the minister should break unjust fetters, undo the thongs of the yoke, and let the oppressed go free, for then will the light shine forth and the wound be healed (cf. Is. 58).

TYPES OF DELIVERANCE

One truth that needs to be drawn out is that all deliverance is not alike. There are three basic kinds or types of deliverance. They relate to the three kinds of situations in which people who need deliverance find themselves, and they all relate generally to the way in which the evil spirit gained entry ("the point of entry"). The three basic types of deliverance are occult, cardinal, and ministering.

1. Occult

The more difficult deliverances are the occult. These are spirits whose source is the occult—whether contracts with Satan, witchcraft or ouija boards. Generally, they are spirits which are stronger and more difficult to dislodge. Two things must be kept in mind when ministering in these situations. First, the person usually must renounce and repent of any involvement in or even curiosity about the occult. All bonds to anything occult must be broken cleanly and completely. Second, the person must be ministered to in his or her woundedness. What led to such occult involvement? Anger at God? Desire for power? Insecurity? The positive growth in wholeness and holiness must be the emphasis—a deeper commitment to Jesus, a greater yielding to his Spirit and more openness to his Will.

People who have strayed into the occult, whether knowingly or innocently, have entered into the kingdom of darkness and have been exposed to the deceits and destruction of hell. To extricate oneself almost always requires deliverance. The reason that the occult is forbidden and dangerous is because spiritual knowledge or power is sought outside the kingdom of God. Fortune telling, mindreading, ESP and astrology are examples of seeking knowledge not allowed a Christian. Witchcraft, both black and white magic, voodoo and astral projection are examples of occult power that also are not allowed a Christian.

Another principle that is important as a rule of thumb is the danger involved in any technique, method or parapsychology that invites the person to "blank the mind." Nature abhors a vacuum. The same rule applies in the spiritual domain. A blank mind is exposed to infernal infestation not easily undone. While not necessarily occult themselves, these methods involve dangers and risks that are not to be taken lightly.

Also, in the process of ministering to people, we encounter the reality of curses, spells and hexes. These are easily broken by a simple command in the name of Jesus Christ. In more complex, deeper cases, the power of a priest may be needed.

Use of this authority when exercised with confidence is very simple: "In the name of Jesus Christ I break any curse, spell or hex placed on you from any source. By the power of his blood I free you and consecrate you to the Lord Jesus."

Under the heading of occult deliverance we include hereditary bondage, curses and spirits. These run in family lines and are very serious. We sometimes must begin a deliverance by praying about the moment of conception. The priest, especially, should know his power and authority and exercise it with confidence. The sacrament of baptism always contained an exorcism that could be effective against the hereditary evils mentioned if the priest were aware of his authority. The deep traditions of the Church are aware of these realities.

There is a deeply mysterious world of the occult that has a fascination all its own. The danger is to be caught up in that fascination. Our focus is ever the Lord Jesus before whom every knee bows—including the netherworld (cf. Phil. 2:10). Our attention is drawn to his victory over all dark powers and forces. Our proclamation is ever the fullness of life contained in him. What is known of the occult is only enough to be wary of the dangers involved and to set captives free.

2. Cardinal

A cardinal spirit is one that entered through the person's own will or lack of it. Repeated acts of sin build a pattern of behavior and invite a spirit to enter. Lust and gluttony are good examples of cardinal spirits. After a while the person loses what freedom there was and is no longer capable of resistance. If the spirit entered through the will, it must be the person's conscious choice for it to leave. Ministry must center on the person's woundedness, especially the wounded will. Sincere repentance must have priority as the person turns away from sin and renounces habits of sin. Exercise of will power is also a necessity. Unless the person is possessed—an admitted rarity—there is still free will that can be exercised. Discipline, fasting and a patterned prayer life are all important. Sacramental life, especially reconciliation and the Eucharist, is a necessity. Ministering should focus on the wounded person who tried to fill some need or void by the patterns of sinful behavior (overindulgence, lust, etc.). Healthy patterns of behavior must replace disordered ones. Ministering and a use of authority over evil in Jesus' name are both needed to bring such people to freedom and wholeness.

3. Ministering

By far the largest number of cases encountered are those spirits that are present which entered through and are hooked on a person's own woundedness. The point of entry is a trauma or repeated hurts in a person's life. A spirit of fear, for example, is not unrelated to the person's own disorder and brokenness, his own wounded emotion of fear. The same can be said for spirits of anxiety, lack of self-esteem, self condemnation, etc.

The ministry is basically one of inner healing aimed at touching the deep pains of hurting memories and disordered emotions and feelings with the healing love of Jesus. If the inner healing is effective, a gentle and simple rebuke is enough to cast out the spirit. It no longer has a "right" to be there; there is no woundedness in which to root.

BINDING

"How can anyone make his way into a strong man's house and burgle his property unless he has first bound up the strong man? Only then can he plunder his house" (Mt. 12:29).

One of the reasons for criticizing the work of deliverance is the emotional—sometimes hysterical—behavior often associated with it. It is not unknown for the person being prayed for

to exhibit loud and uncontrolled reactions, sometimes border-
ing on the bizarre. There is no necessary connection between
deliverance and such behavior. Behavior of this type is demonic.

It is essential to stand on the principle of Jesus' authority
over the demonic. These kinds of reactions should not be allowed. The spirits should simply be bound in the name of Jesus. Only when they are properly bound can the work of
healing take place. If they are not bound, there is the risk of
reacting to the demonic activity both by the minister and by
the one being ministered to. By not exercising one's authority
we allow the evil to have control and authority over the situation. Jesus taught the principle of binding the strong man before plundering his house.

There are two kinds of binding of the spirits. First is what
is called "binding off from." The aim of this binding is to sever
all bonds, interconnections and interactions. First of all, the
spirit should be isolated, bound off from:

• any other spirit or hierarchy. No spirit is isolated from
all others. They all exist in something of a network, interlock-
ing and interconnected. To avoid any possible interplay or interaction, the spirit one is working with, must be bound off
from all others.

• the emotions, mind, will, memories, imagination or any
other locus where the spirit seems to be operating within the
person. In the case of an emotional reaction, binding the spirit
from the person's emotions gives the person the opportunity to
regain control.

A simple command suffices. "In the name of Jesus Christ I
bind you off from any other spirit, power or hierarchy," or "In
the name of Jesus Christ I bind you off from this person's emotions, memories, etc."

Second, there is what is called "binding in" of some aspect. Each spirit has a personality—a makeup of certain qualities known as *aspects.* A spirit can be deceitful, rebellious,
disobedient, angry, hateful, tormenting, mocking, etc. These
are ways that a particular spirit acts and reacts. It acts upon the
person (e.g., torments) and reacts in a deliverance situation

(e.g., disobeys). Each aspect must be bound in the name of Jesus Christ. With each aspect that is bound, a facet of the spirit is eliminated—another dimension is cut off. The spirit loses its ability to act on the person and to react in ministry. Once again a simple command suffices. "In the name of Jesus Christ I bind you in your deceit, disobedience, etc." Once bound, the way is open to minister in love to the wounds of the person without demonic interferences or uncontrollable emotional reactions.

ASPECTS

An important insight into the inner world of spirits is an understanding of aspects. Aspects give us the inner nature of the spirit, insight into the healing needed, and the ability to remain in control of the evil spirit and deliverance. From our experience, we find that the common spirit usually has six aspects—the more aspects present, the more involved will be the deliverance and healing. More than ten aspects indicate that there is a hierarchy present (throne, power, principality, etc.). There is much more probing to be done in this matter. The basic insight, however, is clear. A spirit is not a simplistic entity but does have an inner nature, a personality. There are facets to a spirit's makeup which are manifest as various dimensions of its being. This is something of the same insight of Revelation 13 when it describes the one beast as having many heads and horns. Understanding the demonic personality gives the ministry a greater effectiveness in controlling the situation and in healing the person.

There is a process to deliverance that brings to it an order and focus.

1. Isolate the spirit being dealt with by proper binding

Many mistakes are made because more than one spirit can be manifesting at one time. Chaos sometimes results when a spirit is interacting on the person's emotions, resulting in uncontrolled reactions. Binding the spirit off from other spirits and from the person's own emotions will isolate it and keep the situation under control.

2. Pray for healing

This should always be the focal point of the process—the healing of the person's woundedness, whether it be one's emotions, memories, will or spirit. The person should be involved by making the necessary decisions such as forgiveness, renouncing of the occult, repenting, etc. The ministers are involved in seeking discernment of the root causes and praying for the necessary inner healing.

3. Rebuking and casting out of the spirit

If the inner healing is basically effective, the spirit has no "right" or place to lodge. The resting place is gone and it can only depart. It should be commanded to go quietly and should be sent straight to Jesus.

4. Need for discernment and compassion

Healing is never a simplistic process because we are always dealing with human beings who are complex. Each person and each case must be discerned afresh. Sometimes the problem has a demonic origin; other times we are dealing with a wounded person with many hurts; still other times a personality disorder is causing the problem. Very often it is a combination of factors.

Healing and deliverance must always be a ministry of compassion and discernment. Without these two gifts ministry will not bear abundant fruit.

When the Lord raises up a ministry, he will equip it with the necessary gifts of discernment so that the ministry will be guided by insight, perception and understanding. The ministry will not be simply groping in the dark. 1 Corinthians 12:10 speaks of the ability "to distinguish one spirit from another."

This gift is being renewed in the Church in our day. Combined with good common sense and an appreciation for the complexities of the human factor, discernment is the single most important tool in ministry.

There are many other gifts in the body of Christ, gifts given for the building up of the body—tools available to use in ministry so that the salvific love of God can be effective in the lives of people. Ministry is simply reaching out in the Spirit and in the power of compassionate love to touch the hurting. Deliverance is such a ministry of love—the cross and resurrection being rendered efficacious in the lives of those who are bound, unfree and tormented. One dimension to the life and death of Jesus is to set the captives free. The need is still there; the ministry is being raised up in our time in a renewed way. Certain ones, but not all, are being called to take up the burden of this ministry. They must be well grounded in holiness, firmly rooted in the life of the Church and supported by the community. Compassion must be the distinguishing characteristic of each minister.

God wants his people free and whole. We have experienced the renewal of the healing ministry in the last decade. Although it began in a small way and it grew not without opposition, we see today a general embrace by the Church at large and an acceptance of the reality of God's healing love by the Church. The common experience is that many must be free before they can be healed.

Although some cases of unfreedom are cases of personality disorders, others are demonic in nature and require deliverance. Jesus found the same situation. "He cast out the demon, healed the boy and gave him back to his father" (Lk. 9:43). Sometimes healing cannot be accomplished unless it is coupled with deliverance. Deliverance should never be attempted unless it is coupled with healing.

MARY

Perhaps many errors could be avoided if there were a proper focus on Mary, the woman clothed in the sun (cf. Rev.

12:1). In Genesis there is the promise of a woman who would be at enmity with the serpent (cf. Gen. 3:15). She is the model of the work of deliverance. Under her patronage, the ministry retains a balance and a perspective.

It is the many-faceted role of Mary that draws our attention. Against the serpent she is the fierce, unyielding foe. For her children she is a tender compassionate mother. Toward Jesus she is an obedient disciple reflecting his glory. To the Spirit she is an open vessel. For the Church she is the model of a victorious, full life in Christ, the complete integration of human and spiritual life lived in and for Jesus. We will do well to place all ministry under her mantle. Like her, we must stand implacable against the cunning enemy. Like her, we must never lose a compassionate concern for the individual and a sensitivity for the ways in which people are hurt and wounded. Like her, we must remain always at the disposal of the Lord Jesus, never grasping a work that is truthfully his, never closed to the new surprises of his Spirit, always open to be taught, led and corrected. After her example, we must keep sight of the goal of full union with God in Christ and of the human wholeness of an integrated, balanced and harmonious spiritual life that is grounded in the human and permeated with the divine.

The Church has the mission of Jesus entrusted to her. That mission is not so very different from the very one Jesus claimed for himself:

"The Spirit of the Lord has been given to me, for he has anointed me. He has sent me to bring good news to the poor, to proclaim freedom to captives, to give the blind new sight, to set the downtrodden free, to proclaim the Lord's year of favor" (Lk. 4:18–19).

8
Deliverance Within the Total Ministry of the Church

by James Wheeler, S.J.

Editor's Note: *For years Fr. James Wheeler worked full time at a spiritual direction center he founded in Long Island, New York, and he presently works full time doing spiritual direction in Albuquerque, New Mexico. While many people praying for deliverance have little opportunity to prepare a person or follow up after a deliverance, Fr. Jim Wheeler has an opportunity to do both as he sees people month after month in spiritual direction sessions.*

In his article Fr. Wheeler focuses on the preparation, the actual process of the prayer, and the follow-up for five types of bondage that he frequently prays through with those he directs. The five types are:

1. Negative forces in the human spirit: guilt, resentment, jealousy.

2. Bondage from a possessive relationship to another person, either living or dead.

3. Harassment from a spirit through temptation.

4. Oppression where an outside person or evil controls part(s) of the personality. (In other articles this fourth area is the only area included under the term "deliverance or private exorcism." But Fr. Wheeler uses the word "deliverance" in all five areas because a prayer of command is used to drive out evil.)

5. Possession when total control of the personality by a force not identifiable as the person's or that of another human being has taken place. (This is termed exorcism or solemn exorcism.)

Fr. Wheeler finds that over a period of months or years with his directees he will pray with almost all of them for one of these types of bondage. He leads most of his directees through prayer of the first type, ten percent through the second type, five percent through the third type, and one percent through the fourth type. He has dealt with only one person of the fifth type. But more important is that in the long-term perspective of spiritual direction, these prayers for freedom from bondage are but an instant in a total process of growth involving daily prayer, the sacraments, nurturing God's word within one's heart, deep conversion, and a personal commitment to Christ lived out in his community of the Church. Without this process, Fr. Wheeler finds that deliverance prayer sometimes becomes a technique that temporarily sweeps the evil spirit out only to have him return with seven others through the unhealed doors (Mt.12:43–45).

To keep prayer for bondage from becoming a technique, this article helps focus on some key questions: How can the sacraments be administered and approached for greater healing? How often are we dealing not with an evil spirit but with psychogenic bondage, bondage to people living or dead, or some other bondage masquerading as an evil spirit? But perhaps the central question this article raises comes from the perspective of Fr. Wheeler and the two-year course that he teaches in spiritual direction. Of the fifty-six sessions in this course, only three deal with these five types of prayer. Are we leading people only to deliverance prayer or to all the riches that lead us to a personal love of Jesus Christ that gets lived out month after month through the peaks and valleys of the spiritual life?

*   *   *

Since the time of Descartes, there has been a tendency among philosophers and humanists at large to see the world more and more exclusively from the viewpoint of an unaided human reason. What can be known by analysis and induction is true; what cannot be known by the process of human reason is untrue. Though this is a gradually unacceptable position for the human mind to take, it nevertheless is a view—a rational mythology—that governs the thinking processes of the modern world. Such a vision of reality tends, in Bultmann's terms, to demythologize the supernatural. We are subject to a form of analysis that can have the effect of rationalizing out of existence large areas of the kingdom of God. Instead of the growth of human knowledge and insight being guided by grace and the gift of understanding, the truths of our Christian heritage came under an all-too-critical light of reason. The supernatural aspects of Scripture and the gifts of the Holy Spirit became subordinated and accountable to the achievements of human reason.

I. FIGHTING EVIL FROM EVIL SPIRITS

Included in the overall downplay of the divine power of God entering the human race through the power of faith is the vast Christian tradition beginning with Jesus and Paul, that has been handed down through the spirituality of the Eastern and Western Church. That tradition maintains that there is something else besides ourselves that we have to fight in the pursuit of salvation. That "something else" is not only our own sin and evil; it is the evil that comes from outside, from Satan and other evil spirits.

Meanwhile, we are confronted with the most outrageous examples of human brutality and degradation. Perhaps they have been with us before, but the use of the media has driven home to all of us the rather macabre aspects of the human spirit. We know and are aware of the depths that the human will can reach as its own measuring rod and by its own means— how we are capable of sin and capable of the use of our own nature to turn against ourselves. Each one of the commandments seems to provide the opportunity for negative choices that undermine the human spirit and turn it directly into its dark side.

It would seem normal to expect the development of a form of mendacity, a series of untruths that ultimately break down human relationships. That someone would choose to kill his brother and spread the poison of fratricide through the human race, or that parental life would be discarded and thus produce a basic disorientation in the life of children and a future fraught with anxiety might also be anticipated by the violation of the Fourth Commandment. There are numerous examples of the possibility of human evil engulfing the soul and turning it toward the perverse warp. One could also easily postulate that the continuance of such crimes through a family, nation, or a race might bring a particular group into a profound alienation and estrangement from itself and that that alienation might similarly affect those who would follow. It might be somewhat rational to say that the human race is responsible for its own indignities to itself.

Yet the quality of such evil would seem to point to something greater. How does one pass from simply abusing a child to malicious degradation of that child? When we consider our own involvement in Vietnam, how did we pass from the simplicity of defending a people's freedom to the systematic attempt to destroy the very fabric of that people's life? People suffer greatly when they lose a war. There is almost a natural sense of revenge to regain a lost dignity that overwhelms and motivates them. But how does the human mind turn this moment of revenge into the adulation of a human god of malice, such as Hitler conceived and fostered in World War II? When does that sense of such bitter vengeance enter into the people of the South, who lynched and brutally executed blacks in the century following the Civil War?

In the story of the murder *In Cold Blood,* Truman Capote describes the motivation of the chief murderer. After he and his partner had captured the four people in the farmhouse and were about to steal from them, this man walked briefly outside the house. He was a man with a more than difficult background, so one could see, perhaps, a sense of revenge becoming an underlying motive for what he was about to do. But the experience that he had—one of being transported out of himself—indicated that this might be a case where more than his own motivation was at work. After that experience, he, with his companion, reentered the house and murdered the four members of the family. What was an essential part of the experience was this moment of transition from the experience of repressed anger to the moment of murder. Many of us have repressed anger as the result of terrible childhoods but we do not end up committing homicide. Undoubtedly, there are numerous unconscious forces at work, and it is the choice of the individual to cooperate or not to cooperate with these forces. But it is, first of all, the slow movement leading the personality to move from resentment or hatred to the actual perpetration of a heinous crime that indicates something more sinister and supernatural in the leading. As many people have testified, the few moments before one commits suicide, or steals, or rapes someone, there is a suggestion made or an experience of a motivating force to commit the crime or sin that the person was totally aware of antecedent to the action. Some of this can be explained by the finding of some unconscious psychological factor previously unknown to the person. Some of it can be attributed to the weakness or corruption of the human will. But in all of this, a third factor cannot be denied. It is a factor of evil quite beyond ourselves that does not control us—but given our cooperation with, or our lack of, self-understanding, this intelligent force can lead us to, or over, the brink of destruction.

There is, it seems to me, this transition in all of human actions that verge on the precipice of evil. Paul Tillich made the distinction between the demonic and the diabolical. A turn is made, mysterious though it may seem, from sickness, weakness, or downright sin into something that can only be called outright malice. Witness the recent events in Iran. What begins as something called "revenge" turns into a wholesale slaughter, where revenge is lost in the senseless desire to kill. One does not condone revenge, but the indulgence in revenge seems to leave the human spirit open to a form of unbridled destruction that goes quite beyond the original intent. The original motivation is to get back at the allies of the Shah and the henchmen of Savah. What starts this way blossoms into wholesale murder of the innocent as well as the guilty.

We are truly aware of this process in the myth of the Garden of Eden. Sin was possible for Eve because she thought the fruit desirable. This sin is perhaps within her even before the tempter comes. But the sin is converted into evil by the voice of the serpent who adds to her desire the *idea* that God is not telling her the whole truth. In taking the apple, she not only commits a sin of disobedience, but a sin in which she disbelieves the truthfulness of God. What began as a simple movement of desire ends as disobedience and a form of blasphemy.

This might make more sense than all of the rational explanations of human failure. By this I do not mean that there is not a continual discovery of the roots of human evil and the way to combat it. It is not just that the quality and enormity of the crimes we have committed against ourselves seem beyond our capacity. The underlying sin is there, but the power that changes sin into a form of dedicated hatred or outright willful disobedience is a force induced not only on the matter, the fabric that is there. It is a power that comes from without. We listen to the voices that have survived Auschwitz. We know the capability of the human heart to tend toward evil and even to incorporate the image of the devil within. But we know that then something else was present besides the conception of the man who proved forever that redemption cannot come from man himself. That power had a great deal to use within us— but the power was motivated and instructed by some influence quite beyond man himself.

We are confronted with a culture that has attempted to explain all things in rational terms. Nowhere is the paradox between rationality and evil more apparent than on the local newscast. Pictured before us are all the calamities of the world around us. Killings, robberies, murder, wars, genocide, incest—all get their play. And they are interpreted by a group of logical, rational reporters, secluded in a homogenized room that seems totally aloof from the variety of violence that is offered to the audience. The commentators speak in the language of reason and logic. The whole atmosphere is one of organized control, yet the world they depict is a world of violence, activity, and human slaughter.

Nowhere does the application of the rational as the total cause and total solution of human events appear more incongruous and ineffectual. But it does not seem to bother our newscasters. They are locked into the rational salvation of the world. It would not appear to them to see that man has to confront both the depth of his own sin and his alliance with evil—the reality of Satan—before humanity can begin to hope.

Often our theology is influenced by our culture. One would not want to return to a point where the legitimate achievements of science and human reason are relegated to the rear of the theological barn. But the tendency to place human rationality as the primary interpreter of reality would seem to exclude the basic mythology of Christianity, and that mythology makes more sense in interpreting reality than the feeble attempt of human reason to interpret a reality much larger than itself. Reality makes no sense without the presence of Jesus Christ. My life gives little explanation outside of the presence of my Father. The monstrosity and perversity of evil makes little sense if there is not some calculating personality capable of leading the weakness and sinfulness of humanity astray. What reason can legitimately come to under the guidance of the word of God is essential to us. But human reason alone leaves much to be desired as a total interpretation of our experience.

Of course, such a way of observing our reality can lead us to another mistake. We cannot view the human spirit as a simple battleground between ourselves and Satan, with each being given an almost equal force and the humanity of the person as a simple plaything whose freedom is negligible. Such an outlook undermines the dignity of the person whom God has created for love and good and truth. Only a weakness in the person or his ancestry can permit the actual intrusion of evil. That weakness may be sinful or the mysterious drifting of good and evil that seems to be concomitant with some forms of mental illness. It may have its origin in a close relationship to a parent or brother who was involved in witchcraft. Or it may be the result of an affliction that comes from the use of ouija boards, the extension of a spell or curse upon another person. Whatever it may be, some weakness or power of the human being is involved.

The human soul is the natural domain of God. We are created to praise, reverence and serve God. The intrusion of our own evil proceeds from our own personal or corporate weakness or sin. Cynical intervention of evil likewise depends on some flaw in the human spirit that is sometimes not the fault of the person so caught and harassed. But it can be, also, the result of patterns of sin and continued delight in sinful motivation without any tendency to fight it that can bring the subtle entrance of an evil spirit. What is needed is the redemptive action of Christ and the Holy Spirit or the recognition of the psychological or physical weakness that can free a person.

Even the application of a deliverance or exorcism procedure, when it is effective, must rely on strong measures in the natural, sacramental, personal prayer and the healing power of God's overall grace to bring about the full healing of a person. To perform a deliverance and not treat the person in the human area of weakness is simply to invite a recurrence of the same form of attack.

What I would call "deliverance mania," the attempt to solve all illnesses by some form of deliverance, would be a more than questionable procedure. I am not here speaking of a ministry of deliverance that is a necessary or ancillary part of a healing ministry. It is the attempt to indulge in an exclusive deliverance ministry that sees all illnesses as being solved by a direct and often dramatic confrontation with Satan. Such a ministry more often than not results in a paralyzing anxiety on the part of both the one ministering and the one ministered to that prevents any real healing from taking place. Perhaps some good can come from such a process, but the results are a tendency to look upon oneself as the home and hostel of the diabolic entities from which one perpetually needs to be divorced. It also produces an anxiety about evil that can become more the tool of the evil spirit than the actual evil itself.

Any form of deliverance ministry must always be secondary to the primary ministry of the Church to an individual. The ministries of prayer, word, and sacrament are the primary ministries of the Church to an individual. In these he is sustained, strengthened, and finds his real home in union with Christ. Flowing from these ministries is the ministry of healing to restore the afflicted part of a human being—either in a spiritual or psychological dimension. Though giving the psychological its own growing dimension within the human spirit, the spiritual ministry of healing should be the prevalent ministry. In any case, all of these ministries should predominate, in both the ministry to the ordinary person and the ministry to an afflicted person. In this, the full power of the Church is brought to bear upon the individual and not centralized on a negative or debilitating action which may at times be necessary. Even in an unusual case where wisdom might dictate the use of a deliverance procedure first, it should always be seen as supplementing the main and secondary ministries of the Church.

In the process of dealing with this ministry, a rather delicate balance must be struck. Some would say that the evil spirit does not exist at all. In effect, others of a more radical extreme make him, by fixation, anxiety, or simple concentration on him alone, the only reality. While we cannot affirm someone who would deny the existence of the evil one, I find it extremely unwise to confirm a ministry that deals solely with deliverance. C. S. Lewis' dictum that the evil spirit encourages equally those who would deny his existence and those who would give him too much attention seems closer to the truth.

In Jesus Christ we find that balanced convergence, the nexus, the oneness of the human and divine. In the total ministry of his Church to the individual we discover the process of healing and union that leads us home. When we utilize the deliverance ministry, we employ the total power of Jesus' ministry through the Church to the individual. That ministry is both divine and human. It is partially a deliverance ministry, as Jesus made clear in his lifetime. But he also made the ministries of word, sacrament, and healing the center of his ministry. While the deliverance ministry is most clearly there, it is not the center. He, the person of Jesus, both human and divine, is the center.

II. THE TYPES OF DELIVERANCE

In our experience in the healing ministry, there are a number of types of deliverance besides those we would ordinarily refer to by that name. Some really refer to deliverance within the human sphere, from something within the persons themselves. For our purposes we wish to denote five types of areas when a human being is trapped by some negative force, either from within or without. Within the human framework, we have defined two areas of freedom from bondage:

(1) Negative forces in the human spirit: guilt, resentment, jealousy.

(2) Bondage from a possessive relationship to another person, either living or dead.

From a spirit without the person we define three further areas:

(3) Harassment: the use of suggestions, thoughts, exaggerations of what is already there from an outside spirit and that prey upon the weakness of the person. This is ordinarily called temptation.

(4) Obsession or Oppression:

(a) where some person or evil has seized control of an area of the personality and causes an extreme affliction or deep temptation within that area.

(b) where not one but several areas of personality have been affected. This can be closely related to the following.

(5) Possession: when a total control of the personality by a force not identifiable as the person's or that of another human being has taken place.

In all of these areas, the way of approaching the person involved in it is through the total ministry of Jesus.

The term "deliverance" is used in two senses in this article. The first sense is the ordinary sense of deliverance in the fourth mode or second type of deliverance from evil spirits—

that is, deliverance from obsession or oppression. The second sense is that derived from the Our Father's "Deliver us from evil" which refers as a general term to include all five forms of freedom from bondage. Where there would be confusion as to which meaning is to be taken, I have inserted a qualifying adjective or phrase.

Jesus approaches a person in love. We also proclaim his love and the strength of his word. First, the power of freedom will truly be found in a devotion to these two aspects of life through the personal and sacramental life of the Church. Second, a gradual development of self-awareness, of the human powers that are causing the disruption within the personality, will be necessary to any form of deliverance. Third, the deliverance prayer is always said after a strong, positive context has come in and through the Spirit. We might want to utilize a deliverance prayer in praying with someone for resentment. Before that, the discernment of roots of that resentment should have taken place, and then the power of God's forgiveness should be prayed for with calmness, strength, and deliberateness. Only when a strong, positive context has been established can the deliverance prayer be utilized. As we proceed to describe the causes and the possible solutions in dealing with each area of deliverance, the overall context with which we deal with the total ministry to a person must be kept in mind.

1. DELIVERANCE IN FIRST MODE (DELIVERANCE FROM A NEGATIVE FORCE WITHIN THE HUMAN SPIRIT)

Very often people will let a negative area develop within their own personality, or the sin that they allow actually comes from their background or ancestry. Usually it develops or surfaces with regard to a relationship from which guilt, resentment, hatred, jealousy, or any of these insidious emotions begin to gradually well up within the person. In one's ministry to a person, the roots of this negative or sinful emotion should be delineated, if that is at all possible. The prayer should also

stress the power of forgiveness, self-forgiveness, love and freedom that comes through the Holy Spirit. But we have found
that when people are under, let us say, a strong resentment,
this acts like a negative force or energy within the personality.
An energy within the human spirit that might have been employed for the sake of forgiveness has been inverted, turned in
on itself, and channeled in the direction of forms of revenge.

When one discovers the cause of such an emotion and
prays for forgiveness, the positive is stressed, and in many
cases full healing can occur. On many occasions, however, the
simple application of a deliverance prayer after the above has
been completed has, in our experience, released the terrible
force of inverted energy so that a free and powerful act of forgiveness can take place within the human spirit. When we say,
"In the name of Jesus, we command the spirit of resentment to
leave," the persons will often testify that the emotional bondage to which they were subjected was broken at that moment.
What follows is a more full and complete forgiveness.

It must be remembered that this is not a magical type of
process. Each emotion has its own way of being healed. Each
should be subjected to a different type of process and a different type of healing, and each personal emotion will have
unique complexes which surround it and different kinds of relationships which bring it about. The deliverance prayer is an
effective instrument when all of these processes have been
correctly employed. It becomes a magical instrument which
leaves the person open to the same type of affliction if it is
used by itself. The release must be accompanied by an overall
change or resolution within the person's way of dealing with
his or her life.

This kind of inverted energy can often masquerade as a
form of deliverance in the third or fourth modes of affliction,
that is, by evil spirits. One may see the same type of release go
within the personality. Indeed, the evil spirit, as St. Ignatius
warns us in the rules for discernment of spirits, may exagger-
ate the fear, the anger, the guilt, or whatever happens to be
the particular weakness of the person. In such cases, to rebuke
or take a strong stand against the power that seems to over-

whelm one might be in order. But this remains an essential deliverance from a well of negative emotion within the human spirit. It does not erase the marks of an obsession that is beginning to seriously disrupt the person, or has, indeed, already disintegrated a person's behavior in one area. It is simply the development of a long-standing pattern of sin or self-negation that is often unconscious to the person but needs to be released.

We might mention a case of this sort. A woman came to us on Long Island for deliverance. When she came to the prayer center, her case bore all the earmarks of an affliction that can come from the evil spirit. On an outing with her family, she had been overcome with an hysterical fit that was rather unusual in her case. She was usually a rather calm and moderately self-controlled woman, but the family thought it necessary to have her hospitalized and temporarily sedated. Later on, she left the hospital with a diagnosis that there was nothing physically wrong with her. She was not a person who easily jumped to conclusions, but she wondered if this was not a problem of deliverance from evil spirits.

When she came to the center, we prayed with her. As usual, we looked for the causes within the personality that might have brought about such a serious eruption of emotion. Through the word of knowledge, we were able to surface a traumatic event in her early childhood that she had told to no one. When she was a little girl, she had been molested, and, as usual in these cases, she told no one about it. Over the years, the guilt, anger, and fear that had been placed in her by that event continued to build and fester.

At a very young age, she married for the first time—outside the Church. Her husband treated her in a callous manner, showing her little concern and less affection. His only interest was in sex and the things that she could do to see that his meals and clothes were taken care of. Over the years, perhaps as a result of the first event as well, she began to develop an image of herself, in her own words, "as a prostitute." Gradually, within her personality the sense of disgrace built a carefully concealed volcano of shame, guilt, anger, and mourning. She was removed from that scene, married again, and was in the midst of a second, happier marriage. At that point she had received the Spirit, which began the opening of her unconscious. But a remark by her husband further loosened this internal volcano, and all the negative power so carefully suppressed in her for years caused her to go into a severe hysteria. When we were able to pray for the release of these emotions through the inflowing power of God's love, to pray for the healing of memories, and to pray for her deliverance from negative power of these emotions, then she was released. We checked with her some months later, and she said she was at peace. No recurrence had happened.

This could easily have been taken by the novice as a case of deliverance from evil spirits. We have learned that there are many such cases. What is involved is a deep restoration of the image and life of a person and the breaking of the bondage that these negative emotions have over that person.

2. DELIVERANCE IN THE SECOND MODE (DELIVERANCE FROM THE POSSESSION OF ANOTHER)

Some years ago, a sister came to me who was experiencing a series of nightmares that left her without physical rest and her whole spirit in a sense of disturbance. When questioned about her dreams, she told me that her mother, who had died a short time previously, had come to her in a manner that indicated a sense of distress. I prayed with her for forgiveness between her mother and herself, but we both still had the sense that what was there would remain. After praying again, I had the sense that the mother was asking to leave. "Can you let your mother go?" I inquired. By the look on her face, I understood that this was the problem. When she consented, I prayed a prayer that would sever the possessive bondage between herself and the mother. The dreams did not recur, and the person was at peace.

Such a prayer is ordinarily done, at least in my understanding of it, with deep presence of the love of the Lord or, in this case, our Lady. The woman needed a profound power to let her mother go and feel somewhat safe herself. Mary, in her powerful presence to her, enabled her to let go of her mother.

This particular kind of bondage can happen in any type of relationship with the living or the dead. Many people have been held in bondage to serve the needs of their parents. The person who has committed adultery feels the burden of the inner bondage of his companion that will force him to return when he does not wish to do so, seek, and repeat the action. It is the power of God that severs the relationship and, with a period of penance, begins to unknot the bonds. People have to become aware of the freeing action of God that does not leave them alone when they let go of someone whom they deeply love. The giving of life to another person by setting him or her free gives life to the self.

3. DELIVERANCE IN THE THIRD MODE (DELIVERANCE FROM TEMPTATION)

This is the first of what is normally denoted as a kind of attack that is identified not only with the various centers of my own internal spirit, but with someone who is outside myself. We battle, as St. Paul said, with principalities and dominions, and he was very right. The three types of influence normally attributed to the evil spirit are harassment, obsession, and possession. The types of remedies to free the person that are associated with the three types are rebuke, or firm stand against harassment, deliverance for obsession, and exorcism for possession.

This mode can take various forms. One is when a person hears words that he identifies as not being his own. At a moment of despondency, he will hear a voice telling him to commit suicide. Some people will identify this as an inducement from somewhere within the person himself. But a person can, and often does, experience the voice or the thought as outside himself. One may come up with a pattern of thought that would have led to disaster. Sometimes that thought comes from either a product of the ego or the tendency toward self-destruction within a person. Other times, however, it appears as a pattern-thought clearly inserted from without. Discernment and prayer help to ascertain whether these voices are actually our own subconscious or whether they are coming from somewhere else. Probably it is good, after the voice has disappeared, to ask what weakness it was playing on, so that one might be wary in the future, or that, in some way, one might be healed.

The answer to such a voice, once detected, is simply rebuke and a firmness of stand with Jesus. To argue with the voice while one is under attack does not seem a wise procedure. Later on, in a moment of tranquility one might work through the problem presented when the spirit moves under the action of grace. But to be involved in obsessive forms of reasoning can only trap one more in excessive forms of complicated rationalization that only induce what one does not wish to happen.

Perhaps the best place to attain a comprehensive view of this form of attack would come from the Fathers and Doctors of the Church, both East and West. The most compact form of this wisdom seems to me to lie in the rules for discernment of spirits of St. Ignatius. My Jesuit prejudice is more than obvious here, but this is the best I have seen. What seems to be the opinion of the Fathers and of Ignatius is that the inflammation of weakness within the personality is often the work of the evil spirit. And so the exacerbation of these influences such as lust, hatred, bitterness, etc., refers to the action of the evil one who is exploiting these points to his own advantage. The answer to such a sally was often a rebuke to the evil one and a form of deliverance prayer. This seems to me to be still quite effective, especially when one is under an excessive form of attack. We cannot get at the actual source of the weakness when the flames of it are literally being fanned in our face. It seems to me that this form of assault upon the self happens to those who might be in profound danger. When a person comes who is under the vice of pornography, this way of providing seems part of the way of healing.

Some time ago, a middle-aged man came and told me he was under a terrible affliction from pornography, most of which was in the place where he worked. It was a rather large company, so he had no control over the working situation. What I asked him to do was to use an external protection—that is, of asking Jesus to surround him with his light and rebuke the power that seemed to reach so easily into a weakness that he was unaware of. When he did this, it helped him to calm down the immediate problem so that we could take action against the source within himself. After a session, we were able to come up with a time during courtship and early marriage when he was under a severe form of sexual repression. After working our way through this, the internal compulsion seemed to cease. However, since most of us are weak in this area, he still asks the protection of Jesus, and, if the attack ensues again, he occasionally rebukes it in Jesus' name, and the compulsive problem will disappear.

This problem may have, if we may use Tillich's terminology, a demonic source. In the manipulative world of pornography, energy within a young woman is turned into its dark side and uses the power of human lust to draw a lustful or sexually immature man into its orb. But the manipulative power of such a cynical empire points not only to the inflammation of this negative power, but the influence of a diabolic intelligence. Those who catch others in the web are caught in the web of something else.

In the case of a person who is afflicted by the trap of such a ministry, inner healing, the protection of the light and love of Jesus, and—under strong attack or duress—the rise of a rebuke to the power of evil are the necessary ingredients of the remedy.

Every spiritual director has to be aware of the subtle influences that work on the human mind. Sometimes the sharpness of discernment can lead a person into quite a different form of life, and it is the gift of discernment to uncover not only the positive movement of the Spirit, but the subtleties of human resistance and the intrigues which can destroy a person.

4. DELIVERANCE IN THE FOURTH MODE (DELIVERANCE FROM OBSESSION OR OPPRESSION)

What characterizes this particular type of deliverance is really an inability of the person to control his or her reactions. The infestation of evil into the weakness of the person produces an obsessive kind of reaction with which the person cannot cope. This must, of course, be carefully differentiated from the obsessions of a psychological nature, such as our example of the woman and her hysteria in the first type of deliverance. These cases can only be detected with a careful form of discernment, but many of them, to my mind at least, show the outside influence of evil. Let me give several examples from my own ministry.

Uncontrolled Voice

All of us hear voices of one sort or another that speak to us from time to time. They are the voices of our mind, our heart, our subconscious. Some of these are negative voices, such as the ones that tell a person to commit suicide. Some are the normal voices of anxiety and resentment, or other sources of negative energy that tend to drive us in one direction or another, but over which we can exercise a reasonable amount of control. There are also voices over which we have little control, since in a certain set of circumstances we may lash out at the children, go into a fit, or openly walk out on a person we love. In neurotic states, the hysteria reaches a point of loss of self-control that requires treatment and care. But in all of these things, such persons are aware that they are dealing with their own voices. In other cases, such as the man who heard the voice to commit suicide, they are aware of a voice that is not their own. That voice can gain such a power over them that, unlike the suicide voice, the rebuke does nothing for them and the voice returns to haunt them.

A woman came to me some time ago who complained of such a voice. The voice shouted obscenities at her at random times during the day. She recognized that the voice was not her own, and she could not suppress it. We worked through areas of inner healing, and again we discerned that this woman was the victim of a man who had molested her. This incident provides trauma of a rather remarkable degree in anyone's life. But the voice did not stop with the inner healing. On some occasions, such a voice has been silenced simply through the inner healing or through the power of God's love entering that area of a person's life, but this one did not cease.

By the word of knowledge, I asked the woman if she had something in her home. She said she had a ouija board that she played with at home for a period of time. She had stopped using the ouija board, but it was still in her home. I told her to take the ouija board out and burn it. Then I also asked her to go to confession and ask God's forgiveness for such an action. She did, and thus she renounced the use of the board. Then I prayed a deliverance prayer. As we prayed, I also asked the love of God in Jesus Christ to enter her through her home and drive the evil away. In time the voice disappeared.

This is a case where not only inner healing and the sacraments are involved in the ridding of an affliction, but deliverance is needed as part of the overall process. The person is in bondage to evil, and that bondage has to be broken.

In another case, a young woman came to us from another diocese who had a peculiar problem. She lived a relatively normal life, had a job, and was a good member of her community, but there was one thing in her that was eccentric. When she would be in church, a voice would rise within her that would control her vocal chords. She would let out a high-pitched shriek that would resound through the church and literally chill the rafters on a warm day. Since the house she was in was one where the Blessed Sacrament was located, we were the unfortunate witnesses to one of these shrieks. Our experience of these shrieks was that it was not and could not be her voice. She made no attempt to produce such a tone with such a volume to it and the voice was definitely not her own, but of something unearthly, using her vocal chords. It was not a primal scream of agony, but a simple, powerful, terrifying voice.

In this case we questioned her about her background. From her testimony we ascertained that her father was in the ministry of the occult. We applied the sacraments to her—confession, anointing, repetition of the baptismal vows—and then we asked her to renounce the evil that was controlling her voice. We asked her also to renounce any evil, dominating or possessive bond that existed between her and her father. We told her to say the Jesus Prayer and—whenever she was with her father—to place Jesus between herself and her father. Since she was from another part of the state, we were not able to have a series of sessions with her. But she wrote sometime later and said she was doing much better and found it a great practice to place Jesus between herself and another person.

What became clear in this and other cases was that there must be inner healing and the use of the sacraments. Sometimes just the repetition of the baptismal vows will suffice to release the person. More often than not, however, the point where evil has entered the life of a person must be found and the particular bondage must be broken.

Dialogue with Satan

A young man came to me some time ago and told me that he had made a bet with Satan. I don't recall the incidentals of the bet, but the fact was that he had done such a thing. This man was an exceptional young man, with an intuition into the struggle of good and evil that existed within him. He was aware of the consequences of that struggle, and it seemed, within his particular soul, that he was one of those who have to wrestle with God in order that God might gain within him a very decisive victory. In this type of person, I feel that the evil spirit is tremendously active and makes an attempt to forestall the overwhelming victory of God.

The young man made this bet with someone other than himself. He experienced himself in a dialogue with Satan. Some people experience themselves as having a dialogue or relationship with the evil within themselves, i.e., their own hatred, lust, hostility, or simply being in league with something they call evil. Sometimes this evil can be personified as a devil or a demon within. This young man experienced himself in dialogue with an entity outside himself who gained power over him through the bet. After providing him with the sacraments, we simply commanded that the bondage with Satan be broken. A few weeks later, the young man called back and said that the problem with the bondage of the bet had been ended. He was, however, still in a deep struggle on the level of his faith and his relationship with God. We continued to pray for him in that area.

Contact with the Evil Spirit

A young woman had come into the Spirit a few years ago. After that experience, she found a great deal of difficulty in living with her parents. Another Christian woman allowed her to come to live with her for a time. After a while, she was afraid to go to sleep, experienced other presences in the room, and was generally not at peace. She came to see us with the woman who had befriended her. After a period of time of working on areas in inner healing, she divulged the fact that she had once made a contract with evil. We had known of a similar case in which we had not ministered that was quite serious. Though this case had some strong consequences, the bondage involved did not seem as severe. We asked her to go to confession and request forgiveness for the sin, anointed her, and had her repeat her baptismal vows. Then we asked her to renounce the contract and prayed the deliverance prayer over her. We prayed also a special blessing over the home and asked the Lord to enter the home with his great power of love and wisdom. Eventually the girl's symptoms disappeared. There was much inner healing to be done in her case, but she was at least free of the contract. I believe she was freed so easily because she did not really enter into the contract with any degree of will or intensity.

The Implementation of a Curse

Sometimes people come to us and claim that they are under the power of a curse or a spell being projected into them by another person. Very often this can be a mask for not confronting their own emotional problems or dealings with patterns of sin within themselves. Often enough, however, there is some substance to their claim. The reception of the sacraments and the use of simple prayer of protection and deliverance should suffice to deal with the situation. In cases, however, where there is some physical proximity or nearness in relationship to the one projecting the evil, physical distance or separation may be necessary to have complete freedom.

Sometimes people are unaware that they are under such a case. A young man came to us from a neighboring state and had a pathological case of homosexuality. We applied all of the remedies we know for this terrible disease in a person. Some of them were very helpful, but they did not get to the core of the problem. Through the word of knowledge it was discovered that his mother had cursed him while he was still in her womb. The breaking of this curse seemed to get at the source of the problem and bring this man some relief and confidence that he could survive. We do not know whether the mother used this curse as a direct invocation of evil or not, but the effect was the same and seemed to bring a severe power of evil to play on this man who had a sickness that he did not wish for and could not control.

There have been numerous cases of people who have claimed these things have happened to them. This is especially true as we deal more with the Hispanic, Caribbean, South American and Central American cultures. People seem to be more aware of the diabolic forms of evil in these cultures, while the devil seems to work on the weakness of the Atlantic community in an indirect manner through TV, business success, sexual decadence, etc.

Infestation of the Evil One in a Weakness of the Human Personality

If one has a long habit of sin in a particular area, the movement of the evil spirit in encouraging one and helping one along this downhill path can be quite unnoticed, but always present. Similarly, when the person has reached the point of the prodigal son, the amount of repentance, inner healing, and inner forms of penance that are required is enormous indeed. What is needed is also a great deal of support and love from other people in order to help such persons out of the dilemma in which they have placed themselves. There is, however, a supplementary but rather necessary role that deliverance can play in such a person.

A man who was about thirty-five related to me the very difficult story of his life. Raised by an alcoholic mother, with his father unknown to him, he had turned at an early age to the only service open to him for love and affection, that is, to sexual encounters with women. He had repented of this long and dreadful history, and there was much sorrow for sin and a period of inner healing that went on for months within him. He also began to develop stronger community ties that helped him a great deal. The basis of healing in this case is not only in the hands of a priest or the therapist. It is also in the hands of the community. This young man was also a deeply sincere man who had qualities that one might have imagined in Peter or Magdalene. The depth of his sin was more than equaled by his sorrow for it. This gave him the possibility for a profound relationship with Jesus in the long rehabilitation that would ensue.

Part of this process, however, is the use of deliverance. It should always be at the end of the process, when a powerful movement of prayer and healing has taken place within the relationship between the person ministering and the one to whom he is ministering. In this case, the man had been given a powerful gift of prayer by God. The depth of inner healing and his relationship to the Lord grew as the sessions proceeded, but in each of these moments of healing, for example, "in the womb" in his relationship to his mother, and the encounters with various women with whom he had a sexual liaison, there was not only the repentance and the deep healing, but at the end of each process there was a struggle with an evil presence which refused to leave. With the use of a deliverance prayer, the bondage was broken and the healing and union with the Lord would be completed.

It is so important, in a case like this, that the proper balance be maintained. This could easily have been one of those deliverance cases where a great deal of shouting and confrontation went on and the person, though perhaps delivered, was never really healed. Direct confrontation with evil would not have allowed the process of love, repentance, and healing to grow to a point where real healing would take place. On the other hand, repudiation of this use of deliverance would have, in my judgment, allowed the bondage to remain that was actually there. What is actually healing is the love of God, the love of the therapist, the love of the community, and the repentance and sincerity of the Christian who is in such need. What is necessary is that the healing be fully completed in some form of deliverance.

This type of infestation can happen in any area of the personality. There was a woman who came to the Center. Fortunately, as with the man we spoke of above, she had a consistent and deep relationship with the Lord and a background of contemplative prayer. But she had a deep and overwhelming anger within her from which she wished to be released. In inner healing we came back to a very angry child whose father had loved her deeply, but who had suddenly and abruptly separated from the home, for reasons associated with his job. The separation, which lasted a number of years, provoked deep anger. Within this anger the power of evil began to manifest itself. When we prayed for this inner healing, we also had to pray for her release from this power that had gotten into her and was reinforced by incidents from her later life. In this case again, the love of God, the movement of inner healing and the use of the sacraments gradually brought release, but not without a struggle with the evil one in which we needed both the renunciation of the devil in the baptismal vows as well as several specific renunciations. She is now well and on her way to greater healing. Praise God!

In this ministry at St. Joseph's Prayer Center, we have been taught a process to deal with the liberation of people who are afflicted in the way those above have been. The quality of deception involved here can be very great, as well as the anxiety in dealing with such cases. To avoid difficulties whereby the evil one could use someone to produce excessive anxiety—a disturbance to the ministry—the following procedures are an orderly way of dealing with the process:

(1) There should be discernment as to whether the person should be taken or not. If a person calls for deliverance, we have learned not to take that person right away. First, someone should talk with the person over the phone or in an interview to determine whether deliverance is necessary. Perhaps only inner healing is involved, or inner healing complemented by deliverance in the first or second mode. Such cases can be handled more easily than an outright deliverance.

Second, it should be determined as to whether the person should actually be seen or not. Perhaps this is not the time to do this particular deliverance or you may not be ready for it at this particular time. Such a consideration should not be an inducement to cowardice, but the wisdom of the Lord should apply here as everywhere else. If the community is unable to handle the case, more damage than good can come to the individual, as well as to the community involved. It may also be a clear case of exorcism in which procedures besides those used in deliverance should be employed. Finally the person may be used in such a way as to cause great confusion and disruption to the ministry.

(2) If it is still determined that the person will be taken, it seems good that a team be utilized. In simple deliverances, a person experienced in the ministry might be capable of performing it without too much commotion or difficulty. All of the above deliverances in the fourth mode except one were handled by a team. There should be a leader, preferably a priest, who leads the prayer for inner healing, the application of the sacraments, and a specific deliverance prayer. Secondly, there

should be people doing intercessory prayer both inside and outside the room as well as people with tested gifts of the word of knowledge and images both inside and outside the room. The reason for having people both inside and outside the room is that we have found that an appreciable amount of tension develops inside the room. For the accuracy and full power of the use of these gifts in the situation, we have found that people should be outside the actual room as well as in it.

(3) Before the person comes, the team should spend an hour in prayer together for the sake of that person. This should be for the person first. It is basically the love of God and the power of the Holy Spirit that will heal the person, and so the gathering of power for the person is necessary. It also protects the minister and the team from any influence of evil.

(4) In the area of prayer, we should ascertain the background of the person so as to see whether the person needs any inner healing in a proposed or discerned area of affliction. During this time or any time, the whole power of the deliverance will be to avoid any unusual outburst on the part of the person or someone controlling the person. Even the actual deliverance, if it comes to that, should be conducted as peaceably as possible. A lot of disturbance goes to the advantage of the enemy. Peace is a sign, generally speaking, of the activity of the Spirit.

(5) The next step is to go through an inner healing process. In the area of the affliction or related areas, the process should be as comprehensive as possible. If the release of the person can be gotten through inner healing, then that is all the better for the person and for the team.

(6) There should be application of the sacraments. The person should go to confession sometime during the session so that the power of the sacrament can be applied to the wounded dimension of the person's spirit. If any area of sinfulness is uncovered and confessed, this may break any legal hold that the evil spirit might have on the person. The sacrament of anointing will provide power to heal both body and spirit, and repetition of the baptismal vows with the general renunciation of Satan may hopefully break any bondage that is left. It is to

be hoped that the person, especially during this time, will be a frequent communicant after the deliverance is over. The person should be asked to attend the next Mass that it is possible to attend and/or to receive Communion.

(7) By this time the breaking of the affliction may have already occurred. But it is good to have the person renounce whatever the specific evil may have been related in the testimony or through the word of knowledge. I am basically not in favor of getting this information through any spirit that is in that person because I believe that this gives the evil spirit a temporary control over the person's consciousness that is frightening to the person and may be detrimental to that person. Word of knowledge and testimony may take the risk of being misleading, but it does not take the aforementioned risk.

What is done here should be done in a positive manner. If there is a spirit of resentment involved, then a great deal of prayer for forgiveness should occur. Similarly, if Satan himself is discerned, then a great power of worship should prevail in peace before any renunciation of him takes place. If there is any affliction, the opposite should be invoked first, and, as much as possible, the renunciation should take an integral part of the positive prayer or as a footnote to it. After there has been some release, then the positive prayer should be continued. All excessive focus on evil should be avoided.

(8) The session should always end with a prayer of love and peace. Usually the Spirit will give his peace to the person and to the team when the session seems over. It should be on both, because the evil one may possibly be able to deceive with a false peace that has to be discerned from the real peace of the Holy Spirit.

Multiple Deliverance

We have had experience of several cases where the infestation of the evil one had entered into several areas of the personality to such a degree that the evil influence would act almost at will. These have required several sessions of deliverance and inner healing and have in one or two cases been effective. This case borders so much on the area of possession and exorcism that, if the case were to continue, the bishop should be informed of its existence and his power utilized in the process if he so chooses. Certainly, as we come close to this kind of case, the whole power of the Church is needed to bring release to the afflicted person.

EXORCISM: THE FIFTH MODE
(DELIVERANCE FROM DIABOLICAL POSSESSION)

People in need of an exorcism may be able for a time to lead a normal life, but their inner life is dominated by the power of evil and will tend to manifest itself on occasions. Such persons will speak in a vile tongue, and various other entities will enter them and speak through them. They will appear to have little control over themselves and will, after a period of time, have to be incarcerated. For any case of this sort, the bishop's power should be specifically invoked. Also there should be a wide range of discernment as to what to do and how to proceed. Witness the recent case in Germany where the priest, undoubtedly a good and holy man, kept the case of such an afflicted woman basically to himself. What happened involved the death of that woman.

I have ministered to one person of this type. This person did not return and the power that these personalities had over him was said to have increased, though he did renounce them at the time we prayed with him. (This was at an earlier point in our ministry.)

My own experience with exorcism/possession is limited, but there are several questions that are in my mind about such a ministry. I would like to know whether there has been a permanent release and a gradual upward swing in the personalities of the people who have undergone exorcism in their ministry. It is hard to document a person who has been this far gone and has received a full release. Release may occur in a session, but do the habits and the way of life of such a person almost inevitably mean that the power overwhelming the person will return?

RELATIONSHIP BETWEEN THE BISHOP AND THOSE IN THE DELIVERANCE MINISTRY

In my own ministry, I have become aware of some of the dangers involved in this ministry. One should not allow anxiety to touch a work of the Lord, but, as a matter of fact, we are human and we can come, at times, up against powers that are greater than ourselves.

In working this relationship out on Long Island, we have come to an understanding about the ministry. In relating to cases of deliverance we are to use the ordinary ministry of the person and the priest against such involvement with evil—that is, to pray the ordinary sacramental ministry of the Church which would involve the rebuke of evil through baptismal vows, the Our Father in the Mass, the reception of the Eucharist and the renunciation of evil that is the ordinary concomitant of repentance in the sacrament of penance. Fr. John Healey of the Brooklyn diocese has written in another context as to how deliverance is utilized within the sacrament of penance. When, in the course of such a deliverance, it becomes clear that exorcism is necessary, then the bishop should be notified and his discernment and approval requested.

What is just as important is that the relationship with the bishop be an open and free one so that communication and trust is assured. For a priest or lay person to be acting in this ministry outside the protection of or relationship to the bishop is an unfortunate and dangerous position. Yet some people are presented with deliverance cases in which the relationship to the bishop has not been established and they are left with the choice of going through a chancery office that may not be amenable or may, in some cases, be hostile to consideration of such a ministry. The two extremes mentioned earlier in this article—one, that the devil or that area of the supernatural does not exist at all; the other, that it is the only kind of ministry, with a consequent morbid focus on evil—have not contributed to the solution of this problem. If a generally accepted set of norms would be established and proposed to the bishops, then the relationship between a ministry that develops in the wisdom of Christ and an authority that both strengthens and corrects this ministry might be established. More and more, because of the growth of Satanism and the influence of the non-technological cultures, we are becoming aware of the need. To confront that need, the whole source of the Church should be utilized in compatible and strong relationships.

To talk about deliverance it has been necessary to isolate it from other elements in the healing process. This is essential in order to talk about anything, but it is also necessary to introduce those elements into the process that seem to be left out by the focus on the one term: deliverance.

The most significant element is the element of love, the element that is central to all Christian living and all Christian life. We have to be careful, particularly in the area of deliverance, where a hasty sense of loving and caring for a person can bring us into the web of deceit and manipulation that is part of the tactic of the enemy.

Each person whom we minister to in the deliverance ministry should be approached with a special gift of wisdom. We should proceed, in all of these cases, with the cautious care and discernment mentioned in this article. Where we are assured that we are dealing with a sincere and repentant person, we are aware that it is only love, the love of the Spirit of God, that will, in the long run, heal.

Deliverance does not heal; it only provides the avenue through which healing can take place. And that healing is sealed by the action of God's love and the action of my love in Christ for that person. Only that love will convince such persons that they have not been abandoned by God. Only that love will preserve them from a damaging anxiety about themselves that may persist for the rest of their lives. Only that love diminishes the power of evil and shows it to be the sham that it really is.

Often deliverance is separated from the act of healing love and the persons themselves really feel that they are something malignant. Only love for such persons cures them of that feeling and releases them to feel that God loves them and wants to free them. When they realize that God loves them and that they are not some miserable object that cannot be saved, then healing can occur. A ministry that separates deliverance from the word, the sacraments, and the overall ministry of the Church simply leaves the person without the main sources of healing that are within the Church. The ministry that separates itself from the love of Jesus Christ for the person who is to be healed and delivered divides itself from the very source of the Church's healing power, namely, the love of the Spirit in the person of Jesus.

When I think of all the individuals mentioned in this article, it seems to me that the overall power of the Church was the source that healed them. And that power was received when we humbly asked the Lord for the unselfish and non-possessive love of the Spirit for them. When God loved them they were healed and delivered. When God loved them through the total ministry of the Church, we found healing taking place. When we asked God to place in us the love he had for those persons, then that love truly freed, truly delivered, truly healed.

Section Three

Psychological Perspectives on Deliverance Prayer

9

A Trilateral View of Deliverance: Contributions of Psychology, Theology and Sociology

by Rev. Kenneth J. Metz, Ph.D.

Editor's Note: *By now it may seem that there is much more that we don't know than that we know about the world of evil spirits. Not only is much mystery present in demonic bondage but also in schizophrenia. A contemporary authority on schizophrenia, Dr. R. D. Laing* (The Divided Self, *London: Pelican, 1960) is puzzled in seeking a psychological explanation for states resembling those needing deliverance prayer.*

A most curious phenomenon of the personality, one which has been observed for centuries, but (italics mine) *which has not yet received its full explanation,* is that in which the individual seems to be the vehicle of a personality that is not his own. Someone else's personality seems to 'possess' him and be finding expression through his words and actions, whereas the individual's own personality is temporarily 'lost' or 'gone'. This happens with all degrees of malignancy.

To penetrate the mystery psychiatry sometimes needs the help of a spiritual diagnosis just as those praying for deliverance need the psychiatric diagnosis and treatment of any physical and mental illness exacerbated by the demonic. A person may have illness alone, an illness plus the demonic, or the demonic alone. The test for the demonic is not to rule out all oth-

er natural explanations but to find that the manifestations are triggered by prayer or the presence of Christ, and that this checks out with others who have the gift of discerning spirits. Since the most difficult area of deliverance is proper discernment, we need to gather professionals with medical, psychological, and spiritual skills so as to have enough discernment to know if deliverance is necessary and how the Lord wants us to pray. Thus we can more easily listen to his and not just our own diagnosis.

How can we open ourselves more to hearing the Lord rather than our own diagnosis? There are many ways: praying over the gospels until we think and feel like Jesus, taking time to look with the Lord at the day and ask him when we best heard his voice or ignored it, and living in ways that make us want God's will at any cost. To these Fr. Ken Metz, a professor teaching the behavioral sciences and counseling, adds the need to be aware of our psychological, sociological, and theological biases that shape our questions and the answers we hear. As a priest counselor who prays for healing and deliverance, Fr. Metz has had to straddle and integrate many viewpoints on deliverance. In his article he delineates the underlying psychological, sociological, and theological models that form the assumptions behind conflicting approaches to deliverance. If we know our prejudices, then we can ask new questions and seek the truth of another's conflicting view.

Religious people both believe in and deny the efficacy of delivering a person from the grips of a demon. The position of each religious person rests upon belief or disbelief in the very existence of demons. This article offers an analysis of deliverance from three perspectives: psychological, sociological, and theological. It is hoped that light will be shed on this ministry through a rather involved trilateral analysis.

A friend suggested not long ago that the Roman Catholic Church should "get in touch with its tradition and stop making noise about deliverance." His meaning was that the Church has a long tradition of dealing with demons and that the present debate is producing more heat than light. One of the reasons for the debate within the Christian Church is a shift in theological understanding which has its roots not so much in theology as in the adoption of a different theory of personality. Psychology, the study of personality, has had a deep influence on the theological stance in this instance. To merely describe a psychological approach to deliverance would leave the subtleties of the different approaches uncharted and make this article inadequate. Just as there is no one psychological view of all reality or one psychological view of religion, there is no one psychological view of deliverance.

Although the discipline of psychology has much to offer toward an understanding of troubled people, it cannot give the ultimate meaning to the causes of those conditions. In the same way, approaches to interpersonal relationships vary. Sociology cannot give the answer to the problem of evil control over people's lives expressed individually or collectively.

The basic resource for this article is found in Everett and Bachmeyer's *Disciplines in Transformation: A Guide to Theology and the Behavioral Sciences.* A much more complete analysis of the basic positions and relationships can be found there. For our part, we will analyze deliverance using their basic outline in order to fathom some of the complexities involved. It would be a mistake to assume that each discipline has a uniform way of handling its proper object. Each discipline has a variety of approaches and explanations for the reality it studies. Trilateral analysis moves beyond the usual bilateral approaches of theology-psychology or theology-sociology to a deeper, more complex description of the interaction of all three. Each discipline is affected by at least the implicit input of the others. A theological stance is not free from psychological or sociological input and biases no matter how intent the believer is on being "centered" on God alone. Each of the three disciplines can be divided into three tendencies or "ideal types," each of which has its peculiar loyalties, theories, and practices.

At the outset it is good to note some possible outcomes to our interdisciplinary discussion of deliverance. Using a Christian position as home base, these can be modeled. Some Christians will reject the contributions of psychology and sociology because they entertain values which do not allow for natural human inquiry into areas seen as having contact with spiritual realities. Others will add the findings of psychology and sociology onto their Christianity without discerning the ramifications of these additions. In time confusion of their basic loyalties will result. Still others will state that the findings of psychology and sociology are nothing but realities previously discovered in their Christian theology or experience. Still others will utilize the findings of psychology and sociology to bolster a position already held in their Christiantiy.

The most complicated result occurs in what is called transformation. Three possible ways exist for this to occur. (1) Christianity makes inquiries of psychology and sociology in order to modify Christian practices and positions. (2) Christianity discusses psychological and sociological positions in an attempt to change them. (3) Christianity and the other disciplines are both open to change in the process of discussion. This third kind is known as reciprocal transformation (Everett and Bachmeyer, pp. 167–171).

In the first kind of transformation the Christian would look to be changed in the contact with psychology and sociology. In this style, there is an abdication of part of the reality studied by theology. In the area of deliverance this is illustrated by those who see no possibility of deliverance because they think that psychology and sociology have not supported such a view.

In the second kind of transformation the Christian would enter into discussion on deliverance with the view of correcting the psychologists and sociologists who are "misled" or not in possession of the truth. Both of these transformations are inadequate because they limit truth to one discipline or another.

In reciprocal transformation all of the disciplines are open to learning from the others. Our goal in this article is this kind of transformation. Even though the basic definition of evil and of demons lies in the area of theology, much needs to be modified on all sides of the issue.

VARIOUS PSYCHOLOGICAL VIEWS OF DELIVERANCE

A discussion of psychological views on the existence of demons and of deliverance from their influences begins with an understanding of the proper object of psychology. Psychology is the study of intra-psychic operations of human beings in everyday life with a view first to understanding the inner workings of the mind and then to helping persons cope with the struggles of daily life. Psychologists and psychiatrists study the outward manifestations of people seeking the meaning of their actions. After examining someone thought to be possessed by demons, psychologists would say that the manifestations indicated certain psychological realities and then would interpret these realities according to their preferred approaches. These explanations would fall generally into one of three tendencies: conflict, equilibrium, or fulfillment psychology.

CONFLICT PSYCHOLOGY

Foremost among the conflict psychologists is Sigmund Freud. His discoveries and theories have influenced the study of psychology to such an extent that most theorizing on deliverance seems to be Freudian.

Conflict psychologists see the self in a state of constant tension within the self and between the self and others. This conflict is to be managed so that adequate living can occur. Adequate living is achieved in the management of the conflict in a way that allows more gratifying social or personal functioning. The fundamental loyalties or values of this approach lie in the desire to cure a person so that adequate functioning can occur. Freud saw this as the capacity to love and work in the midst of continued conflict. Adjustment to reality is the best that can be hoped for.

The theory of the conflict approach posited an id, ego, and super-ego always in tension. The mismanagement of this tension was called neurosis. The state where the id broke through the super-ego completely was called psychosis. All persons were thought to have defenses which kept the id in check. Sometimes these defenses became too strong and affected the person's ability to cope. The person would then be using the defenses as unconscious ways of denying or ignoring the tensions. In practice the conflict psychotherapist seeks to alter the approach taken by the patient by promoting insight. The therapist's role is one of making interpretations during the sessions.

In his study of a demonological neurosis Freud (1923) pointed out that belief in a demon was necessary in order to believe in a God. He gave the "possessed" man's experience a psychological expression in that "neuroses of olden times were masquerading in demonological shape and that evil spirits were the projection of base and evil wishes into the world" (Fodor, p. 16). Freud maintained this position to the end of his life despite continued arguments with Jung over the existence of demons. Freud's views have dominated the psychiatric scene over the years. In sum, possession by demons was believed to be the expression of the unruly id breaking through the control of the super-ego.

Carl Jung broke with Freud over more issues than are generally recognized. When it comes to demons Jung began by agreeing with Freud. In 1919 Jung expressed the view that spirits were unconscious, autonomous complexes that appeared as projections because they were not associated with the ego. He considered the usual spiritualistic proofs as psychological products dependent on the unconscious of the percipient (Jung, p. 258). In later works he expressed the concern that he was not so sure anymore. He stated bluntly that an exclusive psychological approach cannot do justice to the phenomena in question (Fodor, p. 268), and he discovered that psychological investigation was much easier under the influence of a spirit-guide named Philomon (Fodor, p. 30). Jung finally saw the devil as being one with God through his theory of the conjunction of opposites. "Jung accomplished more than any other twentieth-century thinker to make occult theorizing respectable, finding his concepts of the 'collective unconscious' and 'synchronicity' corresponding in many ways with oriental and occult theories" (Richards, p. 28).

Following a Jungian approach Gross compared demon possession with multiple personality. He believed that "analysis of the religious symbolism in the New Testament to describe exorcism can bring such exorcism into an intelligible relationship with psychiatric theory, and can lead consequently to a hypothesis describing the function of this symbolism in promoting psychic integration" (p. 39).

Lhermitte distinguished various types of possession, listing pseudo-demonic possession states such as epileptic attacks, psychoneurosis, hysteria, and convulsions as being the usual situation where possession was suspected. He mentioned that "the symptoms of the psychoneurosis correspond with a regression toward the infantile state of the moral personality, with a dissociation of the psychological elements which should hold it together" (p. 87). Further on he describes the process:

> Under the influence of subconscious feeling and the pressure of coanesthetic disturbances, the mind may then be capable of creating a system of thoughts and affective elements which, because of affinity and common origin in the depths of the unconscious, unite to form a complex whole, of which the subject, though unconsciously, is the center, and which appears to be a dual personality (p. 102).

If one were to attempt exorcism in this case, one would call up the devil and see "not the devil himself, but a portrait composed according to the patient's idea of him" (p. 102). Summing up the conflict approach Lhermitte notes that the human being becomes the scene of the duel between God and devil, the debate between what ought to be and what is.

> From this conflict springs an anguish, exhausting and insatiable, impelling the subject to eject this Super-ego which opposes his libidinal aspirations and leading him to give it the form of the devil. The sentiment of guilt, the weight of conscience judging itself guilty—that, according to the psychoanalysts, is the source of demonical illusion (p. 116).

Rollo May serves as a bridge to the second type of psychology. He saw the daimonic as residing in everyone, similar to the id, but with a twist in that it is good unless unleashed in a non-integrative way.

> The daimonic is the urge in every being to affirm itself, assert itself, perpetuate and preserve itself. The daimonic becomes evil when it usurps the total self without regard to the integration of others and their need for integration. It then appears as excessive aggression, hostility, cruelty—the things about us which horrify us the most, and which we repress whenever we can or, more likely, project on others. But these are the reverse side of the same assertion which empowers our creativity (p. 123).

The conflict approach to psychology then sees the id as the source of what is known as demonic. In that the resultant behavior is so horrible to sensitive people, it is ascribed to demons which may or may not exist.

FULFILLMENT PSYCHOLOGY

Many of the early fulfillment psychologists received their training at conflict-oriented institutions. Many became disenchanted with what appeared to be a pessimistic attitude arising from the imperiousness of the super-ego as identified in the analytic approach. Rather than live with the conflict, coping with it incessantly, people were thought to be able to transcend the conflicts.

The theories which sprang from these values are couched in terms of growth, not in terms of cure. Basic to the fulfillment approach is the belief that each person has a set of needs that must be met. Society can block this growth. In order to ensure growth, the person is thought to establish defenses as protection against social pressures. The person thus counteracts barriers to growth. The ideal outcome of growth is self-actualization, according to Maslow. In this state a person is nearing all that he or she can become and the "peak experience" is the height of self-actualization.

In practice many techniques are used to help persons meet their needs. Some therapists reflect back feelings (Rogers); others set up conditions where feelings can be expressed freely in the here and now hoping that effects will carry over into daily activities (Perls; Schutz). By discovering incongruence between a person's feelings and thoughts, the barriers to growth are noted and the person is helped to decide the manner in which the barriers to growth will be transcended.

In the fulfillment approach expressions of demonic possession are viewed as a lack of growth, the lack of achievement of self-esteem. The defense against social blocks takes the form of attribution to other external social forces, so that the person might still seek growth. In this view, society is the real demon of today as it would block the free expression of growth and creativity of the individual. Another expression of the demonic would be seen in the misreading of one's feelings.

In Maslow's view all people are good, striving for self-actualization. Anyone can travel the road to peak-experience. These people who decide to take the road can experience much growth together until they reach what Maslow called the "fork in the road" composed of mankind's disagreements. What are they?

> Only, it seems, the concept of supernatural beings or of supernatural laws or forces; and I must confess my feeling that by the time this forking of the road has been reached, this difference doesn't seem to be of any great consequence except for the comfort of the individual.
>
> Not only this, but it is increasingly developing that leading theologians and sophisticated people in general define their god, not as a person, but as a force, a principle, a gestalt-like quality of the whole of Being, an integrating power that expresses the unity and therefore the meaningfulness of the cosmos, the "dimension of depth," etc. (p. 55).

Consequently, there is little room in the fulfillment approach for demons or deliverance except as a "backward" understanding of the reality of the forces of evil within society that thwart personal growth. Certainly, that force is not conceived of as personal.

EQUILIBRIUM PSYCHOLOGY

The equilibrium approach to personality was developed by those who desired to understand people in a more scientific, quantifiable manner. The constructs of id, ego and super-ego of Freud and the conflict psychologists and the centrality of feelings and needs indicated by Maslow and Rogers were seen as being unscientific and unmeasurable. Proponents of this approach valued efficient personal functioning in the context of socially appropriate behavior. Most adherents of behaviorism and cognitive therapy hold to these values. Their concern is not so much with how a person arrived at the present as much as with how a person can adapt, can learn new behavior, in order to conquer inappropriate behavior.

Learning theory provides the basis for understanding this style of psychology. People are seen as having learned various methods of coping with reality. When some new stimulus comes into their lives, the old behaviors may not be sufficient, and tension results. In pairing the new stimulus with some old adequate responses or some new behaviors, a balance is achieved and equilibrium established. In practice, this approach uses many techniques, all designed to manipulate stimuli to achieve desired goals. Some of these techniques include modeling of behavior, positive control through reward for desired behavior, punishment of undesirable behavior, removal of stimuli, and desensitization through the replacement of feelings.

Equilibrium psychologists contend that the behavior which has been called possession is learned behavior. The explanation runs along these lines: the affected person has either heard stories, or read articles, or seen movies which tell of the experiences of those "possessed" by evil spirits. In the face of some conflict or problem, the person adapts that which was

previously internalized to the present situation. The "possession" behavior is the person's way of adapting to the pressures
of daily life, the way of achieving equilibrium within the person. This behavior will continue as long as the person receives
attention as a reward for this behavior.

Virkler and Virkler mention this source of "possession" as
something to be contended with in their analysis of role enact-
ment:

> People continuously are fulfilling a variety of roles—hus-
> band, wife, father, mother, instructor, therapist, et cetera in
> which they behave as they consciously or unconsciously be-
> lieve persons in those roles should act. A person who experi-
> ences unusual mental events and begins to believe that he is
> demon-possessed may act in ways that he understands to be
> consistent with the demon-possession, without conscious
> simulation on his own part. Such persons may readily mani-
> fest all the classical symptoms of demon possession without
> actually being demon-possessed (p. 100).

Another kind of equilibrium psychology looks to health as
a balance of mind and body forces. People are suggestible; indeed, suggestibility is one of the characteristics of being normal. Sargent notes the relationship of persons to culture in this
regard: "It is clear that states of possession reflect and serve to
confirm the beliefs of bystanders and observers, and that they
also tend to confirm or inculcate these same beliefs in the possessed persons themselves" (p. 53). A bit further on he states:

> A person only speaks spontaneously in his mesmeric or hyp-
> notic state if he really believes he is possessed by the devil,
> or by some other spiritual agency able to speak through
> him. If on the contrary he believes that the condition he suf-
> fers from is due to hysteria and is basically his own fault, and
> if he does not believe in spirit possession, and he is not living
> among others who do, he will not only talk about himself
> and his past and present fears and weaknesses. Even if he
> goes into a trance he never discusses the part being played
> by supposed metaphysical agencies (p. 56).

In sum, then, the view of equilibrium psychology is that the behavior identified as possession is learned from some source, probably not extra-human.

In this review of psychological tendencies, possession is throught to be due to a number of different causes. Of importance to note is the fact that many states of possession in the past very well may have been natural states. Some, such as Gildea (1974), put it this way: "There seems to be little, if any doubt, that every single example of the physical symptoms of possession can have a natural cause and explanation" (p. 299). Lhermitte concludes his book on the subject with these words:

> When, in actual fact, a delirium of demonopathic possessions develops, under our observation, according to the same laws which condition a delirium similar in all respects except color and content, and when the same therapeutic treatment proves capable of reducing both kinds, then we must be convinced that the disorder is one whose cause is to be found, not in "supernature," but in nature itself, nature spoiled by a morbid process.
>
> If, on the contrary, the phenomena of possession appear only in a parasitic capacity, or are accompanied by very high qualities of mind and heart, then the doctor must call in the qualified theologian, the exorcist (p. 124).

When Lhermitte asks the question of some cause beyond that which is visible, he answers his question: "It is not for me to resolve this problem, and on this point the reader must form his own judgment according to his beliefs" (p. 124). To an analysis of Christian approaches to deliverance we now turn.

CHRISTIAN APPROACHES TO DELIVERANCE

Within Christianity three basic tendencies based on loyalties, theories and practices can be discerned. The prophetic, cultic, and ecstatic tendencies form popular approaches to Christianity. These basic patterns are held together, according to Everett and Bachmeyer, by "directing our attention to the grounds by which Christian bodies or individuals legitimate their practices and thoughts" (p. 46). Theology is theory explaining religious practices and values, here being Christian.

Each of these tendencies has affinities for particular approaches to psychology and sociology. We have already noted the various psychological approaches. To complete the triad we also consider sociology. Sociology is concerned with any set of interpersonal relationships that individuals enter into rather than create. The main sociological thrusts have not only tried to describe society but have also attempted to prescribe social relations. There are also three main tendencies in understanding society: dualist, systemic, and pluralist. Each of these will be described in detail as it is encountered as relating to the various Christian approaches.

PROPHETIC CHRISTIANITY

The prophetic approach to Christianity holds the Bible as central to Christian belief and practice. The revealed word of God spoken through the ages in the Scriptures calls people to the will of God. Thus, the Bible must be learned and obeyed. The theology found in this tendency generally interprets the Scriptures as the pure message of God to his people. It employs the concepts of covenant, law, sin, imminent judgment of God, and kingdom of God. The Church is a gathering of those who are saved as they await the return of Jesus. God's grace is freely given, saving people from the evils of this world. Jesus is the Savior who brings God's message of salvation to the world. In practice much time is spent in the dissemination of the Scripture message in Bible meetings, crusades and the ongoing memorization of the Word.

According to this theology demons do exist, and the task of the Christian is to join Jesus, the victor over evil, in the battle. In accepting Jesus as Lord and Savior, the Christian enters into the battle against evil and in faith is equipped for the warfare.

Evangelicals such as Virkler and Koch have expressed this viewpoint quite clearly.

Sociologically speaking, prophetics usually adopt the view of society known as dualist. This approach is one in which society is seen to be a place of conflict between two opposing forces, classes or groups. It tends to see society in terms of equality or inequality expressed in dichotomies such as oppressor-oppressed, elite-masses, haves-have nots, and powerful-powerless. Prophetic Christians are usually seen as conservative dualists, those who say that the best way to spread the good news would be to share it with the "have nots." They have the answer which must be given to the masses of unsaved. They see themselves as being called by God to rescue the unsaved from the clutches of the evil one. The devil's influence is seen as influencing the entire world.

Another style of conservative dualist Christian seeks to escape the world, seeing oneself as saved and the rest damned, and desiring to be clear of all contact with evil. Some founders of religious communes have taken this approach.

When it comes to their view of the individual personality some prophetic Christians tend toward equilibrium psychology, and others toward conflict psychology.

The equilibrium motif of learned behavior is seen in the use of Scripture. Since the Bible contains the blueprint of salvation, it is to be learned, even memorized. The impact of this on deliverance teaching is seen in the many biblical injunctions to be utilized in the struggle against Satan. The goal of this style of Christianity is to teach a person how, with God's grace of course, to achieve right thinking and behaviors in order to win the battle and not to be fooled by the devil. The Church is to provide a proper environment for right thinking and acting.

An example of this approach is found in Timmons. Here Scripture is taken as the rule. The dualist theme of warfare takes a prominent place in his approach: "Yet behind these surface struggles is the real battle of life—the spiritual war. Jesus frequently taught about the demonic activity of the spirit world. He referred to demons and the leader of demons, Satan" (p. 3). He notes later that many Christians have problems today with demons because they do not know how to handle their attacks or the rules of warfare. Among the Satan traps he sees as deadly to Christians are the charismatic phenomena and the opinion that Satan's activity is nothing more than the product of sin in people's lives.

There is some incongruity here, however, in that demons are believed to exist from the theological viewpoint, and that "possession" is learned behavior, not caused by demons, from the psychological viewpoint. Most prophetics then follow their Christian loyalties, tending to see possession in a religious context, ignoring many psychological contributions.

Other prophetic Christians have a conflict psychological perspective. One such is Koch who starts from the view of conflict and integrates that with his theology: "The pastor ... desires, if grace prevails, to bring the person before the face of God, before whom the repressed emotions with their consequences are revealed, not only as neuroses, but also on the deeper level as guilt associations, which can only be overcome by forgiveness" (p. 289). True and total healing comes about through God's grace. When there is evidence of demonic bondage Koch sees that medicine can go only so far:

> The therapy of occult subjection reveals itself in the medical aspect as the problem of dismantling the effects of deep suggestion in the subconscious. This medical concern for healing, however, is only a subsection of the transcendent complex of occult subjection, and can therefore contribute only a limited, preliminary basis for further pastoral treatment (p. 293).

The Scriptures will give the mode of action required.

It is apparent from this analysis of prophetic Christianity that the basic Christian loyalties obtain. In terms of reciprocal transformation the theology changed little while the psychology changed much because psychology cannot have the final answers as found in the Bible.

CULTIC CHRISTIANITY

The cultic tendency within Christianity takes its name from the practice of worship. This cultic action is the main vehicle for the cultivation of religious values from early on in the lives of its adherents. It expresses the fundamental belief that God desires communion with his people. This achieves clearest expression in efficacious symbolic actions. Harking back to the sacrifice of Jesus on the cross, the gifts of Jesus to the Father are now communicated to all people through the eucharistic sacrifice. Through participation in this and other sacred actions Christians participate in the divine life of grace. In its theology, the Church is seen as the body of Christ extended in space and time as the vehicle for salvation of the whole world. The Scriptures are not seen as the only source of the revelation of God's word to his people but as the foundation of the Church which carries on the task of revealing God's loving presence to the world. The Church fulfills the message of the Bible. The practices of the cultic Christian center on acts of celebration, liturgy and sacramental rite, according to Everett and Bachmeyer (p. 53). Though found primarily in Roman Catholicism and Episcopalianism, it is also seen in some styles of Lutheranism, popular religious movements and some black churches.

Deliverance is much more institutionalized in the cultic approach. The kinds of exorcism found in the old moral manuals (Noldin and Schmidt) give witness to the beliefs of cultic Christianity in the past. In those manuals specific methods were determined for the priests (and others) to follow in delivering a person from the grip of the evil one. In the first instance solemn exorcism was to be performed by the priest as outlined in the rituals (cf. The Roman Ritual). Second, there was the exorcism of Leo XIII which could be recited without permission by both bishops and priests. Third, there were the simple exorcisms which were part of the blessing in some rites such as baptism and the blessing of salt and water. Listed fourth were private exorcisms which "qui vero non est sacramentale, peragi potest ab *omnibus fidelibus*" (p. 43). It was duly noted that the effects of this exorcism did not derive from the authority of the laws of the Church but by virtue of the name of Jesus. A formula was not prescribed. It would be similar to one given: "In nomine Jesu praecipio tibi, spiritus immunde, ut recedas ab hac creatura Dei" (p. 43). On the popular level, Catholics were encouraged to have their homes blessed and to use sacramentals such as blessed salt and water on a regular basis. Temptations from the devil were to be controlled through the use of prayers and sacramentals.

In the more recent past, some of these concepts have changed. Modras asks if it is "time to say farewell to the devil" (p. 71) and to the possibility of possession. Riga also believes that the form and rites of exorcism ought to be abandoned. It seems that there has been a swing from the cure of souls to the care of souls. To understand this change it is important to note the influence of different psychological and sociological approaches on cultic Christianity.

It appears that most cultic Christians have been systemic in terms of their sociological viewpoint. The systemic views society as a system which is to preserve itself through the introduction of new members leading to the growth and development of the whole social body. In this arrangement each person has a rather well-defined role. The institutions of this society are complex arrangements of roles. The young are educated into a culture which integrates a person into a role, the roles into institutions, and the institutions into the entire society.

In terms of society, the devil is seen as all which would go against that which was cultivated within that society. Entropy is a concept of value in this instance. A general sociological understanding of the systemic model indicates a tendency for the message to be lost, a tendency to distort the message. This would be perceived as a great evil to be fought at every turn. The demon would then be discerned as entropy.

Other cultic persons have adopted a pluralist approach to society. They move beyond the systemics in that they see society as being composed of smaller groups which make up the whole. These groups are joined together quite loosely. In order to preserve freedom for each group, laws are enacted enabling individuals to associate with different groups freely. In theory, the groups that make up the society are self-interest gatherings which may come and go according to the needs of the people. Change will occur often because people change. Social order exists to the extent that consensus can be obtained.

In their practices, pluralists are masters at using political power processes and the mobilization of groups. Those cultic Christians who choose this approach have moved from a ghetto mentality in which their system was a battle with the rest of the Christians and secular society (a kind of dualism) to one in which they have rights to exist in the day-to-day flow of life. The devil is seen in terms of powerlessness, if at all. This approach seems to be the least open to the concept of the demonic because each group has a right to exist, no matter how deeply division is felt between groups.

Many cultic Christians have chosen the conflict personality approach. The cultics who choose this are similar in many ways to the prophetics who chose it. Cultics who tend in this direction view the continued mission of Jesus as that of continued victory over evil, the cure of sick souls. Sacramental rites are the therapy applied. If there were true cases of possession, exorcism was to be applied. If the demon was not directly involved, then the suspected possession was a case of mental or emotional illness. The "doctor of souls" was to utilize other competent help in diagnosing the real illness. Lists were constructed to aid in this task. Those who opted for the cultic/conflict dyad tended to be systemic in sociological orientation. The priest was to help restore the person to his or her proper role within the community.

More recently, many cultic Christians have adopted a fulfillment psychology. As noted above, a basic value in this approach is the inherent goodness of the individual. With this in mind, belief in demons as forces of evil seems to have diminished.

As persons become more aware of their own freedom they tend to note that moral evil does not come from outside a person, but from what Modras calls "the abuse of human freedom" (p. 75). A person would only abuse freedom under pressure from society, since goodness is inherent to the individual. Exorcism needs to be abandoned, if not destroyed as a relic of an unsophisticated deterministic past. In terms of a sociological approach, cultic/fulfillment Christians tend to choose the pluralist approach because of the need for freedom for growth. They will tend to confront the cultic body with new, "enlightened" views gained from psychology.

In the case of cultic Christianity reciprocal transformation has occurred in two ways. For the conflict-oriented person, the reality of demons is noted and is dealt with much in the fashion of the prophetic/conflict persons, only in the cultic style of ritualistic exorcism. For the fulfillment-oriented person, the psychological loyalties prevail, leading to a change in theology. Much can be said for changes in the understanding of Scriptures, etc., but change would probably not have occurred until the psychological/sociological base also changed.

ECSTATIC CHRISTIANITY

Personal experience of the Holy Spirit is a central facet of ecstatic Christianity. Each religious activity is to be informed by the Spirit much as it was experienced on Pentecost and in the early days of the Church.

The experience of the Spirit is almost more important than, although it leads to, meeting Jesus in the Bible or in ritual action. Worship of God must come freely from the heart and ought not to be circumscribed by law as found in a book or by the rites of a particular church. God's love for his people takes on the highest imperative as it is shown in his bounteous gift of charisms to them. The theology of the ecstatic approach is hard to pinpoint because of the very nature of the personal ecstatic experience. Reflections on this experience assume autobiographical shapes which are at times integrated in a previously held loyalty, such as in the Catholic charismatic renewal, or reject that loyalty. The personal regeneration which can happen after being transformed by the Spirit affects people greatly. Rituals and other previous practices are not enough. In practice the ecstatic personal response runs the gamut from the quiet meditation of the Quakers to the more expressive meetings of the pentecostals. Prayer groups are the usual meeting places for these Christians. Charismatic practices such as healing and discernment flourish in great freedom because the "Spirit blows where it wills."

As one becomes aware of the Holy Spirit, one also becomes aware of that which "opposes" him, the presence of evil. In looking to the Bible which speaks much of demons and deliverance, the ecstatic realizes that his or her own experiences parallel many of the accounts found therein. It follows that one should deal with the world of evil in the same way. Experience then becomes central. One is seen to have the power to free people from the grasp of the evil one when the evil is confronted.

The ecstatic Christian usually tends toward fulfillment psychology in that the person is being equipped by the Spirit to grow into the creature God intended from the beginning. In doing this, all of one's needs will be fulfilled—self-esteem as being loved by the Creator, self-preservation in the sure knowledge of eternal life, etc. This use of fulfillment psychology differs from that of the cultic noted above in that the immediacy of the Spirit is so much greater that it dominates the scene. From this view follows a pluralistic sociological view in which God is seen is leading each person and each group in a very unique way. The freedom to follow the Lord is to be preserved. Deliverance assumes a minor role in this configuration.

Some ecstatics have banded together quite strongly and have founded institutions adopting a systemic approach to society. They ritualize their deliverance services. Many of these have adopted conflict motifs in their psychology.

A most involved triad is that ecstatic Christian whose psychological position is conflict and whose sociological tendency is dualist. It seems that many writers in the charismatic renewal have adopted this configuration. Their beginning point is the personal encounter with the Holy Spirit. They see that as their arming stage where they are equipped to do battle with

Satan, personally or in society. The warfare motifs of the dualist come into focus as they are "being trained" for battle. Their
commands have a decidedly prophetic tinge as the Scriptures
are used to support their battle against evil and to share the
truth with the masses, defeating evil wherever it (or he) is to
be found operative.

This last configuration has a number of competing elements. A value held by ecstatics is love, and yet a value of the
dualist approach is warfare. This is dealt with by calling the
love "tough love." Another value of the ecstatic is emotional
experience of God while the value of the conflict psychology is
rational control of the id. This is handled by placing the intel-
lect under the control of the experience of the Holy Spirit. The
dualist practice is to share with those who "do not know,"
while the ecstatic practice is to allow freedom. This is dealt
with by stating that it is more important to share because salvation is so important. Undoubtedly the stresses of the various
pulls take their toll.

In reciprocal transformation most ecstatic Christians have
placed their Christian loyalties over their psychological and sociological tendencies. Yet some impact of these disciplines can
be seen. For instance, some ecstatic Churches have recognized
"ordained" ministers and have gone in for elaborate rituals.
Some have violated their direction toward freedom by impos-
ing rules on who really has the Spirit and who does not.

From this analysis it is obvious that one's theology or
Christian expression is never quite culture-free or bias-free.
The differing psychological and sociological tendencies have
profound effects on Christian loyalties, theologies and practices. Each person will feel more or less at home on one or another type. We must, I think, allow others the freedom (my
ecstatic loyalty?) to follow the Lord as he is found in their lives.
One final note: each of us needs to know where he or she personally fits into the wide spectrum of Christianity. This for two
reasons: first, in order to appreciate how God has touched our
lives, and, second, to be able to speak kindly and intelligently
with those whose approach is different from ours. In a sense, it
is like knowing our own language and being able to speak

someone else's. And this is true, not only of differing orientations within Christianity, but also toward disciplines like psychology and sociology.

One final note for the Catholic Church which arises from the above trilateral analysis needs to be addressed. In an article in *Commonweal* Ronald Modras addressed the Church concerning the supposed exorcism of Klingenberg where a young girl died. He wrote: "There are lessons to be learned from Klingenberg not only by bishops in Germany and leaders of the charismatic movement here in America. Demonology is dangerous. If there are demons to be exorcised in the Church, their twin names are dogmatism and fundamentalism" (p. 65).

It is apparent from his analysis that he has adopted a fulfillment view of reality in which personal demons have no place. The basic problem to be faced is: Where does our understanding of evil spirits arise—from our psychological understanding or from revelation? Perhaps it comes from both.

The current experience of charismatics is such that the existence of a variety of supernatural principalities and powers is established. The Church needs to weigh *all* the input, not only that of one or another observer.

BIBLIOGRAPHY

R. D. Anderson, "The History of Witchcraft: A Review of Some Psychiatric Concepts," *American Journal of Psychiatry* 126 (1970), pp. 1727–1735.

J. Benjamin, "Satan: Alive and Well?" *Saturday Evening Post* (April 1977), pp. 56–57.

R. Elwood, "Strange Things Are Happening," *Satanism, Witchcraft, and God* (Elgin, Ill.: Cook Publishing, 1973).

W. W. Everett and T. J. Bachmeyer, *Disciplines in Transformation: A Guide to Theology and the Behavioral Sciences* (Washington, D.C.: University Press of America, 1979).

N. Fodor, *Freud, Jung, and Occultism* (New Hyde Park, N.Y.: University Books, 1971).

J. D. Frank, *Psychotherapy and the Human Predicament: A Psycho-Social Approach* (New York: Schocken Books, 1978).

S. Freud, *A Seventeenth-Century Demological Neurosis* (1923), in *The Complete Psychological Works of Sigmund Freud,* Vol. 19 (London: Hogarth Press, 1961), pp. 69–105.

P. Gildea, "Demoniacal Possession," *Irish Theological Quarterly* 41 (October 1971), pp. 289–311.

D. H. Gross, *A Jungian Analysis of New Testament Exorcism,* unpublished doctoral dissertation, Harvard University (1963).

M. D. Hopkins, "Satan of the Evil Within Persons," *Bible Today* 88 (February 1977), pp. 1058–74.

C. G. Jung, *Contributions to Analytical Psychology* (London: Kegan Paul, 1928).

F. J. Kobler, *Casebook in Psychotherapy* (New York: Alba House, 1964).

K. E. Koch, *Christian Counseling and Occultism* (West Germany: Evangelical Verlag, 1972).

I. M. Lewis, The Anthropologist's Encounter with the Supernatural, *Parapsychology Review* 5 (March 1974), pp. 5–9.

J. Lhermitte, *True and False Possession* (New York: Hawthorn Books, 1963).

E. Luissier, "Satan," *Chicago Studies* 13 (Spring 1974), pp. 3–9.

M. Martin, *Hostage to the Devil: The Possession and Exorcism of Five Living Americans* (New York: Reader's Digest Press, 1976).

A. Maslow, *Religions, Values, and Peak-Experiences* (New York: Viking Press, 1964).

R. May, *Love and Will* (New York: Norton, 1969).

J. T. Meigs, "Pastoral Care Methods and Demonology in Selected Writings," *Journal of Psychology and Theology* (Summer 1977), pp. 234–246.

R. Modras, "The Devil, Demons, and Dogmatism," *Commonweal* 104 (February 4, 1977), pp. 71–75.

J. Navonne, "Possession and Exorcism," *The Way* 15 (July 1975), pp. 173–75.

J. J. Nicola, *Diabolical Possession and Exorcism* (Rockford, Ill.: Tan Books, 1974).

H. Noldin and A. Schmidt, *Summa Theologiae Moralis,* Vol. III, *De Sacramentis* (Innsbruck: F. Rauch Verlag, 1960).

F. Perls, R. F. Hefferline, and P. Goodman, *Gestalt Therapy* (New York: Julian Press, 1958).

D. Prince, *Expelling Demons: An Introduction into Practical Demonology* (Fort Lauderdale: Prince).

J. Richards, *But Deliver Us From Evil: An Introduction to the Demonic Dimensions in Pastoral Care* (New York: Seabury Press, 1974).

P. J. Riga, "To Hell with the Devil," *U. S. Catholic* 39 (July 1974), pp. 12–13.

C. Rogers, *Client-Centered Therapy* (New York: Houghton-Mifflin, 1951).

The Roman Ritual, translated by P. T. Weller, Vol. III, *Christian Burial, Exorcisms, Reserved Blessings, Etc.* (Milwaukee: Bruce, 1964).

M. Sargent, *The Mind Possessed: A Physiology of Possession, Mysticism and Faith Healing* (New York: Lippincott, 1974).

F. J. Scheidt, "Deviance, Power, and the Occult: A Field Study," *Journal of Psychology* 87 (May 1974), pp. 21–28.

W. C. Schutz, *Joy* (New York: Grove Press, 1967).

H. A. Virkler and M. B. Virkler "Demonic Involvement in Human Life and Illness," *Journal of Psychology and Theology* 5 (1977), pp. 95–101.

K. Vogl, *Begone Satan: A Soul-Stirring Account of Diabolical Possession: A Woman Cursed by Her Father, Possessed from Fourteenth Year til Fortieth Year* (Collegeville, Minn.: C. Kapsner, 1935).

A. Weisinger, *Occult Phenomena in the Light of Theology* (Westminster, Md.: Newman Press, 1957).

R. J. Woods, "The Possession Problem: Or Everything You Always Wanted To Know about Exorcism But Were Afraid To Ask," *Chicago Studies* 12 (Spring, 1973), pp. 91–107.

Section Four

Conclusions and Guidelines for Deliverance Prayer

10
Pastoral Guidelines for Deliverance Prayer

by the National Steering Committee for the Diocesan Liaisons

The modern intellectual world view has been formed by a high degree of rationalism and materialism. These forces tend to diminish a spiritual assessment of reality. The supernatural world of God, angels and demons seems quite remote from such a perspective. It is such prejudice that has diminished awareness of the work of the Holy Spirit, angels and devils in the spiritual life of men. This has in one way or another affected the piety of today's Church. Whereas in the past we might have prayed to be delivered from the power of the devil, today that might seem an outmoded remnant of a medieval piety.

Within the charismatic renewal in the United States there has arisen the pastoral practice of praying for deliverance from evil spirits. As awareness of the Holy Spirit grows it is almost inevitable that the question of evil spirits must be confronted as well. Deliverance prayer is not public formal exorcism. The term is used to designate simple private prayer to overcome a partial demonic influence or partial control in a person's life. This control would be more than ordinary temptation and less than the total control of full possession by the devil.

Exorcism should never be done without the knowledge and permission of the local bishop. This requirement has evolved in the Church through centuries of experience and expresses the great caution with which the Church views the matter. It is with cautious wisdom, yet full confidence in the power of Jesus, that we should approach praying against the power of the devil.

In the New Testament the Synoptics witness the important place that deliverance from the power of Satan had in the ministry of Jesus. The writings of the great saints also give ample testimony to the necessity of prayer for deliverance from the power of the evil one. By drawing this to our pastoral attention we want to steer a course between the tendency to deny any practical effect to the presence of the devil and the equally dangerous inclination to find demons everywhere. Our people need the full power of the Gospel to free them from the slavery of their sins and the oppression of evil. Prayer invoking the power of Jesus to set free and heal can and should be a normal part of our pastoral practice. It is out of concern for the right practice of this ministry that we offer these guidelines.

WHO MINISTERS DELIVERANCE?

1. Everyone may pray self-deliverance prayer just as we do in praying the Our Father focusing on the Father's love and not on the fear of evil spirits. Christians can always exercise their baptismal power by silent prayer for others. Ideally the person receiving prayer should not be told that he has an evil spirit but simply that he is receiving silent prayer for the Lord's healing and blessing. Generally, silent deliverance prayer is sufficient.

2. If *vocal deliverance prayer* for another is necessary, it should be prayed by a team whose ministry is recognized and discerned as valid by the local Christian community and its pastoral authority. Those who engage in this ministry should be formed by a daily life of prayer and service. They should be compassionate and loving people who are concerned enough to prepare and follow up the deliverance prayer. A team must be cautious in maintaining their own health and support of one another in a balanced Christian life. Such support is the best preparation for their ministry. We might point out too that

those ordained to priesthood and diaconate have been given special power against the power of evil through their ordination. We want to encourage priests and deacons to participate in the deliverance ministry.

3. Exorcism prayer for those possessed should continue to be done only by those explicitly appointed by the bishop as an exercise of the power received through ordination for the good of the faithful.

PREPARATION

It is important to note that prayer for deliverance is an aspect of the healing ministry and should be seen in the context of the healing of the whole person. This means that complementary means of healing should accompany the ministry of prayer:

1. Medical

The mystery of the incarnation affirms that God works powerfully through the human. Thus, often the beginning of the process of healing is the physician. God can and does utilize medical science for healing. Consultation with a physician can be supported by spontaneous prayers for healing and the sacrament of the sick.

2. Psychological

Counseling, psychiatry, forgiveness of people who have hurt us, and prayer for inner healing all address the emotional dimension of the human person. Counseling and psychiatry are especially helpful for bringing about growth and freedom. Moreover, not everyone who claims to be harassed by the demonic is necessarily so subjected. Pseudo-possession may be an introjection or projection of what one cannot face and a desire to exorcise what needs integration. If there is indication of suicide or the person gets worse, professional help should be obtained.

3. Social

In order to assist a person in the healing process and personal growth, it is often necessary to make certain environmental changes. For example, community support systems of significant family members, close friends, neighbors, prayer group members and parishioner friends are very helpful. Alcoholics Anonymous is one group that stresses the importance of the support group in healing and restoration. In certain cases, some people may have to break certain patterns of relationships that are not helpful for them.

4. Spiritual

The goal of the healing ministry is fourfold conversion, that is, religious, emotional, intellectual and moral conversion. This goal is not simply human freedom but a total commitment to live for Jesus and others. On the spiritual dimension of the person, both the action of the Spirit and areas of resistance are discerned. Daily prayer, reading of the Scriptures, the sacraments, especially Eucharist and reconciliation, and Christian service are means of fostering this life with Jesus and others.

If a person has been involved in occult practices in the past, there may also be a need to renounce such practices and the objects connected with them, to break all curses and pacts, and to consecrate the person again to Jesus by the renewal of baptismal promises and reception of the Eucharist. If the person is experiencing the influence of the deceased, the Eucharist of the Resurrection should be offered for the deceased. If a place is disturbed, it should be blessed while the Eucharist of the Resurrection is offered for the deceased and necessary ministry offered to the living.

DELIVERANCE PRAYER

The total impact of the deliverance prayer session should not be to emphasize deliverance from evil spirits but deliverance into the total healing of a life lived for Jesus. The prayer session should involve the six elements listed below:

1. Prayer of Praise and Protection

It helps to begin with prayer of praise and thanksgiving asking for protection on all present and over all we love. Ideally, a group of intercessors should also be at prayer during the session. The group should have a sense of peace and unity before continuing.

2. Prayer for Discernment

Once there is peace, unity and a focus on Jesus, he will reveal the next step and the presence of any spirits.

3. Binding of Spirits

To insure that the healing and deliverance prayer are not blocked, all spirits should be bound from drawing upon any evil assistance. They should also be bound whenever they act upon the person such as stirring up fear, confusion or agitation of any kind. Though it helps to identify the areas for healing and repentance, it is not necessary to name the spirits to participate in the power of Jesus to overcome them.

4. Prayer for Healing

The healing of the woundedness of the person is the focal point of the deliverance process and should take the most time. It is usually necessary to get at the root cause of the difficulty and pray for its healing. The person may need to forgive, renounce occult practices or repent of sin. The person should be led to choose the opposite of what he has fallen into.

5. Deliverance Prayer

When healing takes place, the spirit of evil has no resting place. It can be commanded to go quietly in the name of Jesus.

6. Infilling Prayer

It is well to end with the following prayer: prayer for thanksgiving for all that has happened and will happen, prayer for a new outpouring of the Holy Spirit, prayer for the gifts especially needed by the person, prayer for the needs of the team and prayer for protection for all. Ideally the Eucharist should be received soon and frequently.

FOLLOW-UP

Follow-up is important because a person is not fully delivered until he or she is delivered into living a full Christian life. Praying with others for deliverance bears with it the responsibility that someone will continue contact with them as they work through the struggle with old temptations and feelings that may prompt them to turn back. The delivered person also has a new dimension of life in Christ that needs to be encouraged by prayer alone and with others. Spiritual growth may lead to the Spirit touching further areas in need of healing and deliverance. This should not be seen as regression. If there is more need for deliverance prayer the person should be helped to focus on totally giving oneself to Jesus, not on the presence of evil spirits.

These guidelines have been the result of much consultation with scholars and practitioners. It is our hope that the fruits of these efforts will bring greater freedom to God's people.

Afterword

As the articles explore the interface between theology, psychology and experience, they raise more questions than they answer. We understand only a fraction of the demonic realm and need the expertise of one another. One unanswered question was Bishop McKinney's query on how deliverance prayer can influence whole communities and social structures. Perhaps future research should focus here, for there is great power in praying for communities. For example, a parish community in Houston after a series of neighborhood murders had a Mass and all-night exposition of the Blessed Sacrament to bind the spirits of evil and murder and to fill Houston with peace. On the two Saturdays that they prayed in this manner, there were no Houston murders in twenty-four hours even though Saturday night is usually the heaviest night for murders in Houston which has over one thousand a year. The parish priest, Fr. Jack McGinnis, said, "I wonder what is going to happen if someone does it every night. We could have no homicides in Houston." Perhaps that is hard to believe, but communities are slowly discovering the power of community prayer to free not just individuals but even other larger communities and social structures.

But the most basic area for future research is a better understanding of how a person grows closer to Jesus Christ. The power of freeing others and staying free does not come as much from learning better prayer techniques as from living a life more surrendered to Jesus Christ, the source of power and life. The fathers in the desert handed on the story of Herman, an anchorite whose life was totally surrendered to Jesus Christ. One day a woman seeking deliverance went out to the desert for help but none of the monks were holy enough to drive away the demon. They finally took her to Herman who was leading a balanced life and taking his day off to relax with a glass of wine under the desert's one tree. The demon in the woman immediately shouted, "You wine drinker, you will never get me out." But Herman, who had a heart totally given to Jesus, trusted in the Lord's power and simply held up the glass of wine while saying, "You see this glass of wine? Before I finish drinking it the power of the Lord will drive you forth." He began to drink the wine and the demon dramatically fled to free the woman. To the degree we are like Herman with a heart totally surrendered to Jesus Christ, the evil one will be defeated even as we drink a glass of wine!

Appendices

Appendix A
Exorcism in Catholic Moral Theology

by James McManus, C.Ss.R.

Editors' Note: *While the American Roman Catholic Church hopes for more hierarchical understanding and direction in the areas of exorcism and deliverance, the Anglican Church is already experiencing this and opening the way to more lay deliverance prayer. Twenty years ago the Anglicans viewed deliverance prayer as a form of exorcism needing a priest who had explicit permission of the diocesan bishop for each case (Canon LXXII of 1604). The next step of decentralizing came in 1964 when the Bishop of Exeter's Exorcism Commission of pastoral, theological and psychiatric experts prepared their report, openly published in 1972. This report recommended that each diocese should have its appointed and trained exorcist and also recommended guidelines so that the bishop would not have to give explicit permission for each individual case. But in practice priests brought only the more difficult cases to the exorcist and prayed on their own for the others. With the advent of the charismatic renewal, lay people also began praying for those bound by evil spirits. Anglican bishops were encouraged to delegate deliverance prayer to "selected presbyters and others deemed competent."[1] In England this practice had worked out so well that British Anglican theologians such as Rev. John Richards advised that the laity gifted by the Holy Spirit be recognized to pray for deliverance.[2] Thus in England Anglican bishops are delegating deliverance prayer not just to exorcists or to priests but also to laity.*

The Anglican Church then asked if the present practice of

lay deliverance was new or firmly rooted in the tradition of moral theology. In researching this question, Fr. McManus, a British Roman Catholic moral theologian, came to the surprising conclusion that laity praying for deliverance is not a new practice but a return to his own Roman Catholic tradition.[3] The following summarizes his presentation to a conference of British experts on exorcism.

NOTES

1. "Concerning Deliverance," *The Book of Occasional Services* (New York: Church Hymnal, 1979), p. 155.
2. This summary of Anglican changes relies on John Richards, *But Deliver Us From Evil* (New York: Seabury, 1974), pp. 179–181.
3. The Roman Catholic spirituality tradition also allows for priests and laity to pray for private exorcism (deliverance). Cf. Adolphe Tanquerey, *The Spiritual Life* (Baltimore: St. Mary's Seminary, 1930), pp. 720, 725.

*   *   *

In his general audience on November 15, 1972, Pope Paul VI asked the question: What are the greatest needs of the Church today? This is how he replied: "Do not let our answer surprise you as being oversimple or even superstitious and unreal: one of the greatest needs is defense from that evil which is called the devil." And he concluded his allocution by asking these two questions: "Are there signs, and what are they, of the presence of diabolical action? And what are the means of defense against such an insidious danger?"[1]

In the same year a commission convened in the Anglican Church reported, "In Western countries today, the widespread apostasy from the Christian faith, accompanied by an increasing recourse to black magic and occult practices, is revealing the presence and the power of evil forces. . . . The need, therefore, for the restoration of the practice of exorcism to its proper place is becoming more urgent and more evident."[2] This commission, in effect, answered both questions asked by Pope Paul, viz., there are signs of diabolical action, and exorcism is the Church's means of defense.

THE CATHOLIC TRADITION

In Catholic moral theology since the Council of Trent, we find very consistent teaching on the role of exorcism in the pastoral ministry. St. Alphonsus Liguori speaks for the tradition when he writes:

> Private exorcism is permissible to all Christians; solemn exorcism is permissible only to ministers who are appointed to it, and then only with the express permission of the bishop."[3]

These notes were originally prepared as a follow-up to a workshop on deliverance held at Hawkstone Hall. The workshop was conducted by the Rev. Christopher Niel-Smith. The author of these notes was asked to investigate the traditional moral teaching of the Church on the place of exorcism in the pastoral ministry.

TYPES OF EXORCISM

The basic distinction is between solemn and private exorcism. Noldin, however, in his moral theology makes a further distinction between solemn and simple exorcism. In his view there is a fourfold division:

Solemn exorcism: for the purpose of driving out the devil.

Simple exorcism: for the purpose of curbing the devil's power lest he harm people or things.

Public exorcism: by ministers of the Church, in the name and with the authority of the Church.

Private exorcism: when the exorcist acts in his own name.[4]

In Noldin's view the distinction between solemn and simple exorcism is based on *pastoral needs.* Solemn exorcism is needed if a person is possessed; simple exorcism suffices for curbing the power of the devil. Noldin's distinction between public and private exorcism is based on the *authority being used.* In public exorcism it is the authority of the Church; in private exorcism the person acts in his own name as a Christian.

THE REALITY OF POSSESSION OR INFESTATION

The moral tradition bears striking witness to the Church's belief in the reality of demonic possession and attack. In his *Praxis Confessarii,* a handbook for confessors, St. Alphonsus discusses at some length the possibility of demonic infestation. He warns confessors not to be too incredulous. (Even in the eighteenth century this warning was necessary!) Possessions do take place, and they should not be dismissed as "fantasies or corporeal infirmities." The Church, says Alphonsus, teaches us to pray to the Lord to be delivered from the spirit of fornication, and when this spirit infests a person he will not be able to resist temptations. "In these cases," says St. Alphonsus, "the confessor, before everything else, should pronounce an exorcism against the demon, at least privately, which is certainly lawful, in this way: 'I, as a minister of God, command you, unclean spirit, to depart from this creature of God.'"[5]

Several provincial councils and synods of bishops discussed exorcism during the last century. The Council of Prague in 1860 stated that the devil can not only possess but can also cause disease in men. Exorcism is the Church's weapon against these attacks, and, states this Council, the Church uses this weapon so that the power of Christ the King might prevail against Satan.[6] The Council of Vienna in 1865 expressed the view that possession, while it does take place, is rare in these times.[7]

Moralists like Lehmkuhl, Scavini and Genicot in the last century repeated St. Alphonsus' warning against dismissing the whole idea of possession. Both Lehmkul and Genicot stress the need for caution and for working, when possible, in consultation with a Catholic doctor. In our own time we find moralists like Visser, Häring, McHugh and Callan drawing attention to the role of exorcism. Tanquerey, in his classic *The Spiritual Life*, devotes a whole section to possession and exorcism under the heading "Extraordinary Mystical Phenomena."

In the past three hundred years the great moral theologians of the Church have always stressed the need for exorcism in the pastoral ministry. This need was recognized by St. Alphonsus, whose authority in moral theology is unique. St. Alphonsus was declared a Doctor of the Church in 1871 and in 1959 he was declared the heavenly patron of confessors and moralists.

WHO CAN EXORCISE?

St. Alphonsus stated the Catholic tradition when he said that everyone may exorcise privately, but only the priest, with permission of the bishop, may exorcise solemnly. Since this is the Catholic tradition we have to ask ourselves how we lost sight of it and why it is that exorcism has become such a bone of contention in the modern Church. We lost sight of our own tradition, it seems to me, because we lost sight of the basic distinctions that the moralists of the past made. We reduced all exorcism to solemn exorcism, for which the permission of the bishop is required, and as the bishop appoints only holy and prudent priests for such an exorcism, most priests simply presumed that they would never have to perform an exorcism. Let us look again at our own tradition.

SOLEMN EXORCISM

Solemn exorcism is restricted to those who have "both the power of orders and the power of jurisdiction."[8] The power of orders is needed because, as Suarez pointed out, "solemn and public exorcism pertains to an act of the ecclesiastical order and can only be performed by a consecrated minister."[9] As well as the power of orders the power of jurisdiction is also required, because the law of the Church (Canon 1151) requires the priest to seek special permission from the bishop. (This law goes back to Innocent I in the fifth century.) The Synod of Naples strongly reaffirmed the need for special permission, decreeing that if a secular priest exorcised without the bishop's permission he would be automatically suspended *a divinis,* and a religious priest, if he acted without the bishop's permission, would lose his faculties for confession forever.[10]

The reason for restricting the power of the priest is "in order to take precautions against abuses."[11] This law applies to "exempted religious" in their own churches "in case abuses arise."[12]

The jurisdiction of priests in cases of solemn exorcism has been restricted by the law, for the common good, to safeguard the faithful and the reputation of the Church. The bishop approves only prudent and virtuous priests for the exercise of solemn and public exorcism.

PRIVATE OR SIMPLE EXORCISM

However, solemn exorcism is only one form of exorcism in the Church. Confessors have been urged to make use of exorcism privately. As we have seen, St. Alphonsus says that "before everything else" the priest should exorcise privately when faced with what he believes to be demonic infestation.

Noldin urges confessors to frequently exorcise:

> It is much to be desired that ministers of the Church should perform simple exorcism more frequently, remembering the words of the Lord "In my name they shall cast out demons." This exorcism can be performed without the knowledge of the person."[13]

Prummer writes:

> Experience teaches that sometimes in the confessional exorcism can be used secretly, without the penitent's knowledge, wth good results.[14]

Marc suggests that priests should imitate the example of the venerable Pallota, "who privately exorcised when penitents were not sorry for their sins, or when they were remaining silent about sins."[15] And McHugh and Callan write in their textbook:

> It is recommended that priests frequently use private exorcism, at least secretly, for persons who are vexed by temptations or scruples, for which they may use the form "In the name of Jesus Christ, unholy spirit, I command you to depart from this creature of God."[16]

Where did these moralists get this teaching from? Prummer answers this question with the words: "Experience teaches." In his own confessional ministry Prummer obviously witnessed "the good results" of private exorcism. And because he was aware of the value of private exorcism he was able to instruct confessors in the need for this ministry. Personally I have to admit that for six years I taught moral theology and never even noticed this teaching on the need for private exorcism. It was only when I discovered in my own ministry the effect of the silent prayer of command that I began to notice what the moralists had been teaching!

By losing sight of this basic distinction between solemn and private exorcism the confessional practice of priests has often been lacking in power and the sacrament of reconciliation has not been an experience of liberation and joy. The moralists quoted above—and they represent the tradition of the Church, being the "auctores probati"—were aware that absolution is not always enough. As well as absolution the confessor must use the power of exorcism to free people, to defend them, and to bring them joy. This ministry belongs to the priest, especially in his role of confessor, and consequently no permission of the bishop is required. It would be against the whole tradition of our moral theology for the priest to seek permission of the bishop to perform simple exorcism privately, especially in the sacrament of reconciliaion.

THE LAITY AND EXORCISM

The laity may certainly use private exorcism. Suarez pointed out that in the early Church the power to cast out demons was given to the faithful, to both women and men. This power of casting out demons, when the demon bodily possesses the person, pertains, according to Suarez, "to the order of miracles" and therefore should not be attempted "without the special inspiration of the Holy Spirit and with faith inspired by him."[17] Suarez recognizes the charismatic nature of lay exorcism, while, as we saw above, he sees solemn exorcism "as an act of the ecclesiastical order."

The fact that lay exorcism is a charismatic ministry in no way impedes the lay person from understanding it, nor does he need any permission. Marc stated: "Private exorcism is lawful to all, especially priests, nor is there any special permission of the bishop required."[18] And Prummer writes: "Nowhere is it forbidden to the laity to use private exorcism."[19] Lehmkul held that if a lay person is prudently convinced that demonic infestation is present he may recite the Church's prayers against the devil privately. Noldin also states that private exorcism may be performed by all the faithful. The right of the laity to make use of private exorcism is clearly established in the moral teaching of the Church.

SIMPLE EXORCISM AND DELIVERANCE

The question will surely be asked: Is simple exorcism, as defined and described by the traditional moralists, the same as what writers like Francis MacNutt call deliverance? The purpose of simple exorcism is to curb the power of the devil. Priests, according to the traditional teaching for confessors, should use this power frequently. The assumption was that demonic interference would be a frequent occurrence.

Francis MacNutt takes the view that such interference is a relatively common occurrence: "I find that possession is rare, but people who are "demonized," who are attacked or oppressed by demonic forces, are a relatively common occurrence. If a person is oppressed by evil spirits, then an informal exorcism, a prayer for deliverance, is in order."[20]

It would seem that Francis MacNutt is really putting into practice the traditional teaching of moral theology and that what he calls "informal exorcism" or "prayer for deliverance" is the same as simple or private exorcism. Instead of being something new, the prayer for deliverance is a return to the pastoral wisdom of the Church.

CONCLUSION

Our moral theology has been very clear on the need for and the use of exorcism in the pastoral ministry of the priest. However, we have lost sight of the basic distinctions that the moralists made. The result has been that most priests, when they think of exorcism, are in fact thinking of solemn and public exorcism, for which the bishop's permission is required, and not of simple and private exorcism which they are encouraged to use frequently. By presenting the deliverance ministry in terms of the traditional moral teaching on exorcism we will avoid needless misunderstanding and allay fears.

NOTES

1. *L'Osservatore Romano* (Nov. 23, 1972).
2. *Exorcism*, ed. by Dom Robert Petitpierre (London, 1972), p. 10.
3. *Theologia Moralis*, III, t 2, p. 492.

4. Noldin, *Theologia Moralis*, III, 57–59 (1903).

5. St. Alphonsus, *Praxis Confessarii*, n. 113.

6. *Acta et Decreta sacri concil, Recentiorum*, Vol. 5, p. 483.

7. Ibid., p. 186.

8. Aertnys, *Theologia Moralis* (1918), Vol. 1, p. 476.

9. Suarez, *Opera Omnia*, Vol. 14, p. 741.

10. *Acta et Decreta*, Vol. 1, p. 197.

11. Sabetto-Barretti, *Theologia Moralis*, p. 1803.

12. Scavini, *Theologia Moralis*, Vol. 3, p. 542 (1867).

13. Noldin, *Theologia Moralis*, Vol. 3, p. 59.

14. Prummer, *Theologia Moralis*, Vol. 2, p. 363.

15. Marc, *Institutiones Morales Alphonsiane*, Vol. 1, p. 622 (1927).

16. McHugh and Callan, *Moral Theology*, Vol. 2, p. 365 (1958).

17. Suarez, *Opera Omnia*, Vol. 14, p. 742.

18. Marc, *op. cit.*

19. Prummer, *op. cit.*

20. MacNutt, *Healing*, p. 216.

Appendix B
Gender Identity Change in a Transsexual: An Exorcism

by David H. Barlow, Ph.D.,
Gene G. Abel, M.D.
and Edward B. Blanchard

Editors' Note: *Although this paper was not presented at the Houston conference, it is being reprinted with permission from the* Archives of Sexual Behavior *II:5 (New York: Plenum Press, 1977) because it professionally answers a key question constantly raised: How deep and lasting are changes that come with deliverance prayer? Although some with improper readiness or follow-up seem to lose the progress made through deliverance, many have changes as deep and lasting as the following scientific report on "John," a transsexual healed through deliverance prayer. What is unique about John is not his healing of sexuality through prayer but that at every stage it was scientifically verified. The conclusion states that through prayer "a patient who was very clearly a transsexual, by the most conservative criteria, assumed a long-lasting masculine gender identity in a remarkably short time following an apparent exorcism."*

This too raises questions: What proportion of sexual deviations and emotional illnesses are caused in whole or in part by evil spirits? How to discern the demonic factor? How can those praying for deliverance work closely with professionals so that there will be many more clients finding John's freedom?

*   *   *

INTRODUCTION

The most effective treatment for the relief of suffering in transsexuals would seem to be sex-reassignment surgery (Green and Money, 1969). This radical and irreversible treatment for what is basically a psychological problem is indicated since the suffering of transsexuals is considerable and all efforts at treatment through psychotherapy have been ineffective (Pauly, 1965; Benjamin, 1971; Green, 1974). Post-surgical reports from transsexuals have suggested a relief of suffering and moderate to good adjustments in approximately 75% of patients during the first few years of follow-up (e.g., Randall, 1969; Van Patten and Fawzy, 1976), but surgery is costly and not always available.

Although the prevention of transsexualism is the ideal, work in this area has been fraught with ethical problems, and data on the possibility of prevention, or even what to prevent, are not available (Qualls *et al.*, in press; Rekers and Lovaas, 1974; Green, in press). In lieu of effective preventive measures or psychological treatments, an emphasis has been placed on increasing opportunities for surgery. However, two recent developments raise some questions about this approach. First, reports are beginning to appear describing patients so dissatisfied with sex-reassignment surgery that they discard their new gender identity and return to living in their biological gender role despite the physical irreversibility of the surgery (e.g., Money and Wolff, 1973; Van Patten and Fawzy, 1976). Second, a recent report suggests that behavioral procedures were effective in changing gender identity in one patient (Barlow *et al.*, 1973). Although these procedures were relatively complex and the treatment was lengthy, the implication is that mistaken gender identity, which has been considered fixed and irreversible by the age of 3 (Green and Money, 1969), may be altered by psychological procedures. The following case strengthens this preliminary conclusion in a most dramatic fashion.

CASE REPORT

Information described below was obtained from the patient and verified, in most instances, in a separate interview with the patient's mother. Essentially the same information was obtained from the forwarded records of two psychiatrists who had independently interviewed the patient, 1 and 3 years, respectively, prior to our evaluation.

CHILDHOOD

The patient, hereafter referred to by the pseudonym "John," was born in 1952 and always thought of himself as a girl. At the time of his birth his father was 45 and his mother 32. The marriage was unhappy and the father was seldom home, and, as a consequence, a permanent separation occurred when John was 8 years old. John had one brother, 5 years older, and a sister 2 years older. He reports being the baby of the family and more frail and delicate than his older sister, who was something of a tomboy. He thought that his mother compensated for his sister's tomboyishness by preventing him from engaging in any rough-and-tumble games or other boyish activities. During his early years he stayed in the house and helped his mother clean or do chores in the kitchen, activities that pleased his mother. At age 4 he began applying makeup, much as his mother did, and shortly thereafter began cross-dressing in his sister's clothes. He was very pleased when his sister started school, since she bought a number of new clothes. For several years he made excuses to stay home alone in order to dress in his sister's clothes, an activity in which the family housekeeper acquiesced while warning him not to let his father catch him. At age 6 he broke his leg. He remembers that the most frustrating part of his injury was his inability to dress the way he wanted since wearing a cast made it difficult to change into the feminine clothes.

During grammar school John refused to participate in gym or other related activities. His mother, meanwhile, had obtained a job and he assumed the role of housekeeper. He remembers being the object of scorn and criticism in elementary school for effeminate behaviors, but in the early years of school his brother was somewhat protective of him. Although his family identified themselves as Southern Baptists, they seldom attended church. During his childhood he continued to sleep in the same bed with his mother. He envied his sister and mother as females and loathed his maleness. Thus his childhood was marked by a history of spontaneous cross-dressing before age 5, early cross-gender identification and fantasies, very early development of feminine activities, and absence of masculine activities or interests. These features are stated by Stoller (1968) to be prerequisites for categorization as a transsexual.

ADOLESCENCE

John attended school, performed marginally, and remained socially isolated. He occupied himself with housekeeping and cooking. At 15 he read about transsexualism in a national magazine and began corresponding with The Johns Hopkins Hospital and experts of whom he had learned.

Shortly thereafter he dropped out of school and began intensive reading on the subject in the library. A woman with whom he was acquainted mentioned a doctor who treated hormonal problems. Based on his readings, he was aware of the effects of female hormones and told the physician that he was on female hormones for an endocrine disorder and needed additional prescriptions, which he obtained. He remembers the estrogen as producing a tranquility which he had not experienced for some time and eliminating his unwanted erections. From oral estrogen he progressed to occasional self-injection of estrogen, but was concerned lest his mother find his medication.

In 1969, at age 16, he was involved in a serious car accident and medical treatment for resulting conditions led to discovery of the effects of the hormone (some breast enlargement and thinning of body hair) and the specifics of his cross-gender

identity. He was subsequently referred to a psychiatrist, whom
he saw periodically in years to come. His mother became extremely upset on learning of his cross-gender identity, blaming
it on the automobile accident. This began a very stormy period
in the patient's life, where his mother would attempt to manipulate him with frequent suicidal gestures and other histri-
onic behavior in an attempt to force him to seek psychiatric
care. At his mother's insistence, he was admitted to a state hospital for evaluation. A psychiatric examination and psychological testing, later forwarded to our offices, revealed no
psychosis but mild situational depression, presumably due to
family pressures. Physical examination revaled breast enlargement. He was discharged on no medications with a diagnosis of
transvestism.

Several months before this hospitalization, he had successfully begun working a fried chicken stand and was considered
dependable and a good worker. He resumed this work upon
discharge from hospital and was referred to our offices for the
first time by his present psychiatrist, where one of us (D.H.B.)
diagnosed him as a transsexual. He noted that he enjoyed his
work, was saving money for sex-reassignment surgery, a por-
tion of which he had received as a settlement for his automobile accident, but was continuing to have difficulty with his
mother and thus had moved into his own apartment. He was
started, once again, on oral doses of estrogen by his private
psychiatrist and reported during this time that his voice
heightened and that he again felt calm and relaxed. He would
often dress as a female when away from work and reported
that he was extremely comfortable, did not attract attention,
and was never apprehended for cross-dressing.

John rose to the position of manager in his job but continued to have difficulty with his mother and her friends, who in-
sisted that he "make a man of himself." To "quiet her down"
he entered the Navy, at their suggestion, in November 1972,
but was quickly medically discharged after a thorough psychiatric examination, later forwarded to us, with a diagnosis of
transsexualism. A buccal smear at this time revealed a normal
male chromosomal pattern and psychological testing revealed

no psychosis, no severely defective judgment, and no abnormal affect. After returning from service, he continued to have difficulties with his mother, and by the end of 1972, at age 20, was admitted to our psychiatric unit after overdosing in response to his mother's attempt to move into his apartment with him. Treatment consisted of teaching him to deal more assertively and effectively with his mother, and the patient decided, with our consent, that it was time to begin the process of preparing for surgery.

TOWARD SURGERY

After discharge, John was placed on full therapeutic dosages of estrogen and he intensifed treatments for electrolysis of facial hair, a process he had begun sometime earlier. As part of the process of preparing for surgery, a variety of assessment procedures were administered to measure gender identity, gender role behavior, and sexual arousal patterns. All assessment remained consistent with a diagnosis of transsexualism, as it had in his previous visit in 1971. Sexual arousal patterns, as measured by rating scales and penile circumference measures (Barlow *et al.*, 1970; Barlow and Abel, 1976), were exclusively transsexual but sexual arousal was relatively low, consistent with his expressed lack of interest in sex. The patient had never had any sexual contact and masturbated very infrequently, because of disgust over awareness of his male genitalia. Sexual attractions to males consisted mostly of feeling "warm and close" to a male and were always fantasized with the patient in the female role.

From this battery of assessment procedures (Barlow, 1977; Abel, 1977), two measures were repeated periodically over the next two years. One was an attitudinal "card sort" measure of gender identity in which statements describing masculine gender identity and feminine gender identity were typed on 3 × 5 cards and rated based on desirability (see Barlow *et al.*, 1969, 1973; Barlow and Abel, 1976). This attitudinal measure revealed maximal femine gender identity. Gender role behavior was measured by a behavioral checklist of gender-specific motor behavior while sitting, standing, and walking (Barlow *et al.*, 1973). This behavioral checklist was filled out surreptitiously by a secretary as the patient walked into the office, stood, and sat down while waiting for his appointments. Feminine gender motor behavior was emitted consistently.

With some assistance from us, cross-living as a female began uneventfully in the winter of 1972 and John assumed the name of "Judy." The maturity with which she approached this transition is evident in that she was able to explain the situation to her employees and continued working at this job, changing only her apartment at this time. By the summer of 1973 Judy was doing extremely well and had reconciled her upcoming surgery with her mother and the rest of her family. Judy passed well as a female, had straightened out most of her legal affairs, such as a change of driver's license, and was successfully wearing a bikini (having progressed to bra size 36B).

In the summer of 1973 Judy requested to commence surgery. In view of her excellent adjustment, we agreed and referred her to a medical center in a nearby state.

THE EXORCISM

After a brief note indicating that she had arrived, we received no word for several months. One day in the late fall, a research assistant who had worked with the case came back from a half-finished lunch of fried chicken and shouted, "Judy is back at the restaurant, but she's not Judy anymore, she's John!" Other reports quickly confirmed this, and John was invited back to our offices for a session which occurred in early January of 1974. He entered the office in a three-piece business suit, with polished shoes, neatly cut short hair, clipped fingernails, and consistently masculine motor behaviors. Even to trained eyes, the only sign of his former feminine role was the almost complete absence of facial hair, which in view of his light complexion and in the context of his total masculinity would normally go unnoticed. He enthusiastically related the following story.

After leaving our offices and journeying to the gender identity clinic in the nearby state where he was expected, he kept a promise he had made to the owner of his fast-food restaurant. He had developed a close relationship with the owner of this restaurant over the years in which he had productively and reliably worked; and, although this woman was quite accepting of his transitions, she did request that he check with one physician in the city to which he was traveling before checking into the gender identity clinic. The physician shared with the owner of the restaurant a fundamental Protestant religion quite foreign to John, who had been brought up as a Baptist but was not religious. The physician administered a total physical exam and said that he could live quite well as a woman, but the real problem was possession by evil spirits. After some discussion of this, John reported a session which lasted 2–3 hours and involved exhortations and prayers over John by the physician and laying on of hands on John's head and shoulders. During this period, John reported fainting several times and arising to the continuing of the prayers and exhortations, resulting in the exorcism of 22 evil spirits which the physician called by name as they left his body. During and after this session John felt waves of God's love coming over him but was physically drained. A letter to us from the physician confirmed this basic process. The physician noted in his letter that he showed John that his life was a fake and that Jesus could redeem him and that a standard prescription of Scripture reading caused the spirit of the woman in John to disappear.

Immediately after the session John announced he was a man, discarded his female clothes (hiding his breasts as best he could), and went to the barber shop to have his long hair cut into his current short, masculine style. After this session John returned home and lived with his mother for approximately two weeks but remembers the beginning of some doubts about his conversion and the reoccurrence of some feminine feelings. At this point he accompanied his employer to services of a very well-known faith healer in another state where the miracles that he saw renewed his faith and reaffirmed the correctness of his decision. After waiting 3½ hours in line, he confronted the healer who told the patient that he was having sexual problems (having perhaps seen his breasts) and began the healing process, including praying and laying on of hands once again. During this period, which John estimated as 10 or 15 minutes, he fainted, regained consciousness, fainted again, and as he stood to step off the platform down into the audience, realized that his breasts were gone.

FOLLOW-UP

John was followed for 2½ years after the exorcism and measures of gender identity and gender role behavior were administered at each follow-up session. All the data presented reflect the clear reversal of gender identity after the exorcism and during follow-up. He reported heterosexual arousal at the first post-exorcism interview but refused measurement of penile circumference changes to erotic slides. His minister recommended that he not view slides of nude males for fear that the devil might once again gain access to his soul. In the confusion, gender-specific motor behavior was not formally scored. Examination revealed no residual gynecomastia, although the interval of time between cessation of hormonal therapy and examination was adequate for this "shrinkage" to occur naturally.

He started dating several months later, and at the last interview in December 1975 reported that he had dated approximately ten girls intermittently but had dated one girl for an extended period of time. He reported some sexual arousal toward these girls but did not masturbate, nor did he consider sexual intercourse because of his religious beliefs. He did admit having some sexual thoughts of males for several months after returning from his faith healing, but attributed these to the devil and has not had thoughts of men for almost two years. He continued to do extremely well in his job, benefiting from several promotions, and was looking forward to getting married.

DISCUSSION

"I can't believe that," said Alice.
"Can't you?" the Queen said in a pitying tone.
"Try again, draw a long breath, and shut your eyes."

With that exchange from *Through the Looking Glass* by Lewis Carroll, Jerome Frank leads off a chapter in his now famous book, *Persuasion and Healing* (1961). With Frank's book, this case raises questions on the nature of the process of therapeutic change and the role of various therapeutic procedures in this process. Although most psychotherapists would not deny the role of suggestion, instructions, and persuasion with many psychological disorders, what is important in this case is that no psychotherapeutic procedure of any kind, with whatever element of suggestion or persuasion, has been effective for transsexualism, with the possible exception of behavior modification in one case (Barlow *et al.*, 1973). But even the most facile operant conditioner would be hard pressed to explain the sudden and massive behavioral change observed and objectively measured in this case. Furthermore, this case would be less impressive without the presence of repeated measures, particularly the behavioral measure independently administered, to bolster our subjective impression of change. It is noteworthy that in the earlier case, where behavior modification procedures were seemingly effective in changing gender-specific motor behavior, and in subsequent cases, a period of several months was necessary to teach these behaviors step by step. In this case, without any instruction and presumably without familiarity with the behaviors in the checklist, all of the components of masculine motor behavior were seemingly acquired in a matter of hours.

Obviously, this case has little relevance for therapeutic intervention at this time since most transsexuals are unlikely to flock to the nearest faith healer. But the fact that it did occur could extend the study of the effects of social influence variables to what has been the most intractable of all psychiatric disorders to determine if it is possible to develop psychological intervention to replace surgical treatment in at least some cases. Fortunately, this type of change is not without precedent, although one must go outside the purview of clinical psychology and psychiatry to find parallels. Anthropological study has yielded data from more primitive cultures where changes in gender role behavior and presumably gender identity result from religious or other tribal customs (e.g., Levy, 1973). A closer study of this process in a number of cultures might yield information of some use in our own culture.

The facts in this case are far from certain in all instances. Despite John's report and corroboration from his employer, it is certainly hard to believe that John's breasts disappeared instantaneously in view of our medical understanding of the time necessary for the physical effects of estrogen to reverse. Furthermore, we were not able to obtain objective measures of John's sexual arousal patterns after the exorcism, although it would seem that if John were fabricating his report he would not have indicated continued sexual arousal to men for several months subsequent to the faith healing. Additional follow-up is also necessary to confirm the stability of the measures and any changes in his life situation over a long period of time. What cannot be denied, however, is that a patient who was very clearly a transsexual, by the most conservative criteria (e.g., Stoller, 1968, 1969), assumed a long-lasting masculine gender identity in a remarkably short period of time following an apparent exorcism.

BIBLIOGRAPHY

Abel, G.G. (1977). Assessment of sexual deviation in the male. In Hersen, H., and Bellack, A.S. (eds.), *Behavioral Assessment: A Practical Handbook*, Pergamon Press, New York, in press.

Barlow, D.H. (1977). Assessment of sexual behavior. In Ciminero, A. R. Calhoun, K.S., and Adams, H.E. (eds.), *Handbook of Behavioral Assessment*, Wiley, New York.

Barlow, D.H., and Abel, G.G. (1976). Sexual deviation. In Craighead, E., Kazdin, A., and Mahoney, M. (eds.). *Behavior Modification: Principles, Issues and Applications*, Houghton Mifflin, Boston.

Barlow, D.H., Leitenberg, H., and Agras, W.S. (1969) The experimental control of sexual deviation through manipulation of the noxious scene on covert sensitization. *J. Abnorm. Psychol* 74: 596–601.

Barlow, D.H., Becker, R., Leitenberg, H., and Agras, W.S. (1970). A mechanical strain gauge for recording penile circumference change. *J. Appl. Behav.* 3:73–76.

Barlow, D.H., Reynolds, E.H., and Agras, W.S. (1973) Gender identity change in a transsexual. *Arch. Gen. Psychiat.* 28:569–579.

Benjamin, H. (1971). Should surgery be performed on transsexuals? *Psychiat. Digest,* p. 37.

Frank, J (1961). *Persuasion and Healing.* Johns Hopkins Press. Baltimore.

Green, R. (1974). *Sexual Identity Conflict in Children and Adults.* Basic Books, New York.

Green, R. (1977). Atypical sex role development: Strategy and ethics of prevention. In Qualls, C.B., Wincze, J.P., and Barlow, D.H. (eds.). *The Prevention of Sexual Disorders: Issues and Approaches.* Plenum Press, New York, in press.

Green, R., and Money, J. (1969). *Transsexualism and Sex Reassignment,* Johns Hopkins Press, Baltimore.

Levy, R.I. (1973). *Tahitians: Mind and Experience in the Society Islands,* University of Chicago Press, Chicago.

Money, J., and Wolff, G. (1973). Sex reassignment: Male to female to male. *Arch. Sex. Behav.* 2: 245–250.

Pauly, I.B. (1965). Male psychosexual inversion: Transsexualism. *Arch. Gen. Psychiat.* 13:172–181

Qualls, C.B., Wincze, J.P., and Barlow, D.H. (eds.) (1977). *The Prevention of Sexual Disorders: Issues and Approaches,* Plenum Press, New York, in press.

Randell, J. (1969). Preoperative and postoperative status of male and female transsexuals. In Green, R., and Money, J. (eds.), *Transsexualism and Sex Reassignment,* Johns Hopkins Press, Baltimore.

Reckers, G.A., and Lovaas, O.I. (1974). Behavioral treatment of deviant sex-role behaviors in a male child. *J. Appl/Behav. Anal.* 7: 173–190.

Stoller, R.J. (1968). *Sex and Gender.* Science House, New York.

Stoller, R.J. (1969). Parental influences in male transsexualism. In Freen, R., and Money, J. (eds.), *Transsexualism and Sex Reassignment,* Johns Hopkins Press, Baltimore.

Van Patten, T., and Fawzy, F.I. (1976). Sex conversion surgery in a man with severe gender dysphoria. *Arch. Gen. Psychiat.* 33:751–753.

This article originally appeared in *Archives of Sexual Behavior,* Vol. 6, no. 5, 1977, Plenum Press, New York. Reprinted by permission of the publisher.

Notes on the Contributors

Frs. Dennis and Matthew Linn, S.J. have tried to integrate physical, emotional, and spiritual wholeness by working as hospital chaplains, psychotherapists, and retreat directors. They have taught courses on healing in many countries and universities, including a doctors' seminar accredited by the American Medical Association. They are the authors of four books on praying for wholeness: *Healing of Memories, Healing Life's Hurts, To Heal As Jesus Heals* (with Barbara Shlemon) and *Healing the Dying* (with Sr. Mary Jane Linn, C.S.J.) (all Paulist Press).

Fr. Dennis Hamm, S.J. is a member of the department of theology at Creighton University, Omaha, Nebraska. He did his doctoral work in biblical languages and literature at St. Louis University. A member of the Catholic Biblical Association, he has been an active participant in its task forces on "Healing in the New Testament" and "Luke-Acts." His reviews and articles have appeared in *The Way, Catholic Charismatic, Emmanuel,* and *Catholic Biblical Quarterly.*

Fr. Robert Faricy, S.J. is professor of spiritual theology at the Pontifical Gregorian University and also an active member of the charismatic renewal. He is a member of the renewal's Italian National Service Committee and editor of *Renewal in the Spirit,* an international newsletter for religious men and women in the charismatic renewal. He has authored many books on prayer and spirituality, the two most recent being *Praying for Inner Healing* (Paulist, 1980) and *Praying* (Winston, 1980).

Fr. John Healey is liaison to the bishop of Brooklyn for the Catholic charismatic renewal. He received his S.T.L. degree from the Gregorian University in Rome and has served as a priest for forty-three years. He is a columnist for the *Tablet* and is author of *Charismatic Renewal: Reflections of a Pastor* (Paulist, 1976).

Fr. **William J. Sneck, S.J.** is assistant professor of clinical psychology at Georgetown University in Washington, D.C. His doctoral disertation from the University of Michigan focused on studying a charismatic community; it will be published by University Press of America. His work as retreat master, spiritual director, and counselor led to a theoretical and experential integration of psychology and spirituality.

Francis MacNutt was one of the first to be involved in the Catholic charismatic renewal. He is author of the best-selling *Healing* and *Power to Heal* (Ave Maria, 1974, 1977) and has been active in the healing ministry for over ten years. During this time he has traveled all over the United States and to all continents, ministering to the sick and crippled, and working directly with those in the healing ministries. He has a B.A. (with honors) from Harvard, an M.F.A. from Catholic University of America, and a Ph.D. from the Aquinas Institute of Theology.

Fr. **Richard McAlear, O.M.I.** studied for the priesthood in Rome where he was ordained in 1970. Presently he and Mrs. Elizabeth Brennan, who is a mother of three children, form part of the leadership team for Our Lady of Hope's healing and deliverance ministry. Mainly as a result of the gratitude of those receiving their ministry, Our Lady of Hope Center daily reaches out to feed and shelter the homeless of the Newburgh, N.Y. area.

Fr. **James Wheeler, S.J.** serves as director of two spiritual direction centers, St. Joseph's Center in Long Island, N.Y., and St. Joseph's House of Prayer in Albuquerque, New Mexico. Besides directing these two centers, Fr. Wheeler gives individual direction to about two hundred people each year. In addition he teaches a two-year course aimed at training spiritual directors. An integral part of the training involves learning about inner healing and deliverance prayer. Fr. Wheeler has prayed inner healing with his directees for the past sixteen years and deliverance prayer for the last six years.

Fr. **Kenneth Metz** was ordained in 1965 and received a Ph.D. in counseling from Marquette University in 1979. Presently Fr. Metz teaches theology and behavioral science at St. Francis Seminary School of Pastoral Ministry in Milwaukee. During summers he teaches counseling in the Christian Spirituality program at Creighton University in Omaha. Fr. Metz has been active in the Catholic charismatic renewal since 1971 both in conducting healing workshops and in serving as charismatic liaison for the archdiocese of Milwaukee.

Fr. James McManus, C.Ss.R. studied his moral theology at the Alphonsianum in Rome. For six years Fr. McManus taught moral theology to seminarians. Presently he teaches renewal courses for priests and religious at the Pastoral and Study Center located at Weston, Shrewsbury in England. He is the author of *The Ministry of Deliverance in the Catholic Tradition* (London: National Service Committee for Catholic Charismatic Renewal, 1980).